Microeconomics and the Public Economy: A Defence of Leviathan

John G. Cullis
and
Philip R. Jones

Basil Blackwell

Copyright © John G. Cullis and Philip R. Jones, 1987

First published 1987
First published in paperback 1989

Basil Blackwell Ltd
108 Cowley Road, Oxford, OX4 1JF, UK

Basil Blackwell Inc.
432 Park Avenue South, Suite 1503
New York, NY 10016, USA

British Library Cataloguing in Publication Data
Cullis, John G.
  Micro economics and the public economy: a
  defence of Leviathan.
  1. Finance, Public
  I. Title II. Jones, Philip R.
  336   HJ141
  ISBN 0–631–15552–X
         0-631-16893-1 (pbk)

Library of Congress Cataloging-in-Publication Data
Cullis, John G.
  Micro-economics and the public economy.

  Bibliography: p.
  Includes index.
  1. Microeconomics. 2. Finance, Public. 3. Expendi-
tures, Public. I. Jones, Philip R., 1948–
II. Title.
HB172.C85   1987
ISBN 0–631–15552–X
       0-631-16893-1 (pbk)

Typeset in 10 on 12½ pt Times
by Photo-graphics, Honiton, Devon
Printed in Great Britain by
Billing and Sons Ltd, Worcester

Microeconomics and the Public Economy:
A Defence of Leviathan

To Our Families

Contents

List of Figures

List of Charts

List of Tables

Acknowledgements

The origins of this book lie in a shared taught course on the Theory of Public Finance in the University of Bath, and co-authorship of several journal articles on public sector economics broadly defined. In particular, chapters 6 and 7 draw on articles which were published in the *Scottish Journal of Political Economy* and *Public Finance*, and we would like to thank the publishers for permission to use copyright material. The manuscript has been considerably improved by incorporation of many of the detailed comments received from Professor David Collard at Bath and Dr Dieter Helm at Lady Margaret Hall, Oxford – comments for which the authors are very grateful. Other helpful observations have come from Harry Collins and other members of the School of Humanities and Social Sciences at Bath. However as usual the authors are prepared to 'monopsonize' any criticisms of the final effort. Our initial handwritten drafts were expertly 'wodr brocessed' by Eve Penhaligon and later changes were done by Arlene Heckels. We thank both of them very much for their efforts and sense of proportion about 'our stuff'.

J. G. C. and P. R. J.
Bath

Since the appearance of the hardback edition we have received correspondence from Professor Gordon Tullock. We would like to acknowledge both his encouragement and the perceptive comments he made. The debate as to the role of government in a mixed economy is perennial and his comments will serve as a stimulus to further thought and discussion.

Leviathan

The term 'Leviathan' used in this book owes its origins to the famous political philosopher Thomas Hobbes, whose work with that title was conceived in the early 1640s and published in 1651. Hobbes was one of the three great 'social contract' thinkers, the others being John Locke and Jean-Jacques Rousseau. His conception of the world involved only two alternatives: one the 'state of nature' which was an all-against-all state of chaos, and the other the 'civil state' in which individuals were subjected in a state of common subordination. In this bleak choice individuals were seen as sacrificing their individual liberties to the state in a 'contract' whose pay-off was the benefit of security. He envisaged that individuals would give up their power to resist even an oppressive state, and would therefore always be obedient. He believed that life would be 'nasty, brutish and short' in an anarchistic setting. At the same time Hobbes thought that the state, almost as a matter of definition, would *not* be the source of injustice or oppression. Given this apparent 'gain from trade', it is somewhat of a paradox, as Musgrave (1981) notes, that Hobbes titled his work *Leviathan*. In dictionaries the term attracts various meanings but most commonly is described as a real or imaginary sea monster. In short, Hobbes' title seems to allude to the monster state, while the treatise does not really conform to this view. However the paradox is resolved when it is recalled that Hobbes tells his readers that his title is taken from the forty-first chapter of the book of Job, where Leviathan is called King of the Proud. Vain-glory is a source of quarrels among men so that Leviathan apparently refers to the monster in men rather than in the state (see Hobbes, 1967).

Whatever Hobbes had in mind there is no ambiguity about its modern usage in economics. Musgrave (1981) attributes the use of the term in modern public sector/public choice economics to Buchanan (1975). In this recent writing the term is used in a pejorative and damning way – a large public sector is an unpleasant monster to be destroyed, or at least kept in chains. Buchanan (1971) shares with Hobbes the view that 'almost any government is better than no government' but focuses the problem on 'where to draw the line between too much government, too many laws and too little government, too few laws' (p. 2). In so far as too much is predicted by modern public choice economics, it is government that has been identified as a Leviathan. It is this modern literature to which a substantial part of this book relates. This is the sense in which the words 'Leviathan writings' are used below. In a broad way, however, the intention of the book is to move towards the rehabilitation of the original use of the term. The public sector, then, may be perceived as something large, but not *necessarily* so oppressive as is typically implied in the recent public choice literature.

Hobbes' writings were intended to influence historical events to the advantage of the royalist cause, but it seems they had little impact and remained scholarly. The impact of the modern Leviathan scholarship in economics remains to be assessed.

REFERENCES

Buchanan, J. M. (1971), *The Bases of Collective Action*. New York: General Learning Press.

Buchanan, J. M. (1975), The political economy of franchise in the welfare state, pp. 52–77 in Selden, A. (ed.), *Capitalism and Freedom: Problems and Prospects*, Charlottesville, Va: University of Virginia Press.

Hobbes, T. (1967), *Leviathan*, Edited and abridged with an Introduction by John Plamenatz, London: Collins.

Musgrave, R. A. (1981), Leviathan cometh – or does he? pp. 77–120 in Ladd, H. and Tideman, N. (eds), *Tax and Expenditure Limitations*, COUPE papers on Public Economics 5, Washington: Urban Institute.

Introduction

In 1921 Albert Einstein won the Nobel Prize. His contribution was to convince other scientists that time and space were not fixed and immutable characteristics of the physical universe but relative to the position of the observer. Since such non-absolutist positions have been recognized in the 'hard' sciences it has become much easier to accept relativistic positions in the 'soft' social sciences. What you see in the economic, social and political universe depends on where you stand. The beliefs and writings of social scientists stand testimony to the fact that how the world is interpreted depends on the underlying model (or more grandly, paradigm) in which the author is trying to fit the 'facts' or observations.[1] It is not surprising that people, using different models, find themselves at odds with one another in terms of their analysis, predictions and policy suggestions. However, what may be surprising is that those sharing the same methods also find much to argue about. The same tools build different perspectives depending on who is using them. These different perspectives command greater and lesser support depending on a whole host of historical and other factors.

It is against this background of a world that does not come ready interpreted and an underlying model that is, in many ways, a rather forgiving medium in which to work (even once the conventions of the game have been established) that this book considers micro-economic aspects of the public economy or sector. It is the 1986 Nobel Laureate in economics, Professor J. M. Buchanan, who, alongside others of the so-called 'public choice' school, has consistently written on this topic. In this work the growth of the public sector can be equated with the appearance of a monster or Leviathan. Whilst not wishing in any way to detract from the major contributions of Buchanan, his colleagues and followers, the intention here is to question this view while still using the conventions of mainstream micro-economic theory.

Within this framework the basic unit of analysis is the individual. It is individuals who have preferences and are modelled as making utility- (or satisfaction)-maximizing decisions subject to their budget constraints. Despite reliance on isolated individual decisions, this view of the economic world is well recognized by the majority of economists. They employ this mode of analysis (even with problems which appear to require some form of collective action) and thereby establish an apparent rationale for government activity. The basic arguments for looking beyond the isolated individual and the market have traditionally been collected under the three functions of Musgrave's (1959) public household. These functions are: allocation, distribution and stabilization. Government responsibility arises in these areas because certain goods and services do not possess the appropriate characteristics that facilitate the operation of the market and/or because the market is deemed to generate an income distribution that is 'unfair'. In short, markets in some circumstances produce inefficiently and/or inequitably.

In the 1950s and 1960s the 'market failure' literature held sway and the public sector in the mixed economy found much favour. Progress results when individuals question the current orthodoxy and the late 1960s, 1970s and early 1980s have witnessed the development of the public sector analogue of market failure. This may be dubbed 'non-market or government failure'. Here, as noted above, the writings of the Virginia or public choice school of economists have been central and very influential. The basic thrust of this literature involves applying maximizing behaviour to public sector actors as well as to private sector decision-makers. Given the constraints and incentives that confront public sector actors, it appears that governmental outcomes can also be inefficient and/or inequitable. If this is accepted then the cons of the market have to be balanced against the cons of the public sector. Failure is a two-way street. Some related work, however, goes beyond this. It creates the impression that markets on the whole do less badly than many believe, and policies that involve a 'return to the market' are to be recommended. The message offered here is a more specific version of the one outlined in general terms above. That is, the same framework that 'justifies' a resurgence of the market (the current orthodoxy in a large section of both the political and academic communities) can be re-applied to cast doubt on this prescription. The main point is not to suggest that market believers are wrong and non-market believers are right, or indeed vice-versa, but rather to emphasize that they are *'believers'*. With this in mind, the purpose of this text is deliberately to help fill the armoury of the non-believers and, in so doing, emphasize the relativistic nature of economic analysis.

Thirlwall (1986) describes his study on balance of payments theory as 'an unusual (but I hope appealing and convincing) mixture of textbook and polemic' (p. xii). This also captures the nature of our work. The book is divided into two parts containing four and six chapters respectively. Part I is intended to serve an essentially textbook function describing the tools, arguments and contexts which have been the core of the Leviathan debate. The tools are those of neo-classical micro-economics, and the arguments are those collected under the headings of market and non-market (governmental) failure. The context is the current debate over the size and growth of the public sector. More specifically chapter 1 sets up the two-sector general equilibrium model standard to micro-economic theory and then introduces 'technical' and 'value judgement' sources of market failure. Chapter 2 deals in a parallel fashion with governmental failure. Chapters 3 and 4 centre on measuring the size and 'accounting' for the growth of the public sector in mixed economies respectively.

Part II of the book contains the polemic, and subjects certain aspects of the Leviathan attack to closer scrutiny (whilst at the same time offering illustrations of applied micro-economic analysis). Chapter 5 considers the nature of 'over-provision' biases stemming from majority voting mechanisms and fiscal knowledge. Chapter 6 examines arguments concerning the inefficiencies fostered by bureaucrats, especially the claim that bureaucracies 'over-provide' their services. The main argument of these two chapters is that there are considerable checks to over-provision, and that it is much less prevalent than is often supposed. Chapter 7 poses the question that, even if the public economy does over-provide its wares, does it matter for allocative efficiency? If individuals fully adjust in their market behaviour to government expenditure, there may be little of consequence to discuss unless the public economy provision: (a) is less productive than the equivalent private output of a good (chapter 8); (b) involves large welfare costs because of the financial implications (chapter 9); and/or (c) is inimical to individual freedom (chapter 10). In short Part II deals with the four evils laid at the door of the public economy: allocative inefficiency on the expenditure side; X-inefficiency in production; allocative inefficiency on the taxation side and government as a threat to freedom.

Throughout, reference is made to empirical work, but no attempt has been made to be exhaustive. The main reason for this is simply that the debate over *Leviathan* has been predominantly *a priori* in nature. All we attempt to establish on the empirical front is that evidence is mixed and as always is 'up for grabs'. In short, the book is mainly about micro-economic reasoning and the public sector. It calls in question the 'excesses' noted by those who would lay such emphasis on governmental failure that generate almost automatic fear of a Leviathan. We therefore recognize, with approval, contributions by such economists as Richard Musgrave and Wallace Oates. We accept the existence of a failure but question that the public economy is *always* a Leviathan to be rejected in favour of market economy solutions.

The level of analysis is designed to make the book accessible to those with a good first-year UK undergraduate understanding of economics. It is hoped, however, that some sections at least will be of interest to more general readers. Finally, although we have taken mainstream micro-economic theory as our method of analysis, we have tried in places to indicate to the reader where other approaches, e.g. Marxist, have been adopted. No claim is made that these other literatures are adequately captured here. Rather we want to make it clear that there are many other perspectives on the public economy and that we are considering only one; albeit in our view an important one.

Amongst Mrs Thatcher's favourite television programmes are reported to be 'Yes Minister' and 'Yes Prime Minister'. Quotes taken from some of the episodes head some of the later chapters, partly as a source of amusement in themselves and partly as a reflection of how extensively a number of themes of the Leviathan school have permeated popular culture. (These are reproduced with the permission of BBC Enterprises Ltd. from *Yes Minister*, Volumes 1 and 2 edited by Anthony Jay and Jonathan Lynn.)

NOTES

1 For an extensive, accessible discussion of these types of ideas applied to 'real' science, see Collins (1985).

REFERENCES

Collins, H. M. (1985), *Changing Order – Replication and Induction in Scientific Practice*, London: Sage.

Musgrave, R. A. (1959), *The Theory of Public Finance*, New York: McGraw-Hill.

Thirlwall, A. P. (1986), *Balance of Payments Theory and the United Kingdom Experience*, 3rd edn, London and Basingstoke: Macmillan.

Part I

1

Market Failure: A Rationale for Government Intervention?

1.1 INTRODUCTION

The purpose of this chapter is two-fold. First, we hope to introduce and explain the majority of micro-economic concepts which will be employed in this text. Second, we wish to discuss critically one of the basic arguments for government intervention, i.e. improvement of the allocation of resources within the economy. Throughout micro-economic theory a distinction is drawn between the concepts of 'efficiency' and 'equity'. Efficiency is concerned with the 'best' or 'optimum' allocation of resources. If private markets can achieve such an outcome, it may be argued that the role of government, as a consequence, will be reduced. 'Equity' is concerned with the distribution of income. Even if the allocation of resources satisfies the conditions which underlie the concept of 'efficiency', the outcome may not necessarily be deemed 'equitable'.

We begin by examining those conditions which are typically employed to determine 'efficiency'. These are dependent on a number of normative considerations (value judgements) that determine the allocation of resources referred to as 'best' or 'optimal'. If these are adopted it will be argued that perfectly functioning markets can satisfy the conditions of 'efficiency'. The requirements for such a solution are, however, stringent, and in certain circumstances even a 'perfect' market scenario may fail when the price mechanism is unable to deal efficiently with particular goods, services and activities. If such a result can be established, the question is begged as to whether government intervention is then required to deal with the failings of the market. The form that any such intervention should take is a relevant issue.

1.2 'EFFICIENT' ALLOCATION OF RESOURCES

The micro-economic framework which generates the typical conditions for efficiency stems from the work of Vilfredo Pareto. A Pareto optimum is attained when it is impossible to re-allocate resources so as to make one person better off, without at the same time making another person worse off. This Pareto criterion avoids one of the formidable problems of welfare economics, i.e. inter-personal comparison. Thus, 'better-off' or 'worse-off' are descriptions determined by the individual himself. If, in his *own estimation*, a person is better off as a result of some re-allocation, and no-one declares himself to be worse off, a Pareto improvement can be achieved. To employ this criterion, however, is to accept three value judgements (see Nath, 1969). First, that individuals are the basic and only units of analysis. Second, that each individual is the best judge of his or her own welfare. Third, that to make someone better off is only acceptable if no-one else is made worse off. Such value judgements minimize the scope for 'expert' or other opinions in directing or evaluating choices for others. They also suggest that society can adequately be analysed in a 'non-organic' way as simply the sum of individuals that make it up. The concept of the state as anything other than the sum of individuals is not recognized, and the notion of maximizing the interests of such organisms is hence ignored. If you, the reader, doubt the significance of these propositions consider your views of the following three statements, all of which are consistent with these so-called Paretian value judgements:

1 It is a 'good thing' if a rich person is made 'better off' while a poor person is made no worse off.
2 An individual who chooses to be a hard drug abuser is the best judge of his own welfare.
3 The police force exists to protect individual property rights broadly defined, rather than to ensure the health of the body that is society.

These issues may appear provocative but, as such, they emphasize that it would be wrong to consider the definition of Pareto 'optimality' or 'efficiency' as in any sense sacrosanct. Even so the approach may be attractive. It may be argued that, at least to begin with, the Pareto criterion would be accepted by individuals who stand behind a Rawlsian 'veil of ignorance', where they neither know the hand of cards they are to be dealt in life or the details of the game to be played (see Sugden and Weale (1979) for an account of the Paretian value judgements along these lines). In so far as individuals are uncertain about the changes to be proposed, and, when the initial income distribution is not specified, there may exist an acceptance of the Paretian criterion when individuals feel that they can veto changes which make them worse off.

In this way the appeal of the Paretian approach may be explained. It is difficult to over-estimate the importance of this framework for standard literature in public economics. Buchanan (1959) notes 'This Pareto rule is itself an ethical proposition, a value statement, but it is one which requires a minimum of premises and one which should command wide assent' (p. 125). Here we emphasize the value judgements which underlie Pareto optimality and its importance to the existing literature. It should be noted that we do not infer that it is 'sacrosanct' or indeed necessarily 'obvious'. Certainly its acceptance has been called in question (see, for example, Rowley and Peacock, 1975).

The Paretian efficiency criterion may appear at this stage nebulous with respect to the issue of resource allocation. How should resources be allocated so as to satisfy a Pareto optimum? Here we pursue this question, first within a general equilibrium framework and second within a partial equilibrium framework. Both approaches are utilized in later sections of the book.

Pareto Optimality: a General Equilibrium Analysis

By general equilibrium we mean a framework which encompasses all markets and hence captures interrelationships. By contrast, partial equilibrium tends to focus specifically upon one market. Here, to employ a diagrammatic framework, we begin by studying resource allocation in the provision of two goods X and Y, and examine the implications of price changes in both markets. It is assumed that the goods are produced by two factors of production, capital (K) and labour (L), and it is important to understand both the product and factor market requirements for optimality. Moreover, as there is more than one individual, the question of how goods are allocated between individuals is crucial to the Paretian criterion. Below, we adapt a two-person society, *A* and *B*. If the state of technology is given, then a relationship can be defined between output and any good (e.g. *X*), and the factors (*K* and *L*) required for production. Such a relationship (e.g. $Q_X = f(K,L)$) is referred to as a *production function*. This may be illustrated in terms of an *isoquant*, i.e. a locus of points of identical output quantity attained by the use of different combinations of capital and labour. In figure 1.1, such alternative combinations (K_1, L_1 and K_2, L_2) are identified for a given output of 100 units of *X*. It is clear that K_1, K_2 can be substituted for L_1, L_2 and the same output can be achieved. Hence, the slope of the isoquant at any point may be considered the marginal rate of technical substitution of capital for labour in the production of *X* [i.e. MRTS$_{KL}^X$].

If an economy has a fixed quantity of capital and labour with the state of technology given, the first problem that must be confronted is how to allocate capital and labour between the production of *X* and *Y*. This question of *production efficiency* may be resolved by reference to an Edgeworth box diagram. Figure 1.2 presents such a box. The fixed quantities of capital and labour available determine the dimensions. From origin O_X the isoquants for good *X* are illustrated in the normal way, whereas from O_Y the isoquants appear inverted to form the box. Initially, assume that of the total capital in the economy,

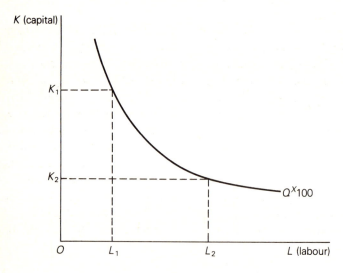

Figure 1.1   Production isoquant

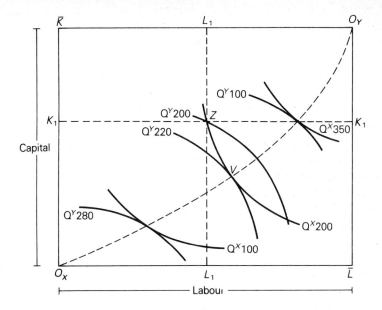

Figure 1.2   Production efficiency

O_XK, an amount O_XK_1 is allocated to the production of good X and of the total labour available, O_XL, O_XL_1 is allocated to the production of good X.

Clearly, at point Z, 200 units of X can be produced. If the remaining labour (O_YL_1) and capital (O_YK_1) is allocated to the production of Y, output of Y is similarly 200 units. Can capital and labour be re-allocated so as to increase the output of one good without at the same time reducing the output of the other? If both goods are valued by the residents of this economy, such a re-allocation may be recommended against the Paretian (efficiency) conditions. If capital was switched from X to Y and labour from Y to X so that a movement from Z to V in the Edgeworth box took place, it is clear that output of Y might increase by 20 units without a reduction in the output of X. At V the essential point to notice is that the slopes of the X and Y isoquants are identical, i.e. $\mathrm{MRTS}_{KL}^X = \mathrm{MRTS}_{KL}^Y$. At this point it is impossible to increase the output of one good without causing a fall in the output of another.

Whilst it is still not resolved as to how much X and Y should be produced, it is clear that a range of options is demarcated by the

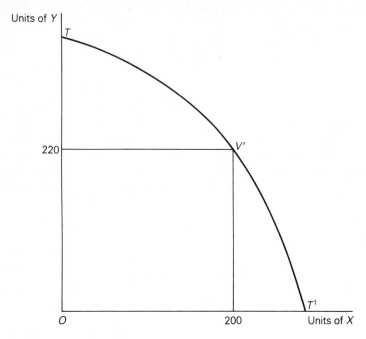

Figure 1.3 The production frontier

contract curve $O_x O_y$. These may be illustrated in figure 1.3 in the form of a production frontier. Any point on the frontier (such as V') accords to a point on the contract curve and indicates that the condition $\text{MRTS}_{KL}^X = \text{MRTS}_{KL}^Y$ applies. From any point within the frontier it is clearly possible to increase the output of one good without a fall in the output of the other good. The frontier shows how much X would be gained if resources were moved from industry Y and full employment maintained. The slope at any point on the frontier reflects the marginal rate of transformation of one good into the other, i.e. MRT_{XY}.

In figure 1.4 we look more closely at the output level V' on the production frontier. If this output level were produced, how would the goods be allocated between two individuals, A and B? Considering the origin of the Edgeworth box O_A, the vertical axis measures units of Y and the horizontal axis measures units of X. The curve I_A^1 is an indifference curve, i.e. a locus of points which stipulates those combinations of X and Y that provide an identical level of welfare for individual A. Any such curve to the right of I_A^1 will imply consumption of the same amount of one good but more of the other (or more of both), and hence will be associated with a higher level of welfare. The slope at any point on an indifference curve will indicate the rate (at the margin) that the individual is prepared to substitute one good for another, i.e. MRS_{XY}. Here in the Edgeworth box we have placed the origin of B's indifference curves at V'. At V' on the production frontier, 220 units of Y and 200 units of X are produced. If these were allocated at random between A and B it is unlikely that Pareto optimality would be attained. Following exactly the same reasoning as applied to figure 1.2, an allocation of X and Y as indicated at point Z in the Edgeworth box is inferior to one such as Q which leaves A no worse off but makes B better off. Indeed, a movement from Z to any point within the shaded ellipse reflects a Pareto improvement. Once again, only at tangency points on a contract curve will a Pareto improvement be impossible. Thus, for any production level of X and Y, *exchange efficiency* demands that $MRS_{XY}^A = MRS_{XY}^B$.

To determine whether or not V' on the production possibility is the optimal quantity to be produced demands further analysis. If the MRS in consumption of X and Y were not equal to the MRT, it would be possible to effect a Pareto improvement. For example, imagine that the MRT_{XY} was two units of X for one unit of Y and the common MRS_{XY}^{AB} was one for one. It would be possible to move capital and labour to reduce the output of Y (by one unit) and hence increase X (by two units). For any individual who had lost one unit of Y, one unit of X may then be substituted and that person's welfare would not decline. This would leave one unit of X by which a Pareto improvement might be effected, should it be given to either A or B. Hence, $MRS_{XY}^{AB} = MRT_{XY}$ is a necessary condition for Pareto optimality. It constitutes the third, or *top-level*, consideration which together with conditions for *production efficiency* and *exchange efficiency* determines Pareto optimality.[1]

Determining the income distribution at any point along the exchange contract curve in figure 1.4 implicitly means picking a specific value of the MRS_{XY}^{AB}. If it transpired that this value was equated to the MRT_{XY} at V', then in effect welfare would be maximized here. Clearly, it will always be possible to find one point on each possible exchange contract curve pertaining to each point on the production frontier, i.e. where MRS_{XY}^{AB} equals MRT_{XY}. Thus, the condition of Pareto optimality can be satisfied for *any* income distribution.

Choosing the 'appropriate' welfare distribution (or 'equity' criterion) implies a specific MRS_{XY}^{AB} somewhere on the exchange contract curve. When this equals MRT_{XY}, the total output of X and Y is resolved.

Market Failure

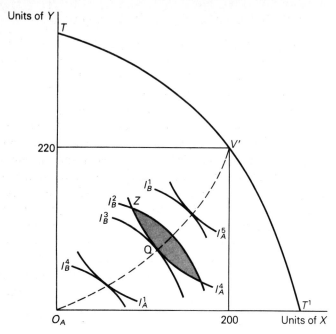

Figure 1.4 Exchange efficiency

The use of capital and labour in the production of X and Y is similarly uniquely determined once the appropriate point on the production frontier is indicated.

It should be clear that a perfectly competitive market will satisfy the requirements for Pareto optimality. Provided there is no price discrimination in either factor or product markets, the production and exchange efficiency requirements are likely to apply. Each producer, in an effort to maximize profits, will equate $MRTS_{KL}$ to the factor price ratio[2] and if the same factor price ratio applies for all industries then marginal rates of technical substitution will be equated between industries. Similarly, each consumer equates his MRS_{XY} with the commodity price ratio in order to maximize welfare[3]. Thus the marginal rates of substitution in commodities consumers will be equated if all face identical price ratios. Finally, the MRT_{XY} is equal to the ratio of marginal costs of production[4] and as MRS_{XY} will equal MRT_{XY} when the price ratio equals the marginal cost ratio. As in perfectly competitive markets the firm in equilibrium equates price with marginal cost, perfect competition also satisfies the top-level requirement.[5]

Pareto Optimality: A Partial Equilibrium Analysis

That a perfectly competitive market will generate a Pareto optimal outcome is apparent also as a result of a partial equilibrium analysis. In figure 1.5 the market for good X is considered. The demand and supply curves are also illustrated in figure 1.5.

To the extent that the demand curve represents the marginal willingness to pay for good X, then at a market equilibrium price of P_e per unit, it is possible to perceive *consumer surplus*. Consumer surplus may be defined as the difference between the maximum sum that individuals would be prepared to pay for the good and the amount they actually do pay. Thus, for some units of good X, consumers would willingly pay more than P_e, and it is only with reference to the marginal unit consumed (i.e. q_e) that this is not so. Consumer surplus is the difference between $OAEq_e$ (the integral of the demand curve between O and q_e) and the amount actually paid for Oq_e, i.e. OP_eEq_e. Triangle P_eAE is consumer surplus. By analogy, the supply curve may be equated with the minimum sum producers would accept to incur the costs of producing an additional unit of the good. The supply curve

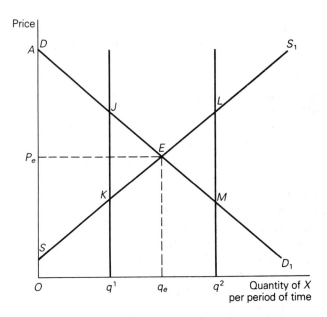

Figure 1.5 Welfare in partial equilibrium

may be interpreted as a marginal cost curve. (When perfect competition holds, the short-run supply curve is determined simply by the horizontal aggregation of the marginal cost functions of firms which produce good X.)[6] Thus, if producers are paid a price greater than the minimum required to increase output by one unit, they enjoy *producer surplus*. This again is true of all units except the marginal unit q_e. The difference between the total paid, OP_eEq_e, and the total costs of producing Oq_e, i.e. the integral $OSEq_e$, reflects producer surplus. Triangle SP_eE is producer surplus.

Taking these estimates as a combined measure of social surplus or welfare confirms the prediction that a perfectly competitive market will perform well. If price equals marginal cost (as predicted for perfectly competitive markets), then output is Oq_e and social surplus ($P_eAE + SP_eE$) is maximized. Any restriction of output (e.g. to q^1) reduces welfare by triangle KJE and generates what are referred to as *deadweight losses*. Similarly, any expansion of output (e.g. to q^2) would create allocative losses as the increased output, q_eq^2, would be valued at an amount equal to q_eEMq^2 but cost q_eELq^2, i.e. a loss of traingle ELM. It is such an argument that lies behind policies which seek to generate outcomes consistent with those of perfect markets.

Of course, once again, there are equity considerations. To accept the output Oq_e as a welfare-maximizing output implies both that social surplus is maximized and that there is satisfaction with the income distribution. Changes in the income distribution will be important for the position and slope of DD_1, and to accept any particular DD_1 curve implies acceptance of the income distribution. Furthermore, there are subtleties that lie behind the interpretation of DD_1 *as a marginal willingness to pay* curve, and it should be noted that here we have interpreted it as relating to that demand which is registered when individuals are assumed to have a constant real income.[7]

The material of this section is repeated in virtually all economic principles, micro-economics and welfare texts, as it represents the economists' theoretical benchmark against which arrangements are to be judged.

One important consideration, however, is the impact of the problem of 'second-best'. The previous discussion implies almost a mechanistic response to the maximization of welfare. The Paretian marginal equivalents appear as a clear set of targets for policy. Thus, for example, if output is provided by the public sector then government should simply price at marginal cost in order to maximize welfare. It can, however, be misleading to interpret the Paretian analysis in this fashion.

The 'first-best' conditions for welfare maximization apply only when, throughout the economy, all marginal equivalences hold. The problem of 'second-best' arises when other Paretian marginal conditions do not hold. The temptation to interpret each marginal rate of substitution that is brought in line with its price ratio as improving welfare must be resisted when it is known that elsewhere these conditions are not satisfied (i.e. when elsewhere additional non-Paretian constraints apply).[8]

Lipsey and Lancaster (1956) discuss the consequences of the problem of 'second-best' and the extent to which it restricts policy-making.[9] While undoubtedly an important consideration, the second-best problem does not completely prohibit piecemeal optimization. For example, in the case quoted, it is not marginal cost pricing *per se* that is the objective, i.e. it is welfare maximization that is the goal (Webb, 1976, p. 46). If it were known that some private sector enterprise output (good i) was not priced at marginal cost, then it would be necessary to incorporate this information in determining the price of a product (good j) provided in the public sector. If good i were priced above marginal cost, then it would be appropriate to consider setting the price of j above marginal cost if the products were substitutes (Mishan, 1982). Intuitively, because good i is priced above marginal cost, consumers in that market value consumption at the margin sufficiently to be able to compensate consumers of good j to reduce consumption and hence release resources so as to enable an expansion of output of good i (Rees, 1976). Pricing good j above marginal cost reduces its consumption and releases resources. The extent to which the price is set in excess of marginal cost may depend upon many factors, including the extent to which i and j are substitute goods.[10]

The reader is then cautioned against interpreting the marginal equivalences as an automatic set of responses to maximize welfare. Whilst it is not possible, *a priori*, to construct second-best rules, it is possible to proceed with piecemeal optimization provided the required information can be found.

In the following sections discussion focuses upon the causes of market failure. Discussion of the response to market failure conventionally envisages a first-best response, i.e. it is assumed that the distortion to be corrected is the only non-Paretian constraint in the economy. When this is not so the problem becomes more complex.

1.3 MARKET FAILURE AND THE ROLE OF GOVERNMENT

In so far as we have shown that perfect markets generate Pareto optimal solutions, the role of the state appears limited solely to the establishment and policing of requisite property rights and the maintenance of perfect market conditions. This conclusion, however, cannot be drawn in a number of instances. Even the most perfect market will fail to achieve allocative efficiency in the event of the existence of the following problems.

Externalities

An externality is said to be present when the utility of an individual A depends not only upon the activities $(X_1, X_2, \ldots X_n)$ that are exclusively under his control but also upon another activity Y_1, which is outside his control (Buchanan and Stubblebine, 1962). Thus an individual may consume goods $X_1 \ldots X_n$ but be affected by activity Y_1 of someone else (e.g. someone smoking, playing a radio, creating litter). It is important, however, to note that an externality implies something more than an interdependency. It is an interdependency that is conveyed *directly* (not indirectly through the price mechanism). Whilst a consumer of good X_1 may exert an influence on his consumption of X_1 by paying a price, it is not the case that he can exert an influence upon Y_1. Externalities may be positive (external economies) and negative (external diseconomies) in their impact. They may operate: between individual and individual (e.g. a consumer of cigarettes may exert an external diseconomy on other individuals); between one firm and another firm (e.g. a firm's effluent may pollute an estuary where another firm depends on clean water); between firms and consumers (e.g. the 'classic' smoky chimney of one firm blackens the washing of a nearby household); between employer and employee (e.g. a firm may improve the human capital of an employee as a result of his employment). In this way it can be seen that externalities are a pervasive phenomenon. If individuals would modify (e.g. by persuasion, bargaining, bribery, etc.) the activities of the externality generating agent, then the externality is *potentially relevant*, and if there are gains from such modification, the externality is *Pareto relevant*. By such a means the externality would be internalized.

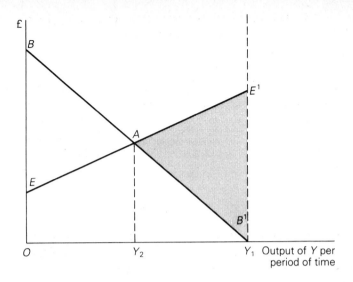

Figure 1.6 Negative externality

In figure 1.6 it is assumed that individuals in a neighbourhood are affected adversely by a firm which produces good Y. The production of Y emits noise and EE^1 reflects the amount (at a maximum) that individuals would be prepared to pay to reduce the output of Y by one successive unit. The line BB reflects the incremental net revenue that the firm receives from the production of Y. A market outcome would lead to a production level of Y at Y_1. However, the market outcome is no longer Pareto optimal. The hatched triangle AE^1B^1 measures the gains to be experienced if individuals compensate the producer for restricting output to OY_2. If individuals pay the maximum, these gains are reaped by the producer, otherwise there are potential gains to the individuals themselves.

It may be noted that, should the state of property rights be such that the producer is liable (and hence must compensate his neighbours), he would still be prepared to do this up to the same output level OY_2, and in this instance the potential gains to be reaped by negotiation would be reflected in triangle EBA.

Ignoring welfare effects of the state of the law itself (Mishan, 1981) the allocation outcome is unique irrespective of where property rights are assigned. Indeed, it appears that with obvious gains from trade, provided property rights are clearly established, the externality will be internalized voluntarily by those concerned. Coase (1960) throws this perspective upon the problem, which therefore implies that the role of the government lies solely in terms of establishing clear property rights. If property rights are clear, individuals will internalize a Pareto-relevant externality. As such the existence of market failure calls for a limited role by government. In response, the following arguments are important. First, time and effort are required for bargaining over externalities, i.e. market correction is not costless (Pigou, 1924). Second, if the individuals concerned are part of a large group, these costs become more formidable when the externality assumes the characteristics of a public good (see the next section). Third, the solution to the externality assumes bargaining over the marginal unit but, in effect, lack of information and blackmailing behaviour on the part of those endowed with property rights may lead to a non-Pareto optimal outcome (Davis and Kamien, 1971; Wellisz, 1964). In short, the transaction costs of internalizing externalities may be formidable, and in this context direct government intervention may yet appear more efficient.

With reference to figure 1.7 there are many alternative, potential responses which the government may take. Merely to indicate broad strategies, we note the following:

1   A tax response. Here a tax may be placed on good Y so as to reduce net incremental revenue and hence shift BB^1 to BB^2. Producers would respond by altering output from OY_1 and OY_2. (It is debatable as to whether or not such a tax only on producers would be sufficient – see Buchanan and Stubblebine, 1962 – but the principle behind such intervention is clear.)

2   Regulation. A noise standard may be imposed such that at any period of time output of Y could not exceed Y_2. Note that this does not imply prohibition of production unless externality costs are E^2E^3. (Unlike the extreme ecologist, the economist can conceive an 'optimal' pollution level greater than zero.)

3   Subsidy. Individuals may be subsidized to move from the area, or the producer subsidized to employ less noisy production methods; the objective being to shift EE^1 towards E^4E^5.

4   Unitization or merger. If the externality generator and sufferer can be engineered into the same decision-making unit, self-interest will lead to the internalization of the externality. If seaside local authority A dumps waste at sea and affects the beaches of local authority B, an externality is present. However, if A and B are

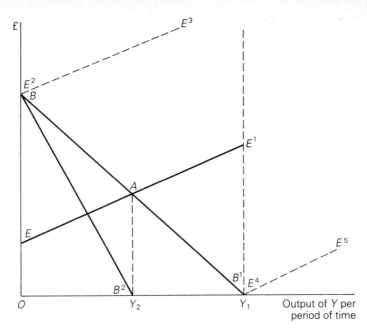

Figure 1.7 Externalities and government intervention

made part of the same authority, the logic is that the externality should now be included as part of decision-making so that the costs A initially placed on B will be taken account of fully.

These non-mutually exclusive alternatives are illustrative of the potential of government intervention. However, this also is not costless. How are the appropriate tax subsidy rates to be determined? How are regulation standards to be established and monitored? The government rejects market prices in dealing with the externality and hence must establish appropriate shadow prices to deal with the problem. Moreover, the costs of agreement between individuals on the proposed action cannot be ignored (and these will be explored in chapter 2). The transaction costs of government in dealing with market failure must then be set against the costs implied by leaving the market to deal with the problem (Arrow, 1971). It is naive to relate market failure to an automatic call for government action (Burkhead and Miner, 1971).

Public Goods

A pure public good has been defined as one 'which all enjoy in common in the sense that each individual's consumption of such a good leads to no subtraction from any other individual's consumption of that good' (Samuelson, 1954, p. 387). It differs then from private goods which 'can be parcelled out among different individuals' (Samuelson, 1954). Indeed, two major characteristics are implied by Samuelson's definition; non-rivalness in consumption and non price-exclusion. The former of these means that if the good is provided for one, it is provided for all individuals. Hence, in figure 1.8, to establish the total demand for the good, in a partial equilibrium context, it is necessary to aggregate vertically (over price), rather than horizontally (over output), as all will consume or value the same output simultaneously. The second characteristic (non price-exclusion) implies, however, that the demand curves shown in figure 1.8 would not be revealed by consumers. If the good is available irrespective of whether or not a price is paid, there is no incentive for consumers to reveal how much they would be willing

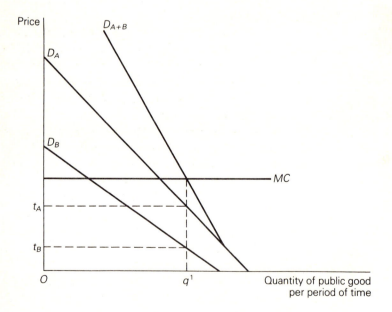

Figure 1.8 Provision of a public good

to pay for units of the good. Narrow self-interest suggests they try to 'ride free', i.e. consume the good without offering to pay.

Abstracting from the problems of the demand revelation it is clear that, in figure 1.8, the optimal output of the public good is Oq^1, where aggregate willingness to pay at the margin is equal to the marginal cost of provision. The clear implication of the characteristic of non-rivalness in consumption is that Pareto optimality requires not simply the general equilibrium condition that $MRS_{XY}^A = MRT_{XY}^B$ but (when X is a public good) that $\Sigma MRS_{XY} = MRT_{XY}$ for individuals 1, ... n. It is aggregate willingness to pay which equals MC in figure 1.8, whereas for a private good, each individual's willingness to pay (at the margin) equals MC. In figure 1.8 each individual would pay according to his marginal benefit from the good. Thus, individual A would pay a tax-price of t_A and individual B would pay a tax-price of t_B and thereby the (constant) marginal costs are covered.

The problems of demand revelation are, however, too formidable theoretically to dismiss. In the extreme scenario, where a large number of individuals are asked to contribute to the provision of a public good, the 'free rider' problem is apparent. In table 1.1 individual A is asked to contribute £1 towards the provision of a collective good, from which he stands to benefit to an amount of £5. The provision of the good depends upon others contributing their share also, and in the pay-off matrix it is clear that, for this individual, a strategy of non-contribution dominates a strategy of contribution. Since the good is non-excludable, the individual stands to gain as much if others cover the costs of provision of the good. If they do not, and the good is not provided, he will lose nothing by not contributing. Provided the individual deems his own action of no significance, his strategy is to attempt to free-ride on the contribution of others. However, if all behave in this way, no one will free-ride, as nothing will be provided (Buchanan, 1968).

If the 'free-rider' strategy is predicted for a pure public good then clearly the market will fail. If preferences are not revealed there will be no incentive to producers to provide the good. The state, with its ability to coerce tax contributions towards public goods, will appear the appropriate mechanism necessary for the financial provision of such goods. Yet once again the equation of public goods with a rationale for government action is naive in the extreme.

First, there is doubt that even in the extreme example described above, individuals would not reveal preferences. Experiments carried out with groups of individuals who are faced with such choices indicate a more honest revelation of preference than that predicted by theory

Table 1.1 Pay-off matrix: public good provision

Strategies	Others contribute; good provided	Others do not contribute; good not provided
Contribute	£(5−1)=£4	− £1
Not contribute	£5	0

(Bohm, 1971, 1972; Marwell and Ames, 1981). This is often termed 'free revelation' to contrast with 'free-riding'. Indeed, so persuasive is the evidence against the under-revelation of preferences that Johansen (1977, p. 147) notes: 'I do not know of many historical records or other empirical evidence which show convincingly that the problem of correct revelation of preferences has been of any practical significance'. Certainly it has been the case that examples of public goods, e.g. lighthouses, have in fact been privately provided (Coase, 1974). Second, the general nature of this response to free-riding is made clear when it is realized that the example discussed above is an extreme one. It is the case in the example that the good is either produced or not produced, and hence the contribution of the individual will have no effect if the latter outcome ensues. Yet, if this 'lumpiness in production' is replaced with the assumption that small contributions permit a marginal increase in output, the prediction for non-contribution is less robust (Chamberlin, 1974). In similar vein, there is the joint contract hypothesis which recognizes that public goods are excludable *ex-ante*. If individuals are told that the good will not be provided unless the funds, including their share, are forthcoming *before* the project is started, then the possibility of riding free diminishes, and they are likely to contribute.

    Finally, one of the most important criticisms of Samuelson's (1954) definition of a public good was that, as defined, no such good actually existed (Margolis, 1955). The ensuing debate indicated that while pure public goods may be an extreme, goods may yet possess elements of publicness (Samuelson, 1969). Thus, goods may possess characteristics of non-price exclusiveness or non-rivalness in consumption. For example, theatres may be non-rival in consumption below capacity limits, but even so are price-exclusive (see for example, Head, 1962; Peston, 1972). When it is realized that such goods can be provided by consumption sharing arrangements, or 'clubs', it is clear that the automatic necessity for state involvement is called into question. Buchanan (1965) outlines the requirement for efficiency of clubs, and Sandler and Tschirhart (1980) review this approach.

The result of these contributions throws doubt on the significance of free-riding and suggests a more pragmatic response for government. When the transactions costs of dealing satisfactorily with such goods voluntarily in the private sector are less than those incurred by government, the intrusion of the state is uncalled for. We take the question of the free-rider problem further in Appendix 1A, where recent literature on solving the 'free-rider' problem is introduced.

Increasing Returns to Scale and Market Structure

The existence of increasing returns to scale poses a problem for market provision. In figure 1.9 the costs of providing a particular good are illustrated. As increasing returns to scale are assumed, the average cost

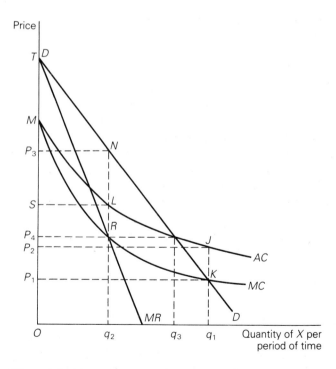

Figure 1.9 Marginal cost pricing and increasing returns to scale

slopes downward and marginal costs are everywhere below average cost. It is clear that, whilst Pareto optimality requires price equal to marginal cost, in figure 1.9 such a pricing policy will imply losses for the producer. A price of OP_1 per unit implies a total revenue of OP_1Kq_1 but a total cost of OP_2Jq_1 (i.e. a loss of $P_1P_2JK_1$). To constrain producers to such a pricing rule is to imply maximum losses, rather than maximum profits, for producers. Such a good would not be provided in this scenario, despite the fact that consumers would benefit by more than it costs in total to produce Oq_1. The cost of producing Oq_1 is equal to the integral of the MC function between O and q_1 (i.e. area $OMKq_1$). The total benefit of Oq_1 is equal to the area under the demand curve between O and q_1 (i.e. area $OTKq_1$).

The alternative response of producers is to re-organize and produce the good at an output level which permits profits to be made. If producers grouped to acquire monopoly control of the output of good X, then an output level of Oq_2 and a price of OP_3 might be selected. It will be clear that such a point is determined by the intersection of the marginal cost (MC) and marginal revenue (MR) curves. Profits are now possible and maximized in this new setting (i.e. profits equal SP_3NL). However, the market has now 'failed by structure' (Bator, 1958). The intervention of monopoly is associated with allocative deadweight losses and these are equal to triangle RNK in figure 1.9. They arise because output of good X falls short of the optimal output. For each successive unit of output between q_2 and q_1, consumers would pay more than the marginal costs incurred by production. A similar objection applies to average cost pricing at OP_4 and Oq_3. Normal profits are made but the output is inefficiently low.

The problem here described may be dealt with by government activity in a variety of forms. For example, the good may be produced by a nationalized corporation and sold at marginal cost. Losses made could then be covered by a government subsidy. Again, however, there are complications. If the subsidy is raised by taxation then, given that taxes distort prices elsewhere, allocative losses in other markets may arise. Again, *a priori*, it is not clear that such government involvement is appropriate if distortions exist in other markets. The example highlights the problem in welfare economics of the 'second-best theorem' which was noted above (Lipsey and Lancaster, 1954). When some of the marginal equivalences are disturbed in the scenario, it is difficult to say, *a priori*, whether this situation has a higher or lower welfare than another situation in which other marginal equivalences are violated.

When a policy of nationalization and correction of the price of X is not possible, the continued existence of the private monopoly in provision of X may call for a response in the pricing policy adopted for goods in the public sector. Indeed, this response of government illustrates how the theory of second-best invokes piecemeal public policy decision-taking. If X is produced in the private sector and, as in figure 1.9, priced above marginal cost (i.e. OP_3) then how should government react when deciding the price of good Y which is a substitute produced in the public sector. The simple advice of pricing Y at marginal cost is redundant in a 'second-best world', i.e. where X is not priced at MC. The solution to this problem (see Webb, 1976) involves an allowance for the degree to which the goods are substitutes. Broadly speaking, if X is priced 'too highly' in the private sector then Y must be priced above MC to correct the distortion of 'too great' a resource allocation to industry Y. The precise response of government in a 'second-best' world demands allowance for distortions elsewhere in the economy. The simple rules generated in section 1.2 need considerable modification. This must take place in response to hard empirical evidence concerning the problem to be dealt with.

The existence of increasing returns to scale, and the implied problems of market structure, produces an apparent rationale for government intervention. However, the form and extent of intervention is once again by no means obvious.

Uncertainty

Uncertainty is an ever-present aspect of everyday life, but not necessarily of economic theory. Arrow (1970) has managed to show that in a world of complete contingency or insurance markets, universal perfect competition will generate a Pareto optimum. Basically, individuals will trade not in actual commodities but coupons that are contingent upon the actual state of the world that happens to arise. With N types of goods and S possible states of the world that can arise, there are $N \times S$ possible contingent claims in which to deal, e.g. sunglasses if sunny state 17 arises, umbrella if rainy state 19 arises. Although markets exhibit some avenues by which individuals can avoid the burden of risk by buying insurance, e.g. life insurance, such markets are not complete. The reasons cited for this are that such markets would be very costly to organize relative to the gains secured. Additionally, the analysis of the effects of insurance on individual behaviour is complex, making the design of insurance policies a far from straightforward matter. Whatever the reasons, the fact that risk is not fully insurable in a market economy may give rise to a case for government intervention.

It has to be noted that some commentators would view this conception of uncertainty as inadequate (e.g. Wiseman, 1980). The major objection to the above is that having S possible states of the world makes the future knowable. True uncertainty, it is argued, is about states of the world occurring that are not expected because they cannot be conceived of in advance. (Hey (1979) deals extensively with the micro-economics of uncertainty.)

1.4   VALUE JUDGEMENT AND MARKET FAILURE

In the section above, what might be termed 'technical' sources of market failure were discussed. The goods, services and activities that generate specific problems for market provision were outlined. However, it is possible that, even in the absence of such phenomena, the market may be considered to have failed if it is associated with an unacceptable distribution of income, or with an inappropriate provision of particular goods which are considered 'merit goods'. Such arguments beg the question of what is the 'right' distribution of income and what are 'merit goods'. In answer to these questions it is necessary to invoke 'additional' normative judgements than those implied by the Paretian framework.

To determine the correct distribution of income is a problem fraught with difficulty. Each individual may have his or her own conception of the 'right' distribution of welfare between individuals (or groups of individuals) in society. We may refer to a *social welfare function* as an explicit statement that welfare (W) is considered by individuals to depend upon a distribution of utilities between individuals, i.e. for individual i, $Wi = f(U_1 \ldots U_n)$ were $U_1 \ldots U_n$ refers to the utilities of n individuals in society. Some individuals, for example, may feel better off in a society which is egalitarian as far as the distribution of welfare is concerned. However, the difficulty of constructing *for society* an acceptable social welfare function by an aggregation of *individuals'* social welfare functions via an appropriate constitution remains a vexed question (Arrow, 1963).

Whilst determining the 'correct' distribution of income remains a challenge, governments in office may hold positions on the existing distribution of income. Whether or not governments adequately reflect individuals' preferences, they certainly express their position explicitly and implicitly in policies which affect the distribution of income. They also express their view on whether goods and activities are particularly 'merit-worthy'. In this way dissatisfaction may arise with market provision because either different or additional normative positions have been taken from those inherent in Pareto optimality. It has been stated that Pareto optimality is consistent with any income distribution. Theoretically this was shown in section 1.2, but in practice the need to attain a certain distribution of income may entail a departure from the efficiency conditions of Pareto optimality. Indeed, maintenance of the efficiency goal via market provision may be to the detriment of the achievement of a specific equity goal. It is appropriate, therefore, to devote consideration to the concepts of 'equity' and 'merit wants'.

(a)   *Equity* is a difficult issue within economic analysis. The Paretian value judgements discussed in section 1.1 define what economists understand by efficiency. They avoided taking a specific position on inter-personal comparison of welfare, which is the heart of the definition of equity. Universal perfect competition (in the absence of technical market failure) generated a top-level efficient economy in which it is impossible to make one person better off with no-one else worse off. Unfortunately, it was also clear that there were a very wide range of allocations that met this condition; one corresponding to each distribution of final utility levels for the individuals that make up society. In short, to determine both an efficient and equitable economy requires the adoption of an additional value judgement about what constitutes equity. However, although there are many suggestions about the 'optimal' distribution of income (utilities) no single principle has found common acceptance. Tresch (1981) points out that 'Economists have all too often assumed away distributional problems in order to analyse more comfortable allocation issues, knowing full well that dichotomizing allocational and distributional policies is not legitimate' (p. 9). Indeed, efficiency and equity issues overlap in a number of fashions. For example, the atmosphere created in society by the existing distribution of income is a non-rival, non-excludable good/bad, i.e. it is a pure public good. Additionally, any unilateral attempt by an individual to alter the distribution of income creates knowledge that the poor have been helped. This is non-excludable, raising the spectre of individuals 'free-riding' in distributional matters. Any attempt by the government to enact redistribution on equity grounds is almost certain to have efficiency costs.

The government does not have the ability to set initial allocations of factors of production to individuals, so that when the competitive process runs its course – and factor prices, etc., are determined – both equity and efficiency are achieved. Instead the government has to work on the income distribution *ex-post*. Taxes and transfers that are not lump sum, however, distort the relative prices faced by the individuals and thereby distort their utility-maximizing choices. This represents inefficiency. Efficient allocation may be unequitable, whereas moves towards equity generate inefficiency; hence these twin criteria are typically at odds with one another and cannot be treated in isolation. If, for example, a government wishes to assist one section of society, it may reject the market efficiency condition of marginal-cost pricing and provide the goods to these individuals at a lower price. It will seek to pursue an equity goal and hopefully minimize the efficiency losses associated with departure from the efficiency conditions.

Introducing equity as a criterion provides a case for in-kind or cash redistribution, through the agency of the government. However, there is little consensus on what equity is or indeed, if actual government policies increase or decrease equity on any given definition. Such equity-increasing policies as exist are generally identified in Western democracies with the operation of welfare states. A major criticism of welfare states as far as the libertarians are concerned is that such activities are inimical to individual freedom. This criticism is considered in detail in chapter 10.

(b) *Merit wants*, a concept introduced by Musgrave (1959), deals with situations 'where public policy aims at an allocation of resources which *deviates* from that which is reflected by consumer sovereignty' (p. 9, emphasis ours). As stated, such wants challenge the value judgement that individuals are the best judge of their own welfare. As Mishan (1981) points out, this proposition may be adopted for several reasons. It may be thought to be a fact. It may be thought of as a moral or ethical statement, involving the judgement that we ought to act as if it were true. Finally, it may be thought of as a piece of political expediency. If democracy recognizes individual voters, should not the market recognize individual consumers as the source of legitimacy? As far as economics is concerned, relatively little attention is directed at this issue. As a guesstimate, the majority of economists probably have the factual interpretation of the consumer being the best judge of his or her own welfare. Although this may appear obvious to many, Mooney (1979) points out that there may be much more involved. He unpacks the judgement into three questions:

1   Does the individual think he ought to be a sovereign consumer?
2   Does the individual think he is able to be a sovereign consumer?
3   Does the individual want to be a sovereign consumer?

Limited or no information may be the reason for answering 'no' to the first question. Potential mental illness or other personal damage may constitute a reason for saying 'no' to the second question, even if the first is answered positively. Decision-making costs, broadly defined to include not only the collection and assessment of information, but also the fear that a decision is 'too big', may make an individual reply 'no' to the third question, even if he/she replies positively to the first two. Hence, information arguments, consumer rationality arguments and/or consumer delegation arguments may support the concept of merit wants and a case for government intervention. Although Musgrave sees the concept as one of imposed decisions, if the individual voluntarily delegates that choice to another (government), then the concept need not be viewed as an imposed one.

However the academic debate as to whether merit wants can be made consistent with the conventional paradigm is resolved, the fact remains that governments do not see its role as simply to reflect individual preferences. The Paretian value judgements define the game only for a certain type of economics. It cannot, therefore, always be expected to be consistent with all that happens in the real world. The implication of merit wants may be that governments constrain the choices of individuals in the market, or that governments pursue a policy of educating consumers.

Stilwell (1975) notes how the twentieth century has been dominated by the (mainstream/orthodox/neo-classical) school of thought identified with the value judgements discussed above. He suggests that a better approach might be to specify a broad set of evaluative criteria and then try and specify trade-offs between them. He quotes four criteria from the literature of the radical political economists, to which he adds two of his own. The list comprises: material well-being; equity; responsiveness of institutions to human needs and historical character-istics of a society; human development; community development and harmony of man in his natural environment. Despite the existence of this broader alternative framework the fact remains that the Leviathan literature which is the subject-matter of this book lies firmly in the mainstream tradition. Failure to develop contrary or modifying arguments within this tradition leaves scope for separate literatures on the same subject to co-exist, and disciples of each never to confront each other. For this reason, if for no other, the current writing is also in the mainstream micro-economic/welfare economics tradition.

1.5   SUMMARY AND CONCLUSIONS

The objectives of this chapter have been to acquaint the reader with concepts and techniques widely used in micro-economics or to revise the reader's understanding, as well as to analyze the causes of market failure. Whilst it is clear that for many reasons markets can fail to determine an 'efficient' allocation, the discussion has, however, left a question mark over the appropriate response of government. The equation of market failure with a rationale for government intervention of a specific form is seldom obvious. The costs involved in government activity must enter the discussion.

In the following chapter the costs of government action are explored in greater detail. The failure of government accurately to reflect individuals' wishes is seen to arise as a result of deficiencies within the constitution, the political party system and the executive branch of government. In addition, derivation of appropriate shadow prices for market correction has been shown itself to be a costly procedure.

Within the literature on resource allocation, attention must also be directed towards the value judgement issues of equity and merit wants, as these may motivate much of government intervention in actual market economics. Although the traditional government reactions to the deficiencies of market failure are now often considered over-reactions, with direct government finance and production of a good or service being particularly criticized, a balance has to be struck. An imperfect market has to be compared with an imperfect government sector. The remainder of this book deals with the imperfections laid at the door of the government/public sector, and tries to argue they have been over-stated in recent years. (In the same way as the initial market failure writing is now viewed as an over-stated case.) In addition, given that the *status quo* in Western democracies is a mixed economy with a significant public sector, the case for increasing the role of the market has to be justified against that background, and it is here that a recognition of an imperfect market is important (see especially chapter 8).

1.1A   APPENDIX: SOLVING THE FREE-RIDER PROBLEM

Until the advent of the 1970s the treatment of public goods was incomplete in that, although their definition and efficiency conditions were well documented, the 'free-rider' problem meant that drawing marginal benefit curves or preference maps for public goods was purely conjecture. However, the recent literature on preference revelation and public goods makes it clear that there is a mechanism by which individuals can be induced to state their preferences truthfully. In the past this was thought to be especially unlikely in the large number case, when individual non-revelation could be predicted to have little impact on the total level of provision of the public good. The purpose of this appendix is to link up simplified diagrammatic versions of what have become known as Clarke–Groves preference revelation mechanisms with Coase's theorem as an exposition of why such mechanisms work (see Clarke (1971), Groves (1973), Tideman and Tullock (1976) and Coase (1960)).

Recent textbooks on public finance and welfare economics contain diagrammatic versions of the Clarke–Groves mechanism along the following lines (see Boadway, 1979 and Ng, 1979, for example). To keep the notation simple, marginal benefit (MB) and marginal cost (MC) curves are designated: 'All' if they correspond to the whole of the society that is concerned with provision of an optimal quantity of public good; 'Others' if they refer to that society excluding the one individual whose Clarke–Groves tax is being determined; 'Me' if they represent the curves of the individual whose Clarke–Groves tax is being determined. The scene opens with all individuals having been assigned a share of the cost of the public good such that MC Me + MC Others = MC All, and the latter covers the full cost of provision of the public good (assumed to be produced under conditions of constant returns to scale in figure 1.A1). Individuals are then asked to (in partial equilibrium) write down their marginal benefit curves in the knowledge they will pay their marginal cost shares plus a Clarke–Groves tax determined by the information they provide. As will be illustrated below, individuals have an incentive to provide honest information. Once the reported marginal benefit curves have been summed vertically to give MB All and equated with MC All, the equilibrium quantity of public good is determined at OQ All in figure 1.A1.

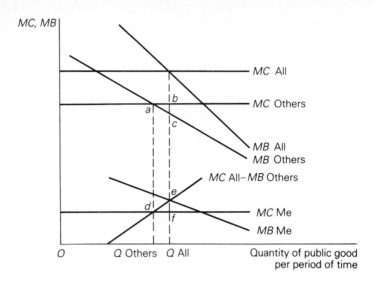

Figure 1.A1 Conventional diagrammatic solution to the 'free-rider' problem

The Clarke–Groves tax for each individual is computed by subtracting *MB* Others from *MC* Others, yielding triangle *abc* in figure 1.A1 as the appropriate tax for 'Me'. It is not to be forgotten that he also pays *MC* Me for each unit of public good in addition.

The determination of the appropriate Clarke–Groves tax can also be seen in the lower part of figure 1.A1 where *MB* Me and (*MC* All–*MB* Others) are plotted. The latter curve is effectively 'Me's' marginal cost curve for the provision of the public good beyond *OQ* Others, the quantity that would be chosen by 'Others' in a world that excludes 'Me' and the need for his tax share. When this effective marginal cost curve is equated with *MB* Me, *OQ* All is again the optimal solution and the Clarke–Groves tax is again the difference between *MB* Others and *MC* Others = *MC* All – *MB* Others – *MC* Me = triangle *def* (= triangle *abc*).

Why does the mechanism of the Clarke–Groves tax lead to honest preference relevation? Consider figure 1.A2 which has the quantity of public good plotted on the horizontal axis and net marginal (dis)benefit curves on the vertical axis. The curve labelled Net *MB* Me is derived by subtracting *MC* Me from *MB* Me in figure 1.A1, whereas the positively sloped curve Net *MD* Others represents the values of the

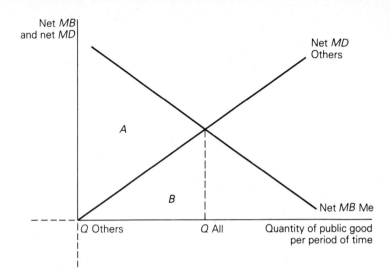

Figure 1.A2 The heart of the matter

net marginal disbenefit to 'Others' of the different levels of provision of the public good and is *MC* Others–*MB* Others from figure 1.A1. The origin is now *Q* Others, the quantity of public good that 'Others' would choose in a world without 'Me' and the need for his cost contribution. The effect of including 'Me' and his tax share in the decision is to move the choice from *Q* Others to *Q* All. This is the optimal solution because the Clarke–Groves tax forces 'Me' to compensate 'Others' for the cost he imposes on them by shifting the collective decision (in either direction).

Below *Q* All he can happily do this, because his consumer surplus gain area *A* plus *B* exceeds the size of the Clarke–Groves tax B. Extending public goods provision one unit beyond *Q* All would involve 'Me' in a marginal Clarke–Groves tax above Net *MB* Me. A similar consequence would follow from over-stating his preference in general, whereas under-statement would lead to 'Me' failing to secure some additional net benefits even after paying the necessary Clarke–Groves taxes, i.e. 'Me' makes himself worse off both by over- and under-statement of his true preferences.

Set up in this way, the correspondence with the familiar 'butterfly' diagram of the Coase's theorem (see figure 1.6) is apparent. The latter states that, for small number externality cases, individual maximizing behaviour will generate the efficient allocation of resources irrespective of the assignment of property rights provided transactions/bargaining costs are near zero. In short, the preference-revealing mechanisms for public goods work because they succeed in placing each individual in a small number externality situation with property rights over the decision as to the optimal level of provision of the public good being assigned to 'Others'. Hence, public good preferences revelation can be interpreted as a series of Coase outcomes with only two parties, 'Me' and 'Others'. It is a question of 'Me' always compensating 'Others' for the external costs imposed by including *MB* Me and *MC* Me in the overall calculation.

NOTES

1   It should be noted that these three conditions for Pareto optimality relate to a *closed* economy. In the case of an open economy reference would be made to the marginal rate of transformation through foreign trade (MRT^f) as distinct from the marginal rate of transformation domestically (MRT^d). The marginal rate of transformation through foreign trade is given by the world price ratio (P_w–P_w). In figure 1.10n the Pareto optimal conditions for a small open economy are illustrated. Production occurs at P_1 on the production possibility curve but consumption occurs at C_1 (with P_1K of good Y exported in return for KC_1 of good X). Welfare is maximized, in Paretian terms, with the fourth condition that $MRT^d = MRT^f = MRS$. In figure 1.10n the community indifference curve is tangential to the world price ratio at C_1 (i.e. $MRS = MRT^f$) and also to the production possibility curve at P_1 (i.e. $MRT^f = MRT^d$). For an open economy Pareto optimality demands that this fourth condition must be added to those of production efficiency, exchange efficiency and top-level efficiency. In figure 1.10n the position of welfare maximum for a closed economy clearly occurs at P,C on community indifference curve I^0. The fact that trade enables the country to move from I^0 to I^1 indicates that trade offers a *potential* Pareto improvement. As income distributional effects would be associated in adjusting to trade (e.g. the movement in production from P to P_1) the movement may not be an actual Pareto improvement but is a *potential* Pareto improvement. (A *potential* Pareto improvement requires that gainers from a change would benefit sufficiently to be able to compensate losers, but such (costless) redistribution from gainers to losers need only be hypothetical and need not actually occur.)

2   Take a typical production function, $Qx = f(K,L)$. The firm which profit-maximizes wishes to produce any output level Q^* as cheaply as it can.

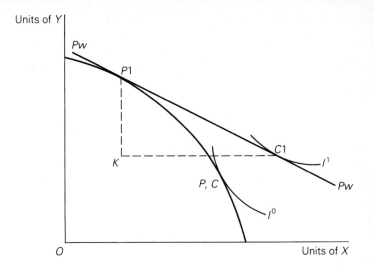

Figure 1.10n Pareto optimality in a small open economy

Total expenditure on inputs equal $p_kK + P_lL$ (where P_k is the price of capital and P_l the price of labour). This total cost M can be minimized by the mathematical procedure of obtaining the Lagrangian expression for a constrained minimization problem, i.e.

$$M = P_kK + P_lL + \lambda[f(K,L) - Q^*] \tag{1.1}$$

$$\partial M/\partial K = P_k + \lambda\partial f/\partial K = 0 \tag{1.2}$$

$$\partial M/\partial L = P_l + \lambda\partial f/\partial L = 0 \tag{1.3}$$

i.e. to minimize costs for producing Q^*

$$P_k + \lambda\partial f/\partial K = P_l + \lambda\partial f/\partial L = 0 \tag{1.4}$$

or

$$P_k/P_l = \partial f/\partial K/\partial f/\partial L \tag{1.5}$$

Hence the firm equates the ratio of marginal products ($\partial f/\partial K/\partial f/\partial L$) or the marginal rate of technical substitution to the factor price ratio.

3   Consumers will maximize a utility function ($U = u(X,Y)$) subject to the budget they have to allocate on the two goods. This budget is $B = P_xX + P_yY$ (where P_x is the price of X and P_y the price of Y so that $B - P_xX - P_yY = 0$). The first-order conditions for the constrained maximization are:

$$Z = u(XY) + \lambda(B - P_xX - P_yY) \tag{1.6}$$

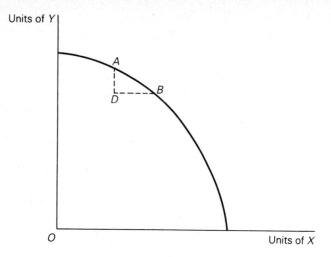

Figure 1.11n   Marginal cost and the marginal rate of transformation

$$\partial Z/\partial X = \partial u/\partial X + \lambda P_x = 0 \qquad (1.7)$$

$$\partial Z/\partial Y = \partial u/\partial Y + \lambda P_y = 0 \qquad (1.8)$$

Hence, to maximize utility $(\partial u/\partial X/\partial u/\partial Y)$ – the marginal rate of substitution – is equal to P_x/P_y – the price ratio.

4   In figure 1.11n consider a movement from A to B. Full employment exists at both points on the frontier. Therefore

AD (units of Y) × marginal cost of Y = BD (units of X)
× marginal cost of X. $\qquad (1.9)$

By substitution:

$$AD/BD = MC_X/MC_Y \qquad (1.10)$$

But AD/BD = slope of the production frontier (i.e. equals the marginal rate of transformation).

5   A standard micro-economic text will confirm that, at equilibrium, the firm in perfect competition will set output such that MC = price. In perfect competition, revenue equals price (p) times output sold (q). Total cost depends upon fixed costs (b) and variable costs (Φq). To maximize profits (π):

$$\pi = pq - \Phi(q) - b \qquad (1.11)$$

$$\mathrm{d}\pi/\mathrm{d}q = p - \Phi'(q) = 0 \qquad (1.12)$$

$$p = \Phi'(q) \qquad (1.13)$$

i.e. price equals marginal cost (see, for example, Henderson and Quandt, 1971).

6 See Henderson and Quandt, 1971, pp. 108–21.

7 The demand curve may be drawn under either the assumption that money income is constant or that real income is constant. If we are to interpret willingness to pay as the maximum sum which an individual would offer for units of a good, then the relevant sum will be the most he can pay and *still maintain his real income*. Hence the assumption that real income is constant. Throughout the money income constant demand curve, real income itself is changing as the individual receives an 'income effect' at being offered the good at successively lower prices.

8 The necessary conditions for Pareto optimality are obtained by maximizing the consumer's utility function subject to the transformation function. Following Nath (1969) let x stand for both goods (i to s) and also factors of production ($s + 1$ to n). From the Lagrangian

$$L = U(x, \ldots x_n) - t(q, \ldots q_n) \qquad (1.14)$$

a necessary condition for a maximum is

$$\frac{\partial U/\partial x_i}{\partial U/\partial x_n} = \frac{\partial t/\partial x_i}{\partial t/\partial x_n} \, (i = 1, \ldots n) \qquad (1.15)$$

But if in the economy,

$$\frac{\partial U/\partial x_i}{\partial U/\partial x_n} = k \frac{\partial t/\partial x_i}{\partial t/\partial x_n} \quad \text{where } k \neq 1 \qquad (1.16)$$

then the first-order consideration for a welfare maximum becomes:

$$\partial U/\partial x_i - \lambda \partial t/\partial x_i - \pi \left[\frac{\partial U/\partial x_n \partial^2 U/\partial x_1 \cdot \partial x_i - \partial U/\partial x_1 \cdot \partial^2 U/\partial x_n \partial x_i}{(\partial U/\partial x_n)^2} \right.$$

$$\left. - k \frac{\partial t/\partial x_n \cdot \partial^2 t/\partial x_1 \partial x_i - \partial t/\partial x_1 \cdot \partial^2 t/\partial x_n \partial x_i}{(\partial t/\partial x_n)^2} \right] = 0 \qquad (1.17)$$

As nothing is known, *a priori*, about the signs of the cross partial derivatives it is impossible to establish general rules about how the original maximization conditions should be modified.

9 Amongst the points noted by Lipsey and Lancaster (1956) are the following:
   (a) there is no point in saying that more Paretian conditions hold in one situation than in another; this has no welfare significance;
   (b) there is no, *a priori*, possibility of evaluating the situation when all departures from the optimum condition are in the same direction;
   (c) second-best may require all Paretian conditions to be distorted.

10 Turvey (1971) defines the new pricing rule as:

$$p_i = m_i - \sum_{j \neq i} \frac{\partial x_j}{\partial p_i} \cdot \frac{\partial p_i}{\partial x_i} (p_j - m_j) \qquad (1.18)$$

j is the substitute for i. If the effect of a fall in demand for x_i is an increase in demand for x_j,

$$\frac{\partial x_j}{\partial p_i} \cdot \frac{\partial p_i}{\partial x_i}$$

is *itself* negative, i.e. good j substitutes for good i. The effect of the last term in the above expression is therefore to lead the optimal p_i to exceed m_i when $p_j > m_j$. The reverse is true if good j were defined as complement to good i. The application of this formula obviously requires particular information beyond that implied by a general rule.

REFERENCES

Arrow, K. J. (1963), *Social Choice and Individual Values*, 2nd edn, New Haven and London: Yale University Press.
Arrow, K. J. (1970), *Essays in the Theory of Risk Bearing*, Amsterdam: North Holland.
Arrow, K. J. (1971), The organisation of economic activity: issues pertinent to the choice of market versus non-market allocation, pp. 59–73 in Haveman, R. H. and Margolis, J. (eds), *Public Expenditure and Policy Analysis*, Chicago: Markham.
Bator, F. M. (1958), The anatomy of market failure, *Quarterly Journal of Economics*, vol. 72, no. 288, pp. 351–79.
Boadway, R. W. (1979), *Public Sector Economics*, Cambridge, Mass.: Winthrop.
Bohm, P. (1971), An approach to the problem of estimating the demand for public goods, *Swedish Journal of Economics*, vol. 73 (March), pp. 55–66.
Bohm, P. (1972), Estimating demand for public goods: an experiment, *European Economic Review*, vol. 3, no. 2, pp. 111–30.
Buchanan, J. M. (1959), Positive economics, welfare economics, and political economy, *Journal of Law and Economics*, vol. 2 (October), 124–38.
Buchanan, J. M. (1965), An economic theory of clubs, *Economica*, vol. 32, no. 125 (February), pp. 1–14.
Buchanan, J. M. (1968), *The Demand and Supply of Public Goods*, Chicago: Rand McNally.
Buchanan, J. M. and Stubblebine, W. C. (1962), Externality, *Economica*, vol. 29, no. 116 (November), pp. 371–84.
Burkhead, J. and Miner, J. (1971), *Public Expenditure*, London: Macmillan.
Chamberlain, J. (1974), Provision of collective goods as a function of group size, *American Political Science Review*, vol. 68, no. 2 (June), pp. 707–16.

Clarke, E. H. (1971), Multipart pricing for public goods, *Public Choice*, vol. 11 (Fall), pp. 17–33.

Coase, R. (1960), The problem of social cost, *Journal of Law and Economics*, vol. 3 (October), pp. 1–44.

Coase, R. (1974), The lighthouse in economics, *Journal of Law and Economics*, vol. 17 (October), pp. 357–76.

Davis, O. A. and Kamien, M. I. (1971), Externalities, information and alternative collective action, pp. 74–95 in Haveman, R. H. and Margolis, J. (eds), *Public Expenditure and Policy Analysis*, Chicago: Markham.

Groves, T. (1973), Incentives in teams, *Econometrica*, vol. 41, no. 4 (July), pp. 617–33.

Head, J. G. (1962), Public goods and public policy, *Public Finance/Finances Publiques*, vol. 17, no. 3, pp. 197–219.

Henderson, J. M. and Quandt, R. E. (1971), *Microeconomic Theory: a Mathematical Approach*, 2nd edn, Tokyo: McGraw-Hill.

Hey, J. D. (1979), *Uncertainty in Microeconomics*, Oxford: Martin Robertson.

Johansen, L. (1977), The theory of public goods: misplaced emphasis, *Journal of Public Economics*, vol. 7, no. 1 (February), pp. 147–52.

Lipsey, R. and Lancaster, K. (1956), General theory of second best, *Review of Economic Studies*, vol. 24, no. 63, pp. 11–32.

Margolis, J. (1955), A comment on the pure theory of public expenditure, *Review of Economics and Statistics*, vol. 37, no. 4 (November), pp. 347–9.

Marwell, G. and Ames, R. E. (1981), Economists free ride, does anyone else? Experiments on the provision of public goods, IV, *Journal of Public Economics*, vol. 15, no. 3 (June), pp. 295–310.

Mishan, E. J. (1981), *Introduction to Normative Economics*, Oxford: Oxford University Press.

Mishan, E. J. (1982), *Cost–Benefit Analysis*. 3rd edn, London: George Allen & Unwin.

Mooney, G. H. (1979), Values in health care, pp. 23–44 in Lee, K. (ed.). *Economics and Health Planning*, London: Croom Helm.

Musgrave, R. A. (1959), *The Theory of Public Finance*, New York: McGraw-Hill.

Nath, S. K. (1969), *The Reappraisal of Welfare Economics*, London: Routledge & Kegan Paul.

Ng, Y. K. (1979), *Welfare Economics*, Basingstoke and London: Macmillan.

Peston, M. (1972), *Public Goods and the Public Sector*, London: Macmillan.

Pigou, A. C. (1924), *The Economics of Welfare*, 2nd edn, London: Macmillan.

Rees, R. (1976), *Public Enterprise Economics*. London: Weidenfeld & Nicolson.

Rowley, C. K. and Peacock, A. T. (1975), *Welfare Economics A Liberal Restatement*, London: Martin Robertson.

Samuelson, P. (1954), The pure theory of public expenditure, *Review of Economics and Statistics*, vol. 36, no. 4 (November), pp. 387–9.

Samuelson, P. (1969), Pure theory of public expenditure and taxation. pp. 98–123, in Margolis, J. and Guitton, H. (eds), *Public Economics*, New York: St Martin's Press.

Sandler, T. and Tschirhart, J. T. (1980), The economic theory of clubs: an evaluative survey, *Journal of Economic Literature*, vol. 18, no. 4 (December), pp. 1481–1521.

Stilwell, F. J. B. (1975), *Normative Economics*, Oxford: Pergamon.

Sugden, R. and Weale, A. (1979), A contractual reformulation of certain aspects of welfare economics, *Economica*, vol. 46, no. 182 (May), pp. 111–23.

Tideman, T. N. and Tullock, G. (1976), A new and superior process for making social choices, *Journal of Political Economy*, vol. 84, no. 6 (December), pp. 1145–59.

Tresch, R. W. (1981), *Public Finance: A Normative Theory*, Plano, Texas: Business Publications.

Turvey, R. (1971), *Economic Analysis and Public Enterprises*, London: George Allen & Unwin.

Webb, M. G. (1976), *Pricing Policies for Public Enterprises*, London: Macmillan.

Wellisz, S. (1964), On external diseconomies and the government assisted invisible hand, *Economica*, vol. 31, no. 124 (November), pp. 345–62.

Wiseman, J. (1980), Costs and Decisions, pp. 473–90 in Currie, D. A. and Peters, W. (eds), *Contemporary Economic Analysis*, vol. 2, London: Croom Helm.

2

Governmental Failure: a Rationale for Market Provision?

2.1 INTRODUCTION

The purpose of chapter 1 was to introduce the basic arguments presented under the collective heading of market failure. This literature suggests that the competitive market place can be inefficient and/or 'inequitable'. By and large the implication was that markets would often produce 'too little' of some goods and services. In contrast the basic implication of so-called governmental or non-market failure is that frequently 'too much' of public sector activities are provided. The literature that deals with this topic comes under the heading of 'public choice'[1] and centres on the inefficiencies and/or inequities that can be traced to collective decision-making and public sector provision. It is the public sector analogue of private sector market failure. Historically, this more recent literature (mainly dating from the late 1960s and 1970s) was developed as an antidote to the belief that, if the market can be shown to be working less than perfectly, then governmental intervention can automatically improve the situation. The fundamental point is that governmental intervention in an economy introduces its own costs, which may outweigh the costs of simply living with an imperfect market. The basic policy question becomes which is the lesser of the two evils; a less than perfect market outcome or a less than perfect government outcome. The sources of the imperfections in the government outcome can be traced to the cost–benefit framework, which individual actors find themselves confronted with in the public sector. The elements in this framework form the substance of this chapter, and are considered under headings relating to the actors involved. Though much of this literature involves the relationship between government failure and 'too large' a public sector, it is conceivable that some aspects of governmental failure might produce the reverse conclusion (e.g. Downs, 1960). At this stage our main concern is the *source* of governmental failure and the implications for public sector *growth* will be more fully developed later.

2.2　VOTING AND COLLECTIVE DECISIONS

Methods of making collective decisions can be viewed as taking place along a spectrum varying from no-one in the collectivity having a say in the outcome to all having to agree on the same outcome. A fully detailed voting rule has at least three aspects: rules about who can vote; rules for determining what issues will be voted on; rules for deciding what constitutes a winning issue. Although casual thought may dismiss a voting procedure as an obvious and neutral mechanism, this is the opposite of the truth. The rules chosen for these three aspects of voting have a very great impact on the final collective decision that is arrived at. It is not surprising, therefore, that voting has both a large and complex literature within economics. Here, there is space only to consider a small part of the results associated with the third of the aspects listed above.

Chart 2.1 is a slightly embellished version of a figure in Hyman (1973). A collective decision that corresponds to zero CVs (consumer voters) taking part might be exemplified by a defeated country whose collective decisions are imposed from outside. An alternative example would be a society that is organized around a set of traditions which are simply inherited from one generation to the next. When all CVs have to agree on the same outcome before it can be sanctioned as the collective choice the unanimity rule applies. Half of all CVs plus one represent a simple majority rule. Between a simple majority rule and unanimity rule are all forms of majority rule, e.g. a two-thirds majority is required in both houses of Congress to propose a constitutional change in the USA, and the proposal then has to be ratified by three-quarters of the states or at a special ratifying convention by two-thirds of states. If half or fewer CVs can carry a collective decision, then a minority rule applies.

The collective decision-making rule that corresponds to Pareto optimality is unanimity. The only collective decisions accepted must make at least one person better off and no-one worse off. In effect,

Chart 2.1   Costs and the degree of inclusiveness of collective decision rules

Efficiency costs	Proportion of CVs	Decision-making costs
Zero	All of CVs: unanimity	Tend toward infinity
	Proximate unanimity	
	$\frac{2}{3}$ CVs: Two-thirds majority	
	$\frac{CVs}{2} + 1$: Simple majority	
	1CV: King, dictator, etc.	
Tend toward infinity	OCV: Foreign power, set of traditions	Zero

every CV has a veto. (For the moment, assume the context is one in which a collective decision involves all CVs knowing what their cost share of any proposal is and what they stand to gain if the vote is carried.) If unanimity has the 'efficiency' property, the question arises as to why it is not a regular feature of modern societies. There are several reasons that are part of the answer. First, although it might be reasonable to assume no-one needs to be worse off for allocative decisions in the public sector, the same is not true of redistributive ones. The object of redistribution is to make some individuals better off at the expense of others. If losers have no concern for the gainers and each CV has a veto, then the prospects of enacting redistribution (in zero sum situations) fall to zero. Second, the power of a veto may encourage strategic behaviour. A CV who is a net gainer from a proposal might vote against it in order to try and secure a greater net surplus from a subsequent proposal. To avoid the possibility of strategic holdouts, Wicksell suggested approximate unanimity might be a suitable rule rather than actual unanimity. Third, there is the problem that even if CVs act in good faith, the time and other decision costs of finding a proposal that commands unanimous support are likely to be very high indeed.

Against this background Buchanan and Tullock (1962) explore the least-cost decision rule. Referring back to chart 2.1, it can be seen that decision costs will rise from zero and tend towards infinity (where the number of CVs in the polity is large) as the decision rule moves from zero to unanimity. Efficiency (or welfare) costs imposed by the collective decision, however, exhibit the reverse pattern; being zero for unanimity and very high when zero CVs make a collective decision. Where the total of two types of costs are minimized depends on the precise shape of the two separate cost curves, but it will be a point that dictates less than unanimity as the least-cost decision rule.

Although there is nothing to stop the least-cost occurring at a minority form of rule, those that favour democratic principles are likely to prefer a form of majority rule. Because of this, and the fact that simple majority is probably the most familiar collective decision rule encountered in everyday life, the properties of this rule are considered here. There are three well-known properties of simple majority rule that cause concern for those who view efficiency and freedom of preferences as important.

Freedom of Preferences and Arbitrary Collective Decisions

Arrow (1963), in his seminal work on the construction of a social preference ordering from the separate preferences of individuals, suggested the constitutional rule should conform with five axioms. One of these axioms was 'unrestricted domain'. That is, if it is considered desirable that a social welfare function be developed on the basis of consumer sovereignty then individuals must be allowed to rank the alternatives in any order they wish. It turns out that, unless individual preferences are 'single-peaked', pairwise simple majority votes may produce a result that is arbitrary in the sense it depends on which vote is taken first.

In chart 2.2 preferences for three CVs are recorded. The issue conventionally illustrated is preferences over budget size with large (L), medium (M) and small (S) being the alternatives. With the preferences of chart 2.2, if the first vote is L *v*. M, then CV1 and CV3 will form a majority and L will win. If the second vote is L *v*. S, CV2 and CV3 will form a majority and S will win. If L *v*. S is the *first* vote, then M will win and finally, if S *v*. M is voted *first*, L will win. The outcome is that *either* S, L or M can win as a result of this sequential voting depending upon the order in which votes are taken. This arbitrariness is not an attractive feature for a collective decision. It can

Chart 2.2   Cyclical majorities

Preferences rank	CV1	CV2	CV3
First	L	M	S
Second	M	S	L
Third	S	L	M

be avoided if CVs do not have preferences like those of CV3, whose first two choices move from one extreme 'small' to the other 'large' forming a non-peaked pattern.

If CV3 alters his preferences to S M L, then they become single-peaked (see chart 2.3) and the reader can verify that, no matter which

Chart 2.3   Single and multi-peaked preferences

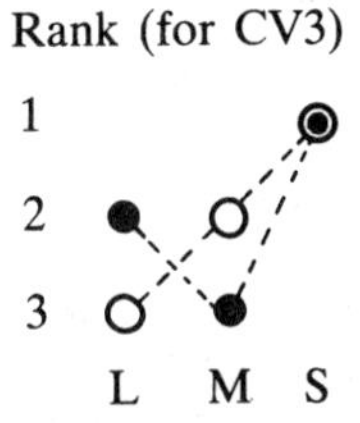

Rank (for CV3)

vote is taken first, M always wins – i.e. the simple majority vote now yields a unique result. At the practical level the doubt about the empirical significance of cyclical majorities does not remove this as a possible source of distortion in collective decisions in the public sector. For a much more exhaustive discussion of voting, see Mueller (1979).

The contents of chart 2.2 can also be used to illustrate the importance of 'agenda-setting'. Suppose CV1 has been delegated to organize the votes on the issue at stake. If he has a good idea of the likely preferences of CV2 and CV3, he may realize that choosing the order of the vote will determine the collective choice. In this instance the ability to set the agenda is, in fact, the ability to make the collective choice. Whilst not suggesting that all collective decisions can be manipulated so easily, it does illustrate the power wielded by those who set the parameters in which a collective decision is to be made. For example, North (1985) suggests that Roosevelt's agenda-setting power allowed him to present his 'social security' legislation as an all-or-nothing proposal, enabling it to pass Congress.

Inefficiency and 'Forced Riders'

Chart 2.4 records imaginary figures for five CVs labelled CV1 to CV5. The proposed measure is a £50 local bus shelter, and it is proposed that equal-share tax prices will be paid if the shelter is built (see column 1). Imagine CV1 to CV3 are regular bus users although CV3, as a pensioner, does not use the bus as much as CV1 and CV2. Given their usage of bus services, their benefit and net benefit are recorded in columns 2 and 3. By contrast imagine CV4 walks everywhere and CV5 never leaves his house. CV4 reasons that on his walks he may occasionally shelter from rain and this is worth £5, whereas CV5 reaps no benefit from the shelter at all. These circumstances give the benefit and net benefit figures recorded in columns (2) and (3). CVs can be expected to vote for the shelter if their unexpected net benefit is positive, and against if it is negative (column 4).

Given the contents of chart 2.4, CV1 to CV3 will vote for and form a majority over CV4 and CV5 who oppose the project. CV4 and CV5 are net losers and are often described as 'forced riders' on the project. They are coerced by the majority into taking part in the proposal. As well as creating 'forced riders', there is a second feature to note about this simple example, and that is that an inefficient project has been accepted. The cost of the project is £50 and the benefits from the project are only £47. The gainers value their gains at £47 from the provision of the shelter. The losers are those who forgo an alternative use of the resources employed in the construction of the shelter. The losers (those who have to be compensated for the labour, raw material,

Chart 2.4   Majority voting and a local bus shelter (see McKenzie and Tullock, 1978)

	(1) Tax price (£)	(2) Benefit (£)	(3) Net benefit (£)	(4) (Vote)
CV1	10	18	8	For
CV2	10	13	3	For
CV3	10	11	1	For
CV4	10	5	−5	Against
CV5	10	0	−10	Against
	50	47	−3	Carried

costs, etc., sacrificed in the provision of the project) need a further £3 over and above this to build the shelter. Hence the project is inefficient. In this instance, gainers cannot compensate losers, and remain better off themselves.[2]

This is not to suggest that all majority votes necessarily involve 'forced riders'[3] or inefficient projects, but rather that both are possible and are unattractive features of a majority rule. In the above example, CV3 (the voter in the middle in terms of net benefit) is crucial. Suppose CV3 inherits a car and, although still using the bus occasionally, his benefit falls to £7 and his net benefit to −£3. CV3 will now vote against the project and will be decisive because he forms a majority with CV4 and CV5. It is this middle or 'median voter' who is determining the outcome of the vote.

The Median Voter Rule and Inefficiency

If a continuous case, rather than the discrete example above, is considered it is easy to show more fully how, in a simple majority vote, it is the median voter's preference that determines the decision. In figure 2.1 the demands of the five CVs for the number of bus services per unit of time at different tax prices are depicted as $MB1$ to $MB5$ respectively. The equal tax price facing all CVs is MC_T and represents one-fifth of the marginal cost of providing bus services per unit of time. The quantities each CV would choose if they could determine the

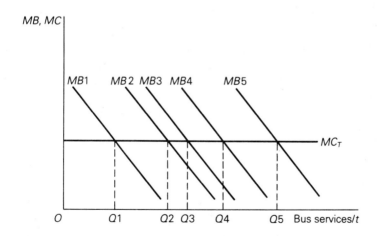

Figure 2.1 Majority rule and the median voter

collective choice would be $OQ1$ to $OQ5$ respectively. However, in a simple majority vote, imagine the proposals begin at zero and are increased by one service per period every time a majority votes a particular proposal down. As the volume of services increases along the horizontal axis in figure 2.1, $OQ1$ will be opposed by CV2, CV3, CV4 and CV5. Similarly, $OQ2$ will be rejected by a majority now CV3, CV4 and CV5, i.e. three of the five voters want more services that $OQ2$. Indeed, it is only at $OQ3$ that there is not a majority to increase the number of services per period. At any quantity below it, CV3, CV4 and CV5 always want more services. The proposal to go beyond $OQ3$ will be voted down by CV1, CV2 and CV3 and hence $OQ3$, the median voter's choice, becomes the simple majority collective choice. Hence in a simple majority vote it is always the median voter whose preference becomes the collective choice, and this is what is meant by the 'median voter rule'.

In public choice literature the provision of public goods is an important element and the question arises as to whether the efficient quantity, determined by $\Sigma MB = MC$, will coincide with the median voter's choice. Figure 2.2 illustrates the marginal benefit curves, $MB1$ to $MB3$, for three CVs for a service that is non-rival. If MC is the marginal cost of this service, then the efficient provision is OQ^* where

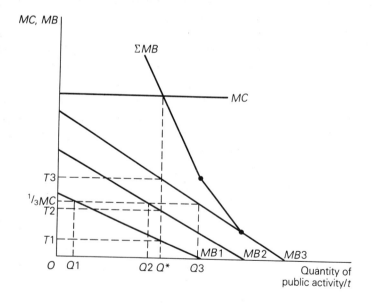

Figure 2.2   Median voter rule and public goods

$\Sigma MB = MC$. If equal tax shares at one-third MC are to be charged then the median quantity demanded, and the majority collective choice, is $OQ2$, which is inefficiently too small a quantity. A different configuration of the MB curves can make the median voter choice too large. Indeed, with equal tax shares it is only by chance that the median voter choice and the efficient quantity will coincide. A distribution of tax prices, that does guarantee the efficient quantity under majority (or any other) rule, occurs when tax prices are determined as the marginal benefits of each CV at the efficient quantity. Tax prices $T1$, $T2$ and $T3$ in figure 2.2 illustrate this proposition. The general point that emerges is that, with tax prices determined other than in line with marginal benefit, majority voting cannot be predicted to yield the efficient quantity as the collective choice. Welfare losses are therefore experienced.

In the brief discussion of voting above, only a single decision has been involved and a majority favouring that decision was required for it to become the collective choice. However, it is possible, where there is more than one collective decision to be made, for 'artificial' majorities to be formed. This process is known as 'log-rolling'. In its explicit form CV's trade support for issues so that 'If you vote for my proposal, I will vote for yours'-type deals are concluded. A more subtle form is implicit log-rolling where a platform or bundle of issues are assembled that can be supported by a majority. Where log-rolling occurs, minority-supported issues become the collective choice. In figure 2.3 a highly artificial situation is constructed which clearly illustrates the principles involved. There are three CVs, and assume there are to be two votes on the provision of goods A and B. CV1 wants neither A nor B and his MB curve ($MB1$) is coincident with the horizontal axis in both parts (a) and (b) of figure 2.3. The second voter, CV2, has the marginal benefit curve $MB2$ for A but does not value B, and therefore $MB2$ in part (b) of figure 2.3 is coincident with the horizontal axis. CV3 is assumed to have the reverse pattern of preferences to CV2 so that $MB3$ is coincident with the horizontal axis in part (a) of figure 2.3 and is illustrated as $MB3$ in part (b). Suppose initially that the social marginal opportunity cost of both good A and B is £30 and the efficient quantities of each, dictated by the demand implicit in $MB2$ and $MB3$, is 20 units. If an equal tax share-pricing rule is announced (£10 each per unit of A or B) and there is to be a majority collective decision on the quantity provided, then: CV2 wants 60 units of A and no B, CV3 wants 60 units of B and no A, whilst CV3 wants zero units of both. In separate votes the majority vote for none of A and B.

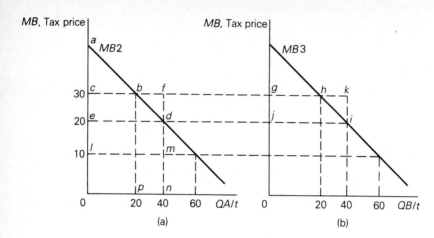

Figure 2.3   Log-rolling and simple majority voting

However, if CV2 and CV3 get together and make an explicit vote trade, then a majority can be found that supports the provision of positive quantities of A and B. Given the illustrative numbers, if CV3 votes for A he must pay £10 in taxes per unit of A consumed, and if CV2 votes for A he must pay £10 in taxes per unit of A consumed. If CV2 votes for B he must pay £10 in taxes per unit of B consumed, and likewise CV3 must pay £10 per unit for B when the motion to place A and B in the public sector is passed. In effect, in this example, the price of a unit of B to CV3 becomes £20, and similarly the price of a unit of A to CV2 becomes £20 as each party cross-subsidizes the other. If CV2 and CV3 appreciate the full implications of providing both goods, then CV2 perceives the price of A to him at £20, and CV3 perceives the price of B at £20. This will be clear if the vote is to provide publicly 40 units of each good. CV2 wants good A, and compared with facing a market price of £30 where consumer surplus would be triangle *abc* he is faced with £20 and consumer surplus is triangle *ade*. Hence, CV2 is better off from the public provision result of log-rolling by *cbde*. Similarly, CV3 is better off in net terms (as a result of log-rolling) by an amount equal to *ghij*. CV1 is unquestionably worse off by an amount equal to *ecfd* × 2. The equity implications are clear, but in so far as income has been re-distributed from CV1, it has been done in a clumsy fashion with high allocative costs. For good A, output has increased from 20 units to 40 units; the social cost of this expansion was equal to area *pbfn*. The social benefit (in terms of willingness to pay) was only *pbdn*. Excess welfare costs of triangle *bfd* have been experienced on product A and similarly triangle *hki* for product B.

In the discussion above, the form of decision was one that involved each CV knowing the costs and benefits to them of an explicit expenditure proposal and then voting on it. This is the process of direct democracy, and is attractive where there are a small number of collective decisions to be made. However, in reality, where there are many decisions, CVs either may not vote, or vote when they have no significant preference, thereby defeating the object of the exercise. Additionally, in complex societies there are so many collective decisions to be made that the decision-making costs in themselves would be prohibitively high. In these circumstances it is representative democracy that has displaced direct democracy as the mechanism through which collective decisions are made. In representative democracies CVs do not vote on an individual proposal; rather they are invited to elect a representative of their interests. The types of policies that potential representatives stand for are announced at periodic elections, and are further indicated by the political party (if any) to which the potential representative belongs.

Explicit log-rolling, as illustrated above, is best thought of as taking place in relatively small-number situations, because this is where explicit 'deals' can be made effective. Given this, it is a process that is also more likely to be a feature of representative rather than direct democracy. Elected representatives pursue their interests by such arrangements when votes for issues arise. Implicit log-rolling is associated with a large-number situation in the context of representative democracy. Musgrave and Musgrave (1976) explain how the selection by a political party of the electoral platform can be perceived as an implicit act of log-rolling which is used to establish that mix of policies which maximizes support. Arguments favourable to log-rolling arrangements have been advanced because it is a means by which strength or intensity of preference can be accounted for. Mueller (1979), however, illustrates that the process can generate non-potential Pareto improvements as well as cyclical outcomes. Everything appears to depend upon the example in question.

2.3　POLITICAL PARTIES AND REPRESENTATIVE DEMOCRACY

The literature on elected representatives (ERs) draws a parallel between their behaviour and that of intermediaries or agents in the private market-place. It seems clear that ERs have an incentive to compose a platform (product) that will carry a majority (will sell) and indeed follow policies (product changes) that will meet with electoral (market) approval. However, the analogy is incomplete in that the ER has 'slack', and is able to do more than simply mirror the majority of CVs' preferences. Competition (election time) in the political market-place is an infrequent occurrence and, once over, leaves the ER with a captive market (constituency) that cannot be competed away. In the political market-place compulsion replaces voluntarism and, apart from the mechanism of forced riding and log-rolling, the ER is likely to foster 'special interests'. This occurs where legislation of benefit to a few (mainly producer and high-income individuals for reasons outlined below) is passed because it secures voting and financial support for the ER from the 'special interest' group and in turn, because of CV rational ignorance, generates little or no resistance amongst the majority. Finally, given that the ER has no saleable property right in his office, which hence does not have a quoted capitalized value, his incentive framework encourages weight being given to the current costs and benefits of any action. Success for an ER relies on being seen to articulate a problem issue and become associated with legislation. In this process the long-term consequences of the legislation have little or no part to play. By comparison, the private entrepreneur has to be concerned with the long-term success of any decision he or she makes. To the extent that the long-term profitability of the enterprise is damaged, it is internalized immediately in a lower capitalized value of the enterprise. It is evident that the position that ERs find themselves in, not only allows them to impose costs on the minority to the benefit of the majority, but also the majority to the benefit of its minority. Any assumption that CVs' preferences are efficiently reflected in the process of representative democracy is a very strong one.

There is also the function of the political party and party leadership to be considered. As alluded to above, for the ER, party membership conveys a great deal of information to CVs about the policies they are sympathetic to. In everyday language it is common to hear the phrase 'brand' of politics, and the role of the party leadership can be viewed as building up and maintaining a brand image. Those that fail to toe the party line are disciplined.

In a two-party system the use of the brand analogy is particularly apposite because parties seeking to capture the median voter may find it difficult to offer more than different brands of the same commodity (political platform). The election-winning calculus is depicted in figure 2.4, where the distribution of preferences between left and right wing is 'thought' given by the shape of the underlying income distribution.[4] This is not necessarily an unrealistic assumption, given the correlation between CV income and political affiliation. Suppose the right wing party adopts a very right wing policy at R1 in figure 2.4. This platform would simply hand the election to the left wing party, as they have only to locate somewhere slightly to the left of R1, say L1, to capture the median voter (and indeed to capture nearly all the voters). The only CVs who find R1 rather than L1 closer to their political preferences (given the two platforms on offer) are to be found in the shaded tail of the distribution. The only way for the right wing party ever to gain office is to moderate the 'rightness' of its platform towards the expected position of the median voter. The word 'expected' emphasizes that the political world, like others, is an uncertain one, where people have to act on their expectations. Positions for the right wing and left wing party, such as R2 and L2 respectively, would make elections closely contested affairs and involve both parties having similar centralist (or moderate) platforms. If the reader has found it both difficult to differentiate the position of the Democrats and Republicans in the USA, or the Labour and Conservative Parties in the UK[5] (and found

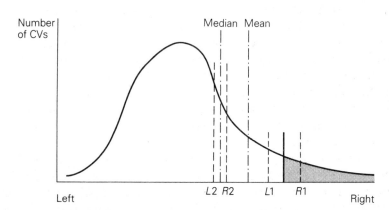

Figure 2.4 Party platforms in a two-party system

their policies consensus ones), then this is one piece of theory that is consistent with that observation.

It has to be recognized that what is making this model tick is the assumption of vote-maximizing behaviour on the part of political parties and their adaptation to the underlying distribution of political preferences as they perceive them. An alternative scenario would view the distribution of preferences as variable, and see parties taking up political platforms and attracting the distribution (and the median voter) to them, i.e. an active rather than passive role as regards political preferences. Which of these models is more comforting is difficult to establish. The passive adjuster approach suggests individuals in government will reflect the middle preferences in any society. Government will attract individuals who are not glued to strong positions at either tail of the distribution but are rather more flexible and pragmatic; shifting position as the median preference is perceived to change. The active majority creator approach suggests the political world would be peopled by individuals of strong opinions and the charisma and leadership qualities to change hearts and minds! A common contrasting claim, however, is that it is not the politicians (in general) and the executive (in particular) that run a democracy but rather the full-time civil servants or bureaucrats. The role of the bureau may, therefore, severely limit the choice of politicians and voters.

2.4 THE INDIVIDUAL WITHIN REPRESENTATIVE DEMOCRACY

The individual consumer voter (CV) is the basic unit of analysis on the demand side of the public sector. As far as the individual CV is concerned, the key difference between the private and public sector context is that, in the private context, all CVs can themselves adjust to their preferences the quantity of any good or service they consume; whereas this is not true of the public sector. The essence of a collective decision is that all CVs must adjust to a given quantity of any publicly provided good or service.

For many commentators the level of knowledge of public sector decisions and variables among CVs is observed to be minimal, and this is the source of disquiet. The 'political market', however, generates imperfections and disincentives for any CV. In the first instance, CVs cannot within representative democracy easily vote for individual policies in the way consumers purchase individual products. Political parties typically bundle policies within manifestos. Hence, for any CV, voting for policy A may imply voting for a party which similarly proposes policy B (and policy B may not be to the interests of the CV). Secondly, even when the CV derives benefit from the policy consequences of his vote, the *expected* benefit of voting is low because, where many voters participate, the probability that any one individual's vote will be decisive is infinitesimally small. In this way CVs are, as individuals, 'optimally ignorant' when the marginal benefit of additional information is equal to the marginal cost of acquiring such information. To the extent that individuals participate politically at all it will be only if associated costs are low (Downs, 1957). Generally the CV is likely to be ignorant of public sector resource allocation, because acquiring information on political programmes is a costly pursuit and the expected benefit from being better informed (in the shape of being able to influence the outcome using a single vote) is minimal.

Whilst the expectation is that most CVs will play a small and ill-informed role, there are potential exceptions. First, high-income individuals may be more able to stand the costs of participation (Jones and Cullis, 1986) and may be more productive in participation (Frey, 1971). They may be more able, for example, to lobby politicians, and more persuasive in this respect. Their greater advantage in the use of information may sustain a higher degree of political participation.

In the second instance, pressure groups are organizations able to mobilize a greater degree of participation. They may be more able to deal with small identifiable groups. Producer groups (trade associations, professional associations, trade unions) may more easily fit this description than groups of consumers of various services. Small numbers are important because of the 'free-riding' problem (outlined in chapter 1). Individuals may wish for legislation which improves their conditions, but associations will not easily become effective in this pursuit if the goals are non-excludable between members and non-members. A piece of legislation may achieve such a result, and pressure groups will arise if they can overcome the free-riding tendency generated by the public good nature of this result. It has been argued by Mancur Olson (1968) that associations overcome this public good dilemma by one of two courses of action. Coercion (e.g. closed shop) may be exercised so that, to be one of the potential beneficiary group, an individual must also be a member of the association. Alternatively, 'selective incentives' or private goods contingent on membership (e.g. cheap insurance, invitations to social occasions) are the mechanism of membership drives. The tendency for free-riding has been shown to increase within a large-number scenario. As such, the prospects for pressure group activity appear more likely for smaller groups. The logic of collective action then implies that such groups (albeit possibly producer groups) may be at an asymmetric advantage to reap benefits for themselves by political activity. Such action may be at the expense of the broader community, which remains ill-informed and immobilized.

Sufficient has been said to throw doubt on the potential of the political market to ape a perfect economic market in generating socially optimum results. The interest and involvement of CVs is dampened by the lack of significance which their own individual action appears to possess upon the end result. When, via the activity of pressure groups, this influence is increased, it is argued that it may be levied in such a way as to increase government spending. Subsidies, for example, may be pursued by industry lobbies. The benefit for producers may be great at the expense of a small increase in taxation for individual members of the broader community which does not keep informed of the nature of the changes. The prospect of vote-loss associated with this action is thereby reduced. To this end, pressure group activity may well suit the aspirations of politicians as well as bureaucrats. It is to the 'standard' economic theory of bureaucracy that we now turn.

2.5   BUREAUCRATIC ECONOMICS AND PUBLIC PRODUCTION

Recent years have seen the economics of bureaucracy become a prominent subject in economic texts and articles. The literature lends some support to the Californian bumper sticker which reads: 'Bureaucracy – a form of organization that converts energy into solid waste'. Less offensively, the mainpoint of the literature is that bureaucracy is both the cause and effect of an expanding public sector. As far as our application here is concerned, one can model civil servants as utility-maximizers whose utility function contains such arguments as prestige, office perks, rank and pay, and the possibilities of promotion. Niskanen (1968 and 1971) would argue that these sources of utility are positively related to the size of the bureau budget, and this can be treated as the relevant maximand for civil servants. It is worth emphasizing that this literature does not suggest that civil servants are a particularly corrupt group in society, rather that they are like all others, motivated to some extent by self-interest and influenced by the cost–benefit environment in which they find themselves.

Having the utility function outlined above is not harmful to society's interests in itself, but becomes so once harnessed to monopoly power. The bureau can be viewed as having a monopoly over the supply of its activities to the government. Equally the party in power, or more particularly the cabinet, are monopsonists in relation to the bureau. The situation is one of bilateral monopoly. The effect of this situation can be described using figure 2.5, which represents the bureau relationship within the government. Using figure 2.5 it is possible to illustrate the output and 'pricing' decisions of a competitor and a monopolist in the market. These may be compared with the situation in the public sector when bureaux have influence. The simplifying assumptions built into the diagram are that constant returns to scale apply, so that long-run average cost is equal to long-run marginal cost ($LRAC = LRMC$) and that D is both the market demand curve D_M and the demand of the median voter (D_V). Within a perfectly competitive market the output provided would, of course, be OQ_C at a price of OP_C and, in a Paretian context, this would be socially efficient. The private monopolist maximizes profit and equates marginal cost with marginal revenue (MR), producing OQ_M units per time period, at a price P_M. The public monopolist, locked into the bilateral monopoly situation described above, may be deemed to have the upper hand. (This follows because they have superior knowledge on where $LRMC$ is located. Also they probably know more about where D_M (and D_V) is by monitoring the daily papers, political speeches, etc., and in general trying to find out

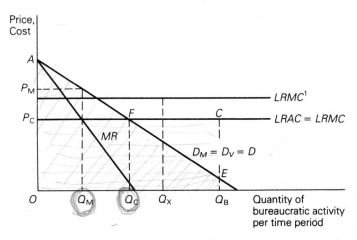

Figure 2.5 The government and the economics of bureaucracies

what voters' desires are in relation to their activity. Finally, politicians will have to spread themselves over many activities and hence not be in a position to monitor in detail the activities of the bureau. Once it is recognized that the monopoly powers of the bureau cannot be translated into cash, like the private monopolist, the utility function outlined above is maximized and the size of the budget expanded to a theoretical limit at OQ_B with an 'all-or-nothing offer' to government. Since total cost cannot exceed total benefit, total benefit ($OAFEQ_B$) and total costs (OP_CCQ_B) are equated at output OQ_B (hence $\Delta P_CAF = \Delta FCE$ since OP_CFEQ_B is common to both the total cost and total benefit areas).

The degree of allocative inefficiency is represented by $Q_C–Q_B$. An elaboration can be built into this model if we allow for the fact that the bureau will not produce its services in a least-cost fashion. In these circumstances $LRMC$ may shift upwards to $LRMC^1$ with output OQ_X being produced in an X-inefficient manner, i.e. producing a given volume of services with more than the minimum inputs. The ability to be X-inefficient is fostered both by the bureau having only vaguely specified duties, and the difficulties encountered in enforcing and policing even those activities that are specified. To summarize, the main thrust of the argument becomes that the bureau has power to exact an inefficiently large budget from ultimately the taxpayer, by being both X- and allocatively inefficient.

The Niskanen account of bureaucracy suggests that each bureau produces 'too much' of a given output (at possibly too high a per-unit cost). An alternative approach has looked at the mix of outputs generated by public agencies. Inasmuch as certain outputs are less visible than others, there exists the possibility of misallocation within the budget allocation. Lindsay (1976) has explored the impact of government enterprise on the mix of outputs produced as compared to a market system. In the latter, the profit motive guides entrepreneurs to produce the quantity and quality of goods and services that conform with individual preferences. Firms exist to capitalize on the gains from long-term contracts, team production and specialization in risk-bearing. Monitoring is facilitated by profits which not only provide a clear indication of success or failure but also act as an incentive to managers to monitor effectively if, that is, they receive a proportion of the residual earnings of firms. Lindsay points out that government enterprise is characterized by zero-priced output. This means that allocative information comes from a legislative process and, even if it was assumed that it could accurately represent people's preferences, these will be followed only imperfectly because of the inability to use profit as part of the monitoring process. In Lindsay's schema there is a bias towards 'visible' outputs, which not only are capable of easy documentation for the government monitors, but also are easily verified by them. An example is illustrated in figure 2.6. TT^1 is a transformation curve and represents the possible combinations of two outputs, one invisible (e.g. counselling activities) and the other visible (e.g. physical aids), that an agency concerned with disability policy could choose to produce. The curves labelled E_0 and E_1 are equiprice curves and represent combinations of the 'visible' and 'invisible' outputs that could command the same price on the market. Given that market managers will want to maximize revenue for any given outlay, these curves can be treated as managerial indifference curves. The market outcome would be point 1 on E_1 with Oa of counselling activities and Ob of physical aids. By contrast, if some outputs are impossible to monitor by government, and are in effect completely invisible, the non-market manager will treat them as 'neutrals' and have vertical indifference curves as with E_2. Equilibrium is now found at point 3. This is a corner solution with the visible output being produced exclusively. In the case where monitoring costs are discontinuous, it may be sensible for the government to monitor for some threshold level of the invisible output

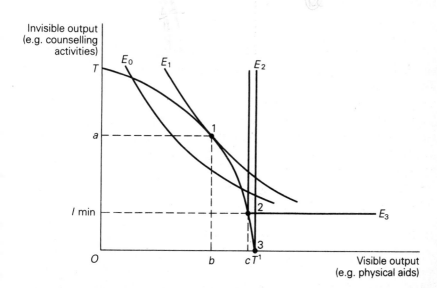

Figure 2.6 Government enterprise and output bias

(I min) only. In this case the non-market manager's indifference curve will take the form of E_3 and equilibrium will be found at 2, with I min and Oc of the invisible and visible outputs respectively. This analysis suggests that provision from public enterprises are skewed towards visible outputs compared with a market situation in which the preferences of CVs rule, and hence is another potential source of governmental failure. Again, the governmental sector appears guilty of failure to generate appropriate shadow prices for allocative decisions.

2.6　WOLF'S TYPOLOGY AND GOVERNMENTAL FAILURE

Wolf (1979) has a complete overview of non-market failure. His typology begins by considering the demand and supply characteristics of non-market output. Some of the features have been described above, whilst others are additions to the discussion. On the demand side, increasing awareness of monopolies, externalities and distributional inequity means politicians in recent years have found active markets for their services. To emphasize a point made above, the successful politician is more likely to be the one who articulates and legislates on specific problems, rather than the one who is cautious and concerned that any policies adopted are likely to be successful. This reward structure makes politicians rationally myopic and hence their activities result in policies that are often the source of further but future difficulties.

The supply side of the non-market sector involves final outputs that are difficult both to define and measure, resulting in inputs being used as a proxy for outputs (and if Lindsay is right, 'visible' intermediate inputs). This picture is further complicated by the government producers being non-profit monopoly suppliers. These latter points are especially developed by the economics of bureaucracy literature summarized above. Given these demand and supply preconditions, the forms of non-market failure isolated by Wolf are:

Internalities and Private Goods

Internalities and private goods are effectively the *standards* adopted by non-market institutions to replace the discipline of the market in metering and monitoring individual and organization performance. These internalities raise the supply curves of non-market providers.

Examples of internalities are provided by the budget-maximizing bureaucrat. Wolf calls this the 'more is better' approach. There is also the 'more complex is better' or technological test of success. Here high technology is all, so that, for example, 'Cadillac' quality is encouraged in, say, health care irrespective of its relative costs and benefits. There is also the reverse syndrome of opposing all changes in technology, irrespective of cost–benefit considerations. A final internality example is 'knowing what others don't know is better'. It is argued under this head that the acquisition and protection of new information may become the internal source of activity or standard performance (again irrespective of the usefulness of the information to the pursuit of the initial policy objective).

Redundant and Rising Costs

That X-efficiency is likely to be a common feature of non-market production is a prediction already described. A more novel feature under this heading is that objectives of some government policies will be unattainable. In the field of disability policy, for example, this may involve seeking cures for certain types of handicap as part of an unrealistic short-run research project or (using Wolf's example) plans to make individuals with IQs of less than 70 into draftsmen. A further source of rising costs may be inconsistency rather than the unattainability of objectives. So, in the disability field, for example, the thrust of government policy may be to minimize the level of acquired disability, whilst at the same time treating all the disabled largely as one group independent of the sources of their disability and the role of their own activities in their situation.

Derived Externalities

This is the name given to 'further' market imperfections induced as unanticipated side-effects of government legislation, or simply the unanticipated consequences of ill-conceived government legislation. An example of the former is provided by Peacock (1980), who describes how a firm eligible for subsidy will adapt by raising its cost structure by deliberately fostering 'slack'. An example of ill-conceived legislation is provided by complaints against section 504 of the Rehabilitation Act passed in America in 1973. Under this section universities and colleges have an obligation to provide handicapped students with expensive special help. The University of Texas, forced to provide a sign-language interpreter for a deaf student, appealed to the Supreme Court on the grounds that the intention of section 504 was not to impose heavy financial burdens on institutions that drew only a small part of their revenue from federal funds. Whatever the rights and wrongs of the objectives of the legislation, the resistance encountered by its implementation suggests it was less than fully thought through by the legislators.

Distributional Inequity

Here the point is that the government activity may be a source rather than a remedy for inequality. This may take place with both cash transfer and in-kind help. Where it is very difficult to police activities, there is scope for deliberate corruption and 'irregularities'. More likely, however, is the exercise of arbitrary power by government servants, not as a result of any corruption but rather because the regulations (e.g. for transfers) are often very complex and elaborate. This makes the achievement of horizontal and vertical equity in treatment in the non-market sector very difficult.

Given this list of possible sources of governmental failure and inefficiency, it is easy to see how government provision of goods or services has become the target of considerable criticisms in recent years.

2.7   SUMMARY AND CONCLUSIONS

This chapter discusses the public sector analogue to market failure, dubbed governmental or non-market failure. The arguments of chapter 1 are generally used to suggest a rationale for the assertion that government or public policy can improve on the market failure situation. More recently, however, commentators have noted that claims that government intervention improve matters are often simply assertions. It has to be shown not only that government could do better, but that it does do better than the unaided market. An increasing volume of literature, briefly introduced here, seeks to show that government activity is beset by inefficiencies of its own. A fully articulated model of public sector resource allocation would consider: the position of the consumer voter (CV); voting as a mechanism for ascertaining preferences; representative democracy and the role of the political entrepreneur and bureaucratic or civil service economics. Clearly, this is a very large topic and all that was attempted above was to bring out the salient predictions for the provision of public sector goods and services.

The economics of voting mechanisms has a large and complicated literature, but a basic prediction, as it relates to majority voting mechanisms, is that public sector activities are 'over-provided'. Downs (1960) is an exception to this rule. He views the benefits of government expenditure as less 'visible' to voters than the costs in terms of taxation, and therefore under-provision is predicted. (This is discussed in detail in chapter 5 below.) Nevertheless, the more general lines of argument above points towards excessive public sector provision. This is because any constitutional rule which is less than unanimity allows a majority to impose net costs on the minority by providing public sector goods and services for which their tax costs exceed the valuation of the benefits. This is so-called 'forced riding'. Implicit and explicit log-rolling creates 'artificial' majorities, and although the income effects may cancel out, the effect of a perceived decreased tax price for public sector activities encourages the tendency to over-provide them. Special-interest effects accentuate this process. As regards the economics of bureaucracy and governmental enterprises, distortions of the volume, cost and mix of their outputs are a prediction of the models reviewed. Taking chapters 1 and 2 together, if 'market failure' is the frying pan then 'governmental failure' appears as a fire!

NOTES

1 For a recent discussion of the public choice literature and its development, see Frey (1985).
2 The project fails against a *potential* Pareto improvement criterion. If gainers *could* compensate losers (given costless redistribution), then it would be possible potentially to pass the Pareto improvement criterion discussed in chapter 1. If gainers actually *did* compensate losers, the Pareto improvement criterion would be met. Since it is impossible even for the *potential* Pareto improvement criterion to be satisfied, the project is inefficient.
3 It might be expected that there are some forced riders in all majority decisions. The closer the costs of a collective project can be tailored to those who benefit, the less forced riding that will occur.
4 This distribution is said to be positively skewed as there is a tapering tail of high-income CVs. With such a distribution the extremely high incomes raise the mean income above the median income.
5 Note this is a feature of two-party systems and the analysis does not carry

over to three-party ones where there is an incentive for parties to differentiate their platforms more (see Tullock, 1972). To the extent the Alliance in the UK can establish itself as a third party, then UK CVs should perceive greater party differentiation if this vote-maximizing theory applies.

REFERENCES

Arrow, K. J. (1963), *Social Choice and Individual Values*, 2nd edn, New Haven: Yale University Press.

Buchanan, J. M. and Tullock, G. (1962), *The Calculus of Consent*, Ann Arbor: University of Michigan Press.

Downs, A. (1957), *An Economic Theory of Democracy*, New York: Harper & Row.

Downs, A. (1960), Why the government budget is too small in a democracy, *World Politics*, vol. 13 (July), pp. 541–63.

Frey, B. S. (1971), Why do high income people participate more in politics? *Public Choice*, vol. 11 (Fall), pp. 101–5.

Frey, B. S. (1985), State and prospect of public choice: a European view, *Public Choice*, vol. 46, no. 2, pp. 141–61.

Hyman, D. N. (1973), *The Economics of Governmental Activity*, New York: Holt, Rinehart & Winston.

Jones, P. R. and Cullis, J. G. (1986), Is democracy regressive?: A comment on political participation, *Public Choice*, vol. 51, no. 1, pp. 101–7.

Lindsay, C. M. (1976), A theory of government enterprise, *Journal of Political Economy*, vol. 84, no. 5 (October), pp. 31–7.

McKenzie, R. B. and Tullock, G. (1978), *Modern Political Economy*, New York: McGraw-Hill.

Mueller, D. C. (1979), *Public Choice*, Cambridge: Cambridge University Press.

Musgrave, R. A. and Musgrave P. B. (1976), *Public Finance in Theory and Practice*, New York: McGraw-Hill.

Niskanen, W. A. (1968), Non-market decision-making: the peculiar economics of bureaucracy, *American Economic Review*, vol. 58, no. 2 (May), pp. 293–305.

Niskanen, W. A. (1971), *Bureaucracy and Representative Government*, Chicago: Aldine.

North, D. C. (1985), The growth of government in the United States: an economic historian's perspective, *Journal of Public Economics*, vol. 28, no. 3 (December), pp. 383–99.

Olson, M. Jnr (1968), *The Logic of Collective Action*, New York: Schocken Books.

Peacock, A. T. (1980), On the anatomy of collective failure, *Public Finance/ Finances Publiques*, vol. 35, no. 1, pp. 33–43.

Tullock, G. (1972), *Towards a Mathematics of Politics*, Ann Arbor: University of Michigan Press.

Wolf, C. Jnr. (1979), A theory of non-market behaviour: framework for implementation analysis, *Journal of Law and Economics*, vol. 22, no. 1 (April), pp. 107–40.

3

Measuring Leviathan: the 'Size' of the Public Sector

3.1 INTRODUCTION

In the 1880s a German economist and one of the founding fathers of public finance, Adolph Wagner, predicted that economic development would be accompanied by a growth in the public sector. This prediction appears to have borne fruit, and has ostensibly involved an expansion in the role of government in the allocation of national output. One commentator has written: 'A striking phenomenon of modern times has been the steady growth of the governmental sector. Despite the hot political debates that have greeted the successive steps of government expansion, there is surprisingly little scientific understanding of the forces tending to bring it about' (Hirshleifer, 1984, p. 529). Before responding to this assertion, some notion òf what is meant by 'the steady growth of the government sector' has to be established, and an outline of the evidence as typically presented is considered. Yet, as with many (all?) areas of life, the closer one is to the issue under discussion, the less certain one is about its interpretation. The same is true for measuring the size of the public sector; hence the ambiguous subtitle, 3.2. What has to be borne in mind is the point made by Peacock and Wiseman (1979) that 'it is possible to classify the data in so many different ways – the *organisation* of data itself presupposes some kind of hypothesis' (p. 18). There is no 'scientific' or 'neutral' measure of public sector size that can be adduced.

The main purpose of this chapter is to consider the ambiguities of estimates of the size of the public sector. However, estimation problems aside, the question might reasonably be raised as to why the particular size of the public sector should be a matter of concern. A recent article by Brennan and Pincus (1983, p. 362) is important for marshalling thoughts. They argue that 'public expenditure growth *per se* has had relatively little effect on the allocation of resources'. Consider an extreme example. In figure 3.1 it is assumed that individuals can privately supplement directly provided units of publicly provided goods. Good Y is a good publicly provided and good X is a composite of all other goods. Initially the public sector provides Oy_0 at a tax cost to the individual of xx_0. The individual supplements such provision and the equilibrium provision of Y is Y_E (with y_0y_E units supplemented from the private sector). Assume government provision expands to Oy_1 at a tax cost of xx_1 then the private supplementation falls to y_1y_E but the same allocation of resources between Y and X pertains. The public sector has grown but the size of the public sector *per se* has had no resource allocation effects. Even if the public sector was large or has grown larger it is questionable that this is cause for concern.

The adjustment mechanism described in this simplistic illustration is examined in greater depth in chapter 7. Of course fiscal regulation may restrict such supplementation, in which case attention should focus on those constraints to supplementation and the possibilities of re-trading

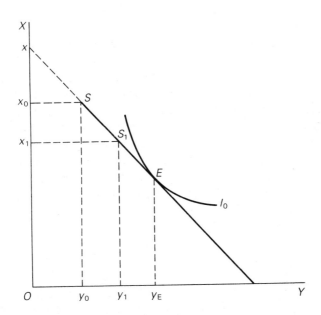

Figure 3.1 Private supplementation of publicly provided goods

publicly provided goods. These appear more relevant than time-series data on the size and growth of the public sector. In effect if the public sector could be correctly measured the significance of its size or growth in terms of resource allocation is clearly spurious. If the argument above has a good measure of truth in it then the size of public expenditure tells us little in terms of misallocation. In so far as existing literature generally imputes to the public sector the argument that 'changes in the level of public provision of various goods automatically involve changes in the levels of aggregate consumption', Brennan and Pincus counter that 'the effects of enormous increases in government spending on the aggregate pattern of consumption in the economy are uncertain, but probably quite small' (p. 352). Yet the size of the public sector is the centre of debate in political, academic and journalistic circles. Why? The answer appears to be that the resource allocation implication of the size of the public sector may be important in so far as it arises through distortions on the tax side (Brennan and Pincus, 1983, p. 362) and this question we address in chapter 9. Also the location of production may be important when one sector is more productive than the other, and we explore this possibility in chapter 8. The size of the public sector is especially important in terms of freedom for those who concentrate on so-called negative definitions of freedom. These definitions focus on freedom from the coercive powers of others including the state. Dasgupta (1986) notes that justification for exclusive reliance on markets has been made on these grounds, and that market transactions are argued to be an expression of negative freedom. Such concerns are discussed in chapter 10.

The size of the public sector and its growth are, then, important if the distortionary impact of taxation, the lack of cost-effectiveness and the threat to freedom rise proportionately with public expenditure growth. This is itself an assumption and one which may be called into question.[1] At present, however, it appears evident that such a perspective exists and in this sense the size of the public sector is relevant. Therefore it is important to ask the question of what exactly is being measured?

3.2   THE BROAD 'FACTS'

Two main features of public expenditure statistics are usually high-lighted, namely the overall long-term trend and changes in its composition. For the UK, Brown and Jackson (1986) provide a convenient summary of the main points under both these headings. Between 1970 and 1980 government expenditure, defined as all public expenditures (excluding nationalized industries[2] and net lending by all levels of government) grew from 12 to over 53 per cent of GNP at factor cost. As regards composition, it is worth noting that between 1953 and 1980 the proportions of total government expenditure going to defence fell from 24.5 to 11.0 per cent. Over the same period, social security benefits rose from just over 13 to 21 per cent. Smith (1982) documents the increasing share of transfer payments in the public sector. He notes that between 1950 and 1978 the overall public expenditure/GNP (at factor cost) ratio rose from 38.3 to 50.0 per cent. For the same period the expenditure on goods and services/GNP ratio rose by 19.2 per cent, compared to a 45.7 per cent increase for the transfer payments/GNP ratio (for further discussion of the UK public expenditure growth, see Heald, 1983).

Rosen (1985) provides a recent discussion of the USA. For government expenditures at all levels of government, the 80 years 1902–82 saw the percentage of such expenditures to GNP rise from 7.7 to 40 per cent. Like the UK, America has experienced a recent decline in defence spending as a percentage of public expenditure from 25.3 per cent in 1970 to 16.6 per cent in 1982. Historically, however, the figure has grown from nearly 10 per cent at the turn of the century. These figures are somewhat higher than for the UK which, since the early 1950s, has seen the break-up of its colonial empire and loss of 'world power' status. Yet, more in line with the UK, has been the growth in transfers in the USA as witnessed in the growth of the social security programme and public welfare spending. More broadly, in the period 1965 to 1983 the major social insurance programmes[3] grew from 3.2 per cent of GNP to 9.0 per cent of GNP. The 1983 figure represents over 37 per cent of federal expenditure.

The prediction of Wagner in the late nineteenth century appears confirmed by the evidence of the twentieth century. Total public expenditure as a percentage of GNP has grown, not only in the UK and the USA, but in many industrializing countries over the period. Bird (1971) confirms that countries such as Germany, Sweden and Japan adhere to a trend similar to that experienced by the UK and the USA. He notes that, while cross-sectional evidence will not necessarily confirm that countries with the highest income levels have the largest public sectors (Musgrave, 1969), time-series evidence is consistent with Wagner's law of 'expanding scale of State activity'.

3.3 THE 'SIZES' OF THE PUBLIC SECTOR: A CRITIQUE

The purpose of this section is to discuss various possible measures of the public sector in fairly broad conceptual terms. The problems of gaining and analysing the statistics appropriate to each measure are ignored, except to emphasize that in themselves they add an additional layer of interpretation and hence scope for dispute, given that one of the main points made here is that the size of the public sector is to a great extent a matter of choice.

The choice revolves around what precisely is to be estimated. Selection of data will be appropriate only when it is clear how public sector or state activity is conceived. To draw inferences about: the influence of government in the economy; the extent of national spending enacted by government; the responsibility of government for welfare, etc., will require emphasis on different data and a clear awareness of their limitations. We begin therefore by reference to estimates such as those quoted above. The ratios typically chosen to measure the public sector are by no means obvious.

Measuring the size of the public sector in real absolute terms gives no sense of scale or proportion; hence it is conventionally measured as a proportion or percentage of national output. The answer arrived at is a quotient and, as such, is affected both by the content of the numerator and the denominator. The contents of each are not self-selecting, so that 'facts' do not arrive in the world unaided. If the numerator is considered first, a number of possible definitions of the public sector present themselves. Beginning with a comprehensive measure (labelled A) this would include:

Measure A

1   The spending of central and local government;
2   the capital of public corporations (nationalized industries);
3   tax expenditures (which covers special provisions in the tax system designed to encourage certain types of activity which involve the government sacrificing revenue that would otherwise be raised on its behalf).

This sum could be amended in several ways that would considerably reduce its size.

Measure B would be as A but excluding tax expenditures. 'Should' this split be made? Once it is recognized that there is no analytical difference between the use of tax revenue to directly subsidize a good X and an equivalent adjustment to the tax code that exempts X from taxation, there is a case for treating these actions alike. Conventionally the subsidy would be measured as government activity but the tax expenditure would be ignored. Rosen (1985) lists some considerations favouring this conventional treatment. First, at the theoretical level, the tax expenditure implies a particular view of property rights distribution. The view is that property rights over private income (and therefore liability for tax) are essentially vested in the government. It is, however, the severe sovereignty principle that individuals have property rights over income, and hence offer the proportion of income up for tax that they deem appropriate; this is more in keeping with the 'democratic' principles underlying Western democracies. If the individual sovereignty model is accepted, then tax-exempt income (or tax expenditure) is not a subsidy offered by the government. A slightly different point relates to the definition of income. If this cannot be defined rigorously, then whether an item is an exemption or not, part of the legitimate tax base in the first place is somewhat arbitrary. At the practical level, computations of tax expenditures measure current expenditures on the exempt items and treat them all as potential taxable income. However, this makes no allowance for individual response in the presence of a tax. Such responses are the mainstay of public finance theory, and cast doubt on the accuracy of measured 'tax expenditure' budgets. To the extent these arguments are found unconvincing, there is a case for including tax expenditures in any measure of government activity. Such a connection would increase the measured size of the public sector in an economy.

Measure C would be as B but exclude nationalized industries on the grounds that they are largely autonomous.

Measure D would be as C but exclude all expenditure on 'financial assets' on the basis of the argument that these expenditures represent loans to private and public corporations and hence reflect the role of local and central government as financial intermediaries.

Measure E would begin to break down the global figure in A(1) above. First, a distinction can be drawn between *transfer* payments and real or *exhaustive* public expenditure. Netting-out transfers would be justified on the grounds that all the government is doing is transferring purchasing power from one group to another, and not deciding on how it is spent. The consumer remains sovereign.

Measure F, the smallest listed here, would net out market-purchased inputs from exhaustive expenditures on the grounds that they are not part of the output that is controlled or generated by government. The 'value added' by government on this line of argument is simply the employment costs involved in central and local government.

Depending on the purpose of the analysis and political viewpoint, it is possible for all these measures to be deemed acceptable, yet they provide very different sums to take as the numerator of the public sector calculation.

Turning to the denominator, there is a consensus that, in principle, net national income or product (NNP) is the best indicator of the output of an economy. Yet, given the unreliability in estimating capital depreciation, the figure of gross national income or product (GNP) is typically used. National income figures are provided at factor costs (FC) and at market prices (MP), the difference being the impact of indirect taxes and subsidies. Market prices are easier data to collect but, given there is more indirect taxation than subsidies, they inflate the size of economy output. Additionally there is a distinction beween national (N) and domestic (D) income or product; the latter only includes the output of residents of the country and deducts net income from the ownership of foreign assets. These distinctions provide eight possible denominators which are, in order of magnitude, beginning with the smallest:

Measure 1   NDP at FC
Measure 2   NDP at MP
Measure 3   NNP at FC
Measure 4   NNP at MP
Measure 5   GDP at FC
Measure 6   GDP at MP
Measure 7   GNP at FC
Measure 8   GNP at MP

With at least six possible numerators and eight possible denominators, it is very easy to see how very differing views on the size and growth of the public sector are readily sustained.

An example of the employment of these estimates and the care required in their interpretation has been outlined by Gillie (1979). He notes that in 1976 Milton Friedman was reported as saying: 'Total government spending in Great Britain (central and local) amounts to some 60% of the national income ... . I fear very much that the odds are at least 50–50 that within the next five years British freedom and democracy as we have seen it will be destroyed' (Friedman, 1976). Similarly, in 1976 Roy Jenkins (then the Labour Party's Home Secretary and former Chancellor of the Exchequer) appears to make the same point: 'I do not think that you can push public expenditures significantly above 60% and maintain the values of a plural society' (Jenkins, 1976). Both statements have an emotive tone and alert the listener to the size of the public sector, but what does 60 per cent mean? First, it is not a satisfactory measure of government influence on the individual. It does not encompass laws and legislation determined by government, e.g. compulsory seat-belt legislation involves little in the way of direct government expenditure or transfer action but nevertheless commits all car-owners to a cost-incurring response. Second, it rests on a numerator which is as large as seems possible. In 1976 total general government expenditure was £58,506 million. This embraced transfers and, if these are netted out, a figure for central government expenditure on goods and services would be 33 per cent of national income (Gillie, 1979). Transfers are spent by private individuals on goods and services in exactly the same way as others spend wages, interest or profit earnings. They are not *spent* by government. Certainly, they pass through government 'hands' to effect income redistribution. However, as pointed out above, this goal could be pursued by tax credits rather than direct subsidy. The size of government measured in public expenditure terms would thereby be smaller than the measure referred to by Friedman, but the involvement of the state need not be reduced. To the extent that a figure for the numerator records transfers it must, of course, always be remembered that there is no logical reason why this ratio could not exceed 100 per cent. The denominator does not incorporate transfer payments.

While the estimate of government expenditure is larger by selecting the appropriate numerator, the public sector appears larger by choosing the smallest denominator. National income in 1976 was £96,676m and hence 60 per cent is recorded, but we realize that, given problems in estimating capital depreciation, GNP rather than NNP is typically used as a denominator. In 1976 Gillie records public *exhaustive* expenditures as 29 per cent of GNP, at factor cost. Of course, if the intention were to minimize government, one might record it as a percentage of GNP at market price, i.e. 25.9 per cent. The emotive impact associated with the statement that public expenditure is 26 per cent of GNP is substantially reduced.

In the early sections of this chapter, public sector growth in accordance with Wagner's Law was virtually unquestioned. One commentator, however, draws attention to some recent doubt. The ratio of exhaustive expenditure to GNP at factor cost may be used to reflect the share of income which is spent by government. Such ratios confirm public sector growth when estimates are considered in current prices, but what of real terms? Beck (1976) has argued that the price (cost) index of government services rose by a greater margin than the price index of GDP or total output. Table 3.1 presents evidence discussed by Peacock (1979). This highlights the effect of constant prices for the size of the public sector measured as the ratio of government consumption expenditure to gross domestic product. In those cases where the elasticity is less than unity this means that G/Y falls rather than rises

Table 3.1 Elasticity of government expenditure for consumption, 1950–74, and the size of the public sector

	Current price data			Constant price data	
		G/Y (%)			G/Y (%)
	Elasticity 1950–74 (1)	1950 (2)	1974 (3)	Elasticity 1950–74 (4)	1974 (5)
Austria	1.39	11.3	15.3	0.48	7.1
Canada	2.00	10.3	19.2	1.27	12.4
Denmark	2.43	10.2	23.2	1.47	13.4
Finland	1.59	11.1	17.2	0.96	10.7
France	1.02	12.9	13.0	0.52	8.6
Germany, West	1.41	14.3	19.7	0.78	12.0
Greece	1.20	11.5	13.6	0.60	8.0
Ireland	1.54	12.1	17.6	1.09	12.9
Netherlands	1.45	12.2	17.2	0.55	8.6
Sweden	1.82	13.7	23.6	1.19	15.4
Switzerland	1.08	11.2	12.0	0.67	9.0
United Kingdom	1.30	16.3	20.5	0.78	14.1
United States	1.74	12.1	19.1	1.23	13.7
Median	1.59	12.1	17.6	0.79	12.4

G = government consumption expenditure; Y = gross domestic product; Elasticity = ratio of percentage change in G to percentage change in Y.
Source: Peacock (1979).

as income rises. Note this reversal of the elasticity for Austria, Finland, France, West Germany, Greece, Netherlands, Switzerland and the UK over the period indicated. Peacock notes that as capital expenditure is relatively 'small', any real rise in aggregate government expenditure as a ratio of GNP over this period would be attributable to an increase in the real value of transfer expenditures. Certainly, the price deflators of Beck beg discussion, but sufficient has been said to caution acceptance of current price data.

Beck (1985), in his last scientific paper before his death, looked at recent public expenditure data for the US economy. He confirms Wagner's rising share hypothesis to the extent that between 1960 and 1982 total government expenditure as a percentage of GNP in current dollars rose from 26.9 to 35.5 per cent. However, the introduction of different price deflators for the numerator and the denominator, reflecting the fact that the price index for public expenditures rose faster than the GNP price index, makes the 1980 figure a more modest 29.2 per cent. The 2.3 per cent increase in the ratio of total government expenditure to GNP in 1960 dollars comprised a 6.1 per cent increase in the transfer share, making the 1980 figure 13.2 per cent and a 3.8 per cent decline in the exhaustive share lowering it to 16.0 per cent in 1980. The constant dollar elasticities with respect to GNP were 2.71 and 0.62 over the 20-year period. Given the differences that can be generated by different treatments of the data it is not surprising that there is debate over whether nominal or real magnitudes are the ones to be concerned with. Beck's position is that in order to investigate public sector growth there is a need for theorists to distinguish between changes in the volume of public services and changes in their relative prices.

3.4 EXPLICIT AND IMPLICIT TAXATION

Two major problems have been noted in discussing the size of the public sector. The first is the difficulty of interpreting such data as already exist in official publications. The second is the problem of estimating government activity for which no obvious estimate immediately exists. For example, government regulation may imply as important an intrusion in the decisions of individuals as taxation, but it is ignored in conventional measures of the public sector. The legislative activities of government constitute an important aspect of public sector activity, but, as they may imply no direct flow of funds to or from the government purse, they are ignored within the conventional ratios.

One approach to this question is to consider other government activity in terms of the *implicit* tax or subsidy that would be required to create the same results. Thus, for example, in figure 3.2 the consumption of a good may be reduced from Oq_1 to Oq_2 by an *ad valorem* tax which causes the selling price to rise by x per cent. Since constant costs are assumed (i.e. the marginal cost curve is horizontal), the welfare loss associated with this tax is estimated by triangle ABC. Tax revenue of $(P(1+t)-P_1) \cdot (Oq_2)$ will be reaped. Such finance will figure in public expenditure and appear directly in the ratios which have been the centre of discussion so far. However, government may have attained exactly the same result, as far as consumers are concerned, by legislating that output of this good shall not exceed Oq_2. The supply of the good would be constrained, and in figure 3.2 would be $P_1B\bar{S}$. Price would rise to $P(1+t)$ though no *explicit* tax were applied. Existing producers would reap an addition to their producer surplus of $(P(1+t)-P_1) \cdot (Oq_2)$. Indeed, if the overall objective of policy were a redistribution via income to these producers, the goal may be as easily effected by regulation as by a tax/subsidy scheme, whereby tax revenues were

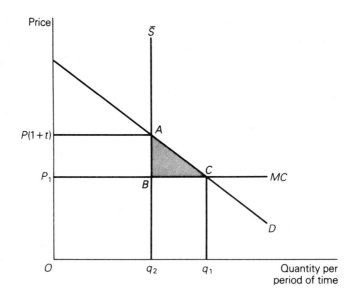

Figure 3.2 Regulation and implicit taxation

redistributed to government. Clearly, the size of the government in terms of the ratios already discussed would be far less if regulation were employed than if a tax/subsidy were applied. In effect, other forms of government can be considered as *implicit* taxation and subsidy.

Much of the Leviathan literature, to which attention is focused, is concerned with the 'intrusion' of government. Hence, it appears that the size of the public sector would be more appropriately estimated if both explicit and implicit taxation and subsidy were estimated. The task is obviously difficult, but it potentially holds significant policy implications. For example, in international comparisons of government activity, Prest (1985, p. 21) notes: 'Nor should it be assumed that explicit and implicit tax burdens are necessarily positively correlated in the sense that countries with higher than average rates of explicit taxation to GNP are likely to indulge relatively more in implicit taxation. Indeed, the reverse is more likely in that taxation by one mode can so readily be a substitute for taxation by the other'.

There are many examples in which implicit and explicit taxes and expenditures can be substitutes. For example, tax expenditures are examples of implicit expenditure substituting for explicit expenditure. When governments conscript labour for national defence an implicit tax is substituted for an explicit expenditure. When protection duties mean that consumers buy domestic output at higher prices, they are paying an implicit tax rather than the explicit tax on imports (e.g. the Common Agricultural Policy of the European Economic Community; see Morris, 1980). Yet they may not always be substitutes. For example, inflation pushes taxpayers into higher income bands and implicitly increases tax rates when taxation is not price index-linked. Here, implicit taxation may be associated positively with explicit expenditure.

Attempts have been made to quantify some of these implicit taxes and implicit expenditures. For example, Prest (1985) notes that the Bank of England (1982) presented a figure of taxation by inflation of £12 billion and the Institute of Fiscal Studies (1983) estimates implicit taxation in the Common Agricultural Policy at £4 billion. In the USA and West Germany, tax expenditure budgets are presented. To examine the size of government it would be necessary to include many other examples. If comprehensive, the idea of estimating government as an implicit tax offers a means of providing in one figure an estimate of the public sector. The problems of estimation are, however, formidable.

3.5 SUMMARY AND CONCLUSIONS

The main point we would make with reference to estimating the role of government in economic affairs is that, prior to selection of data, it is imperative to be clear conceptually about what is actually to be gauged. Government spending as a ratio of GNP is but one estimate. It does not satisfactorily tell us about government influence, since this occurs via many other routes. For example, as already explained, legislation and control may imply reduced spending; income redistribution can be achieved by tax credits. Yet in both cases government affects the welfare of individuals. Moreover, even when the welfare effects of direct taxation are considered, these do not only depend upon total tax revenue. The allocative impact (i.e. interference with consumer decisions) may be lower when general taxes create higher revenue than for selective taxes with lower revenue. Estimates of government spending are precisely that, and are far from adequate proxies for government influence. In different contexts it may be more appropriate to estimate government activity in terms of the ratio of tax revenue to GNP or the percentage of employment within the public sector. The choice of estimate should be tailored to the issue in question. When government spending is precisely the issue in question, it is important to distinguish between exhaustive and transfer expenditure. The latter has been a major force in the growth of government in many industrial countries as redistribution goals have been pursued.

In general, in so far as international comparison is appropriate, it is questionable that the UK or the USA is out of step as far as public expenditure is concerned. Table 3.2 shows that public spending and taxation for the UK by the 1980s hardly appears alarming by comparison with certain other countries. The emotive arguments of pro-market economists in the UK and the USA may be perceived as somewhat spurious, and in need of perspective.

As our theme has been the difficulty of data interpretation, we have purposely avoided providing a compendium of data. Further, it is one thing to measure the size of the public sector; it is another to measure Leviathan or the 'excessive' public sector. Whilst Brennan and Buchanan (1980) are concerned at the growth of government in the twentieth century, they are cautious on interpreting such evidence. Amongst the qualifications raised they note that: 'Nor does the growth of government *per se* imply that government is too large: there is no presumption that government was the "right size" in 1902 or that increases in size do

Table 3.2 General government expenditure and receipts as percentages of GDP[a]

Country	Current expenditure on goods and services (1984)	Current disbursements[b] (1983)	Current receipts (1983)
Australia	17.1	32.4	32.6
Denmark	25.9	58.2	53.1
France	16.4	48.6	47.7
West Germany	20.1	44.4	45.2
Italy	19.4	51.5	45.3
Japan	10.0	28.1	30.4
Sweden	27.8	61.3	60.0
The Netherlands	16.8	58.0	56.1
United Kingdom	21.9	44.3	42.5
United States	18.8	36.9	31.7[c]

[a] At current prices and exchange rates.
[b] Current disbursements = Current expenditures on goods and services *plus* current transfers and payments of property income.
[c] For the United States in 1983 taxation as a percentage of nominal GNP/GDP at market prices comprised: direct taxes (14.5%); indirect taxes (8.5%) and social security contributions (8.3%) (see OECD, 1985).
Source: OECD (1986).

not accurately reflect electoral wishes' (p. 24). If government failure were not pervasive, then large or small public sectors would not be a problem in and of themselves. However, the simultaneous existence of governmental failure and public sector growth has raised the fear of Leviathan, and it is to explanations of growth that we now turn.

NOTES

1 For example, the tax distortion associated with greater public expenditure need not necessarily increase if the tax base were to change.
2 Their exclusion is generally justified by the fact they have to sell their output very much like private sector firms.
3 There are social security, unemployment insurance workers' compensation, veterans' disability compensation, railroad retirement, black lung and Medicare.

REFERENCES

Beck, M. (1976), The expanding public sector: some contrary evidence, *National·Tax Journal*, vol. 29, no. 1 (March), pp. 15–21.

Beck, M. (1985), Public expenditure, relative prices, and resource allocation, *Public Finance/Finances Publiques*, vol. 40, no. 1, pp. 17–34.

Bird, R. M. (1971), Wagner's 'Law' of expanding state activity, *Public Finance/ Finances Publiques*, vol. 26, no. 1, pp. 1–26.

Brennan, G. and Buchanan, J. M. (1980), *The Power to Tax: Analytical Foundations of a Fiscal Constitution*, Cambridge: Cambridge University Press.

Brennan, G. and Pincus, J. M. (1983), Government expenditure growth and resource allocation: the nebulous connection, *Oxford Economic Papers*, vol. 35, no. 3 (November), pp. 351–65.

Brown, C. V. and Jackson, P. M. (1986), *Public Sector Economics*, 3rd edn, Oxford: Martin Robertson.

Dasgupta, P. (1986), Positive freedom, markets and the welfare state, *Oxford Review of Economic Policy*, vol. 2, no. 2, pp. 25–36.

Friedman, M. (1976), The line we dare not cross: the fragility of freedom at 60%, *Encounter*, November.

Gillie, A. (1979), *Measuring the Government Sector: Size and Productivity*, Milton Keynes: Open University Press.

Heald, D. (1983), *Public Expenditure*, Oxford: Martin Robertson.

Hirshleifer, J. (1984), *Price Theory and Application*, 3rd edn, Englewood Cliffs, NJ: Prentice Hall.

Jenkins, R. (1976), Speech to the Anglesey CLP, 23 January 1976.

Morris, C. N. (1980), The common agricultural policy, *Fiscal Studies*, vol. 1, no. 2 (March), pp. 17–35.

Musgrave, R. A. (1969), *Fiscal Systems*, New Haven and London: Yale University Press.

OECD (1985), *Economic Surveys 1985/86, United States*, November, Paris: OECD.

OECD (1986), *Economic Surveys 1985/86, United Kingdom*, January, Paris: OECD.

Peacock, A. (1979), *The Economic Analysis of Government and Related Themes*, Oxford: Martin Robertson.

Peacock, A. T. and Wiseman, J. (1979), Approaches to the analysis of government expenditure growth, *Public Finance Quarterly*, vol. 7, no. 1 (January), pp. 3–23.

Prest, A. R. (1985), Implicit taxes, *The Royal Bank of Scotland Review*, no. 147 (September), pp. 10–26.

Rosen, H. S. (1985), *Public Finance*, Homewood, Illinois: Irwin.

Smith, D. (1982), Transfer payments and public expenditure, pp. 3–40 in Maunder, P. (ed.), *Case Studies in Public Sector Economics*, London: Heinemann.

4

The Growth of the Public Sector

4.1 INTRODUCTION

Leaving aside the debate over the appropriate measure of the size of the public sector, and taking it as an axiom that it has grown (if only because this is a common belief) *what factors account for this growth?* Wildavsky (1985, p. 349) puts it: 'Why does public spending grow? Because, the literature tells us, nations are rich, because they are poor, because their economies are open, because their economies are closed, because there is consensus, because there is conflict.' There has, then, been no shortage of answers to the 'growth' question; however, they cannot be treated as alike in that they involve different types of explanation or rationalization. Following Klein (1976) we have collected our survey of accounts under different heads to indicate their different natures. But before surveying, albeit briefly, these types of explanation it is worth emphasizing why, apart from pure curiosity, there is interest in accounting for public sector growth.

From an evaluative viewpoint the answer normally lies in the two criteria used by economists to assess public policy matters – namely efficiency and equity. Here, however, these are modified slightly to efficiency and freedom. The efficiency criterion has been discussed in chapter 1 and dominates the evaluative statements in chapters 2 to 9, where aspects of alleged public sector inefficiency are explained. Equity has been largely displaced by 'freedom' as a relevant evaluative criterion in chapter 10 for two reasons. First, part of the rationale of public sector intervention is to achieve equity, and although there is much debate about whether the equity of society is increased by actual public sectors it is our perception, at least, that somewhat less criticism has been attracted on this score. Rather the criticism has been that what equity has been achieved has been brought at too great a sacrifice to freedom. Second, there is already a large literature on equity that readers can consult (see for example Le Grand, 1982[1]), and hence more may be gained if a less well-established aspect of the public sector debate is considered. In summary, throughout this work mechanisms described will be appraised against two questions: 'Are they inefficient?' and 'Are they anti-libertarian?' Given this the majority of the book could be described as having a normative purpose. Attention focuses upon the question of whether or not, on either efficiency grounds or on concern for freedom, the public sector has grown to an 'excessive' size. Many, though not necessarily all, of the explanations of public sector advanced below imply a positive response to this question. If these are the dominant causes of public sector growth then there may appear genuine cause for alarm.

Given the above, the work of Musgrave (1985) must be awarded prominence. He tries to establish the efficiency benchmarks for public goods, publicly provided private goods and redistribution, and then to assess if there are clear sources of bias to their over-provision. For public goods, arguments along the lines of those used in chapter 2 section 2.3 are employed, to suggest a necessary bias. For private goods provided in the public sector over-provision is thought more likely. However, two caveats apply. First, private market transactions, if available, will in some cases allow adjustment towards efficient quantities. Second there may be few truly private goods provided by government once externality/merit–want type arguments are considered. On redistribution Musgrave finds the optimal level of transfers a very difficult magnitude to define. After reviewing a number of possible defining approaches he concludes (p. 306):

> The growth of redistributive programs – be they in cash or of the in-kind (categorical) variety – has been a major factor in budgetary expansion. But it is by no means evident to what extent this growth has been the outcome of a 'legitimate process' reflecting changing voter preferences in distributive matters, or the product of a malfunctioning of the political system by which budgetary decisions are reached.

If such a conclusion can be accepted the balance of attention devoted to the various issues in this current work is appropriate.

4.2   A MICRO-ECONOMIC APPROACH

There are a number of reasons for predicting the growth of the public sector that rely on changes in the structure of supply and demand for public sector goods and transfers. Some relevant headings are prompted by the elements in demand and supply functions. In order to set up a 'base' explanation for this sub-heading two strong assumptions are made. First, that private–public sector allocation decisions are carried out in an efficient manner, so that the mix of goods and services produced reflects the quantities of each that individuals demand when each good or service is priced at its marginal cost of production. The consequences of relaxing this assumption are briefly introduced in sections 4.3 and 4.4, and discussed in detail in chapters 5, 6 and 7. The second assumption made is that the production of goods and services is efficient, so that not only are maximum units of output obtained from the inputs used, but the least-cost factor combination is chosen for each level of output. Whether this assumption is more likely to correspond to public, voluntary (non-profit) or private (for-profit) production is partly discussed in chapter 6 and is the specific focus of chapter 7. In these circumstances the size of the public sector over time will reflect a number of influences:

Demand Influences

Tax prices have an important role to play in the micro-economic analysis of the public sector. In analysis they perform the same role as prices in the market sector of the economy, that is locating production of a quantity of a good or service per unit of time that a utility-maximizing individual would voluntarily choose to purchase. However, it must be recognized that, in a market context, prices are a clear-cut, easily understood feature, yet in the public sector they are rather nebulous and difficult to track down. Although for the purpose of analysis it is reasonable to write of tax shares or tax prices it is to be remembered that no individual consumer voter (CV) faces individual prices for publicly provided goods and services, rather CVs vote for bundles of programmes offered by different parties. Each CV may, for example, only be aware of the proportion of his income that is directly taxed away. Any systematic errors in perception of actual tax prices are a cause for concern as they would suggest CVs 'demand' too much or too little public expenditure. This is discussed in some detail in chapter 5.

As regards the 'fiscal connection' between taxation and public expenditure itself, evidence provided by Lewis (1979a), and surveyed by the same author (1979b), leads him to conclude that:

> the results of the studies conducted by Piachaud and Mueller suggest that a realistic appreciation of the relationship between taxation and public expenditure is not a central aspect of taxpayer consciousness. This view is reinforced by the findings of the present author gleaned from a factor analysis of tax mentality calculated from the responses of 200 British taxpayers (Lewis, 1979b, p. 4).

This model does not, of course, preclude the building of models that, for example, embody the seemingly false assumption that the median voter equates marginal benefit with the tax price of any public sector good or service. However, for empirical work there is the problem of devising a reliable proxy for the tax share of the median voter. Some studies, however, have come to grips with this problem. For example, Bergstrom and Goodman (1973) look at the demand for police, parks and recreation expenditures, as well as expenditures on education and welfare. Their price variable for public goods (the tax share of the citizen with the median income for a municipality) is derived by noting that a majority of locally generated revenue comes from property tax, which in turn is largely levied on real property. To estimate the share of the tax on real property which is paid by the citizen with the median income, they assumed that the critical citizen owned the median value house, and this constituted all his property holding. The final step involved computing the tax bill on the house of median value (by finding the tax rate and ratios of assessed to market value in each community) and then dividing by the total property tax for the municipality.

By contrast, Borcherding and Deacon (1972) computed the marginal tax price of the quantity of a non-Federal government good or service by assuming: a Cobb Douglas production function; that production was carried out in a least-cost fashion and that the rental rate on capital was identical over all political units. Given these assumptions the authors derived a horizontal supply function for each state, namely

$$CX = aW^b$$

where CX = the marginal cost of X;

a   = a constant term common to all states;
b   = labour share of income for each state;
W   = wage rate in a given state.

Both studies claimed success with their chosen methods (estimated price elasticities were generally significant and negative). They are reported here simply as illustrative of empirical tax price proxies. For those following a 'positive' methodology, it is the potential refutation of hypotheses derived from abstract models by empirical data that justifies the use of deliberately unreal economic models. For our purposes it is sufficient, first, that public choice debates are conducted, and implications drawn employing tax price analysis and second that, other things equal, there is an inverse relationship between tax prices and the quantities of public sector goods and services demanded.

Income is a variable that alters the position of demand or marginal benefit curves. For so-called normal or luxury goods provided in the public sector, increases in income should shift the curve rightwards, and vice-versa for inferior goods. Although in recent years per capita income has not grown rapidly, historically income has grown so that establishing that publicly provided goods or services have a positive income elasticity greater than unity would help explain Wagner's Law. Broadly speaking the evidence is mixed.

Musgrave and Musgrave (1976) indicate there is no decided pattern in the income elasticities for public sector consumer goods and services. They suggest some will be greater than unity (e.g. health, higher education), others less than unity (e.g. basic education). As for capital expenditure there is also ambiguity. In the early stages of development they suggest social infrastructure justified by natural monopoly or non-private goods arguments (e.g. electricity supply and roads) will dominate. In later stages externality-correcting and human capital investment expenditures might be expected to replace the infrastructure expenditure, yielding no clear prediction on the connection between income growth and public sector investment expenditures per period. A second connection between income and public expenditure arises via income-related (means-tested) welfare state provisions which are triggered by income falling below a certain level. Such transfer expenditures will vary immensely with the state of the economy, and hence the success or otherwise of macro-economic policy in maintaining full employment. As noted above, how this affects the 'size' of the public sector turns on measurement methodology. Additionally, to the extent welfare state provisions are designed to reflect real living standards, then in the longer period the level of such provisions should rise in real terms also.

Complementarity and substitutability relationships within the public sector and between the private and public sectors are also likely to be of considerable significance. Musgrave and Musgrave (1976), for example, suggest that the public sector provides the non-private-good complements of (rising income) individual purchases. Boat marinas and airports are ready examples.

Preferences and tastes are usually taken as datum in economics, and therefore have attracted relatively little discussion. Here two points are worth making. First Galbraith (1962) and his followers argue that individual preferences are distorted away from public sector goods and services by the intensity of market private goods advertising. Second, however, there is the interdependence which revolves around the issue of endogeneity of preferences. Weisbrod (1975) notes the significance of endogenous preferences, and our later discussion in chapter 7, which refers to Titmuss (1970) and Cooper and Culyer (1968), explores this argument.

Population size and structure is an important factor affecting public expenditure. Many elements of public sector provision are directly or indirectly age- or numbers-related. Education is differentially consumed by the younger sections of the population and health care by the older ones. Welfare state provisions are often 'contingent'-based. Being in a certain category (e.g. single-parent family, retired, etc.) may automatically qualify individuals for in-kind benefits or cash transfers. To the extent that such contingent-based provisions are 'freely' given, or at least not readily charged, they put a considerable volume of public expenditure outside the day-to-day control of government. For example, people are tending to live longer than they did in the past; for the period 1953 to 1976 in the UK, the number of people over retirement age increased by some 2.7 million, causing government expenditures on pensions to increase considerably (Smith, 1982).

Supply Influences

Technology and factor prices are two key determinants of the marginal cost of an additional unit of output per period, and therefore influence supply. Technology is embodied as the production function that relates maximum outputs to given quantities of the inputs. Factor prices are simply the rewards that have to be offered factor owners to compensate them for taking part in the production process. Normally they are treated as independent factors but in this context there is a well-known argument that connects the two and produces a prediction of rising costs of public sector provision. This prediction has become known as Baumol's Law (Baumol, 1967). The argument, at its simplest, notes that public services are labour-intensive forms of output (for example, approximately 60 per cent of Britain's NHS expenditure is labour costs) and such activities are less open to productivity increases consequent on changes in technology. Over time the rising productivity of workers in, most notably, the manufacturing sector will be reflected in higher wages for them. Whether because of the power of unions to use the 'comparability principle', or simply the need to compete for workers that would otherwise go to manufacturing, remuneration in the public sector can also be expected to rise, although productivity has remained unaltered. In these circumstances, if the demand for public sector activities (or the political interpretation of it) is price-inelastic, then the provision of a constant volume of activities over time becomes increasingly expensive. Hence this productivity lag argument is consistent with the operation of Wagner's Law.

The welfare interpretation of this 'relative price effect', as it is also known, turns on an analysis of its source. Is it 'natural' or 'unnatural'? Some commentators clearly see the labour intensity of public sector activities as inherent and immutable; so that, for example, nursing is about a sick person having contact with, and help from, another *human* being. It may be possible to have mechanized and/or computerized help, but this is not nursing. The human element is part of the service being provided. Teaching might be another example. Peacock and Wiseman (1979) offer an alternative view. They suggest there are no technical limitations making for labour intensity in the public sector; rather they note there may be institutional barriers. A speculation as to the cause of such barriers is also offered. Bureaucrats protected from competition have discretion and may seek to maximize 'power'. Hence their reluctance to lose labour intensity in the production process. This argument, however, lies outside the scope of this subsection where least-cost production has been assumed. Both bureaucratic decision-making and the relative price effect are pursued further in chapter 6.

Other supply factors have largely been removed by the assumptions made in this section, but are discussed below when these assumptions are relaxed. In particular the objectives of suppliers of governmental activities will be explored.

In a recent article Borcherding (1985) uses an elasticity analysis to attempt to consider the empirical impact of apolitical or institutional factors (relative prices, income and population growth) on government growth. His figures suggest that these factors account for a 1.1 per cent approximate annual growth in US public budgets. On this evidence these factors could explain a government sector of 18 per cent of GNP in 1978 as opposed to its actual recorded value of 35 per cent. Total institutional effects then appear to be clearly significant, but only to the extent of explaining 52 per cent of the US public spending growth 1902–78. If accepted this, of course, leaves considerable room in which other influences can manoeuvre.

To the extent that public sector growth can be explained by an appeal to the 'undistorted' effects of the factors above, then it is a reflection of individual demands and marginal cost prices, and this conforms with the underpinnings of conventional micro-economic analysis. (For a positive micro-model of public sector growth, incorporating factors described here, see Brown and Jackson, 1986). In short the public sector, whether thought absolutely large or small, would be at its efficient size. If these explanations do not hold, or are thought partial, then other explanations must be turned to, and it is then evident that inefficiency, with its implied welfare loss, may be present. However, as outlined below, not all explanations are couched within the conventional economic paradigm and some economic explanations are more macro than micro. Since the concern of this book is micro-economics the remainder of the listed explanations are provided in part simply to isolate the 'inefficient' micro-economic mechanisms that are the centre of the subsequent analysis.

4.3 THE POLITICAL PROCESS

Political process bias, favouring an inefficiently large public sector, centres on the arguments of chapter 2 (namely the position of CVs, the constitutional rule and the role of the political entrepreneur). The arguments are not repeated here, save to stress the implications for growth. It was determined in chapter 2 that voters would be 'rationally ignorant'. Some arguments, however, suggest that they may be 'fiscally illuded' in a specific direction. Some authors expect voters to underestimate the real cost of public expenditure programmes. As a result an excessive level of expenditure is demanded. These views are more fully developed and challenged in chapter 5. Here, however, with reference to a distinctively separate literature, we outline some reasons for a misunderstanding of the costs of public sector programmes.

Bacon and Eltis (1976) have an account of 'too large' a public sector in the UK that, in part, draws on the valuation and/or perception of public sector activities. In essence their reasoning is as follows. The public sector has increased rapidly in size over the 1960s and early 1970s, which has to be financed out of the production of marketed output (overwhelmingly the private sector). Although taxes have been levied on wages to finance the public sector, the wage-earners, so the argument runs, have either not valued the increased 'social wage' or have not perceived any change in the 'social wage', and have tacitly refused to finance the public sector. Their concern with 'take-home pay' has led them to resist tax increases with claims for wage increases. In the Bacon–Eltis scenario this has been achieved by trade unions passing on the taxes to profits following a period of rapid wage increases. Retained profits is the main source of investment funds in Britain, so that ultimately the price of the increased public sector has been reduced investment and consequent economic problems on all fronts. Some evidence relevant to this theory which enjoyed considerable currency is discussed in chapter 9.

Failure to accept the logical tax increases that would maintain the 'social wage' has occurred within this account by the successful resistance to tax increases on the part of an important section of the voting community. Pressure for increased public programmes is therefore not abated. However, there is an argument that suggests that *all* individuals will fail to accept the logical full tax price of public programmes, and this hangs on the question of debt finance. When government finance rests on taxation a sacrifice is apparent to the public. When government makes good its finance requirements by borrowing, creditors purchasing government bonds *voluntarily* enter into an inter-temporal consumption arrangement from which they can hardly be considered to suffer (Buchanan, 1958). *Tax payers* thereby pay less than one dollar for each dollar-worth of public expenditure and the budget deficit is financed by borrowing. This Keynesian heritage appears to delude voters in the specific direction of increased public sector activity (Buchanan and Wagner, 1978). With reference to chapter 2 it soon becomes clear how a specific bias for public expenditure growth can enter the debate. We postpone further discussion of this issue until chapter 9.

Log-rolling agreements can explicitly generate this bias, as explained in chapter 2. However an *implicit* agreement to vote favourably on increased public expenditure is also said to arise within the political process as more and more individuals become dependent upon the public sector for their employment. The livelihood of many families becomes dependent on resisting cuts and promoting increases in public expenditure. To the extent that these may operate as a block-vote there is clearly the potential for a snowball effect. The more the public sector grows, the greater it ties the fortunes of voters to its future and, the greater the dependency, the more favourably voters react to a maintenance or increase in public sector activity (see Busch and Denzau, 1977).

Recent writings by Becker (1985), Linbeck (1985) and Mueller and Murrell (1986) emphasize the role of interest groups in government expenditure growth, especially in the form of redistribution policies. Becker has taxpayer and subsidy groups lobbying for their position to be advanced. Similarly Linbeck has income redistribution being sought for several reasons, of which narrow self-interest is the predominant one. The deadweight costs and benefits of taxation have an important role to play in Becker's analysis because, as they affect the 'price' of pressure, they modify the quantity. Linbeck gives emphasis to so-called 'fragmented horizontal redistributions' as a strong case of government growth in recent decades. Such redistribution seems very close to the special-interest legislation described in chapter 2, i.e. benefits are small-group specific whereas the tax costs are general. Mueller and Murrell test the hypothesis that the relative size of government is positively related to the number of organized interest groups. In a number of cross-section econometric and sample specifications the number of interest groups shows up as consistently positive, leading Mueller and Murrell (1986, p. 140) to conclude that 'interest groups are able to influence public policies in such a manner as to lead to increased government size'. The elasticity at the sample mean of the interest group variable is estimated at 0.18 (other things equal, if the public expenditure is currently 35 per cent of GDP, a 10 per cent increase in the absolute number of interest groups would raise the 35 per cent to 35.7 per cent). The normative interpretation of the argument and finding outlined here need to be considered against the background provided by Musgrave (1985), noted above.

4.4　GOVERNMENTAL EXPLANATIONS

Here the focus of attention shifts to the hierarchical structure and incentive mechanism inherent in the executive or administrative branch of government. A major part of any governmental explanation of Wagner's Law is the literature on the economics of bureaucracy reviewed in chapter 2 and considered further in chapter 6 below. If the analysis has force the implication is that politicians are largely in the hands of the full-time civil servants and, even if they are not, it is clear that a plausible case can be made out for them having similar motivation to that of the bureaucrats. Klein and Sandford (Sandford, 1979) have pointed out that it may be significant that there was only one treasury minister in the cabinet during recent periods of very rapid public expenditure growth. However, beyond this standard bureaucratic model, which questions inappropriate incentives, there lies a literature which casts greater emphasis upon the sheer difficulty of dealing with public expenditure. In the first instance the problem of estimating departmental requirements for the coming year has, it is alleged, been met by an 'incrementalist' rule which explains public sector growth. In the second case we note the difficulties of resisting government growth have been attributed to the complexities of the 'system'.

The simplest approach to explaining government expenditure would rely on the 'incrementalist' model of budgetary determination outlined by Davis, Dempster and Wildavsky (1966) and Wildavsky (1964 and 1975). Here the cabinet government minister responsible for a given expenditure is predicted to request a constant percentage increase in his allocation of funds each budgetary period. The response of the full cabinet or executive would be, in this model, to apply a simple rule that allowed on average only a constant percentage of the claim made (the percentage being less than 100). More formally, the health minister, for example, would claim an allocation of general taxation $H't$ that was a 'mark-up' $\alpha_0(>1)$ of the health care expenditure of the previous year $(Ht-1)$, i.e.:

$$H't = \alpha_0 Ht-1 + u \qquad (4.1)$$

where u is a randomly distributed error term. The actual budget allocation (Ht) would then be determined by the executive as

$$Ht = \alpha_1 H't + v \qquad (4.2)$$

where α_1 is a constant (<1) and v is also a randomly distributed error term. Substituting for $H't$ in (4.2) yields

$$Ht = A\ Ht-1 + E \qquad (4.3)$$

where $A = \alpha_0 \alpha_1$

and $E = u + v$

The major criticism this model attracted, despite its predictive success, was similar to those voiced in the debated over 'mark-up' pricing. That is, critics suggested that α_0 and α_1, and consequently A, would shift over time (see Williamson, 1967) and would in fact reflect conventional economic conditions and arguments. Hence the model was viewed as a generalized political picture of a more complicated economic process. In short the possible determinants of Ht and A remain to be established in this model. In his more recent work Wildavsky (1985) explains differences in public sector growth rates and composition patterns between countries by reference to types of culture (market (bidding and bargaining to reduce the need for authority), hierarchic (institutionalized authority) and sectarian (foster equality to reduce the need for authority)). Myhrman (1985) notes that it would be desirable to be able to define and measure changes in culture over time, which seems to suggest he finds the approach too broadly specified in its current form. However, at minimum, Wildavsky does offer a taxonomy of budgetary strategies under different political systems.

At a more mundane level the difficulties of government decision-making are further illustrated by what might be termed 'the system' approach. This approach would argue that rules, processes and procedures take over from people as organizations become more complex. In terms of the growth of public expenditure this amounts to ascribing the changes that take place to changes in administrative and planning procedures of public expenditure; for example, the Public Expenditure Survey Committee. In this vein Sandford (1979), for example, writes of the relatively recent expansion of UK public expenditure that:

> A plausible case can be made out that, in the period since 1964, a major
> if not the predominant influence on changes in the share of the public
> sector in the economy has been the characteristics of the particular
> methods and techniques adopted to control and allocate resources,
> including the failure to adopt or adapt techniques when required
> (Sandford, 1979, p. 3).

There is, however, a basic weakness of 'the system' approach. This arises in that it has no actors to account for the system that is developed and operated. It seems rather like watching a first division football game and observing that the ball played very well.

Alt and Chrystal (1983) offer a rather different perspective on the public expenditure debate. They note the *stability* of the ratios to

GDP of the annual values of three categories of public expenditure (consumption, transfers and investment) in Britain for the period 1955–9. 'The fact to be explained is not the high variability of government expenditure but rather its *remarkable stability* with respect to the trend growth of national income' (Alt and Chrystal, 1983, p. 220). The explanatory model offered by Alt and Chrystal draws on Friedman's (1957) 'permanent income hypothesis' account of personal consumption spending. The authors hypothesize that public expenditures are planned to grow in proportion to expected or trend national income. The rationale for such an argument is a planning context in which expenditure growth is targeted on the expected growth of national income. Although there are errors in such expectations the broad picture is one of sluggish government expenditure largely independent of short-term income fluctuations responding to changes in trend of permanent national income only. Alt and Chrystal offer supporting econometric evidence for the UK and the USA for three types of expenditure noted above, and emphasize that 'A theory of public expenditure growth should at least start from the assumption that expenditures will take a stable share of national income in the long term' (Alt and Chrystal, 1983, p. 228). Burton (1985) is critical of this permanent income approach to government expenditures, and argues that if it has any validity it is for the period 1790–1905 rather than the post-World War II period investigated by Alt and Chrystal.

4.5   THE DISPLACEMENT HYPOTHESIS AND DEVELOPMENT PERSPECTIVES

By far the most quoted explanation of the relative growth of the government sector over time is that of Peacock and Wiseman (1961). Their essential observation was to note that the public sector, *as measured by government expenditure as a percentage of GNP*, grew over time in a stepwise rather than a smooth manner. Their proposed hypothesis to explain this comprised several elements. In what might be described as normal times, the size of the public sector and the 'tax threshold' remains largely unaltered, but during periods of major social upheaval (especially the two world wars) the public sector grows rapidly. Some peace-related government expenditures are 'displaced', and more than replaced by war-related expenditures, financed by a new higher tax threshold made acceptable by the 'crisis'. With the passing of the crisis it is possible for the old tax threshold to be re-established. However, rather than this occurring, war-related public expenditure is replaced by public expenditure devoted to long-standing problems made more visible by the crisis. This occurs as a result of an 'inspection effect'.

This displacement thesis rests upon an empirical examination of public sector growth in the UK. Figure 4.1 illustrates the growth in public expenditure at times of crisis (e.g. World Wars I and II) with government expenditure on the top path remaining at a higher level after the crisis has passed. The weight of the explanation falls on the financing side of public expenditure and a relaxation in this constraint. Peacock and Wiseman note that together with this displacement effect there is a concentration effect, whereby central government controls a greater proportion of the economy.

The hypothesis has come under criticism. Bird (1972) believes that, over the period of crisis, there is a replacement of peace-related expenditure by war-related expenditure together with a growth in public expenditure as a fraction of GNP. However, after the crisis G/GNP slowly reverts to the same trend rate of increase experienced prior to the crisis. The question is therefore whether Peacock and Wiseman have established a displacement effect of long-run significance. After

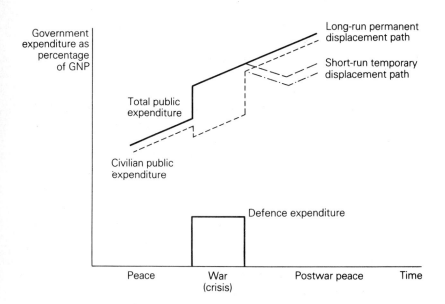

Figure 4.1   The displacement hypothesis

the crisis, does public expenditure continue to grow from a higher ratio, or is there an adjustment such that it reverts to the long-run trend dictated prior to the crisis?

Musgrave (1969), using illustrations, a modified version of which comprises figure 4.1, reviews the possibilities which are further discussed in Brown and Jackson (1986). Long-run permanent displacement, associated with Peacock and Wiseman, is viewed as crisis- (war)-related (defence) public expenditures being replaced by civilian expenditure in the post-war period. There is then a permanent displacement of private- by civilian-related public expenditure. The Musgrave (1969)–Bird (1970) position is that after the crisis defence expenditure falls and overall total expenditure (together with civilian expenditure) returns to the same trend experienced prior to the crisis. The effect is a short-run temporary one. The empirical research does not adequately resolve this issue but is well surveyed by Thompson (1979). Examples of the empirical work carried out can also be found in the Appendix to this chapter.

The essence of the Peacock and Wiseman approach is the limit of taxation that a community is prepared to tolerate. Clarke (1945, 1977) actually set a figure to the limits of taxation for an economy. It was set at 25 per cent of national income and might be breached only with dire consequences for inflation and freedom. It was described as an arbitrary figure (Heald, 1983), and certainly there is evidence that tax finance will breach this limit when availability exists. Musgrave and Musgrave (1976) present an explanation of the operation of Wagner's Law which rests on the availability of tax handles. Their argument applies to the ease of financing a large public sector as an economy develops. A less developed economy will lack the necessary civil service and administration to raise taxation, as well as the 'handles' on which to place taxes. The latter, they argue, come with increased economic specialization and trade, both intra- and internationally. Hence, the argument becomes that the more a country develops the easier it is for the public sector to grow. Also, they make mention of the less hostile attitude towards taxation that may be part and parcel of the development process. The argument that generally it may be easier to find funds for any given programme over time is consistent with findings that spending social security as a proportion of GNP is strongly correlated with the length of operation of the system (see Pryor, 1968). The Musgraves, however, have been criticized as outlining a facilitating process for growth rather than an explanation of the instigating process. The counterpart of the Musgraves' 'tax handles' study may be, for example, the finding of 'spending handles' by bureaucrats.

North (1985) considers the growth in US government from an historical (development) perspective; however the causal factors he isolates are divided into demand and supply ones. The key to his explanation is increasing specialization and division of labour. On the demand side he argues: specialization reduced production costs and potential gains from trade, but raised transactions costs, thereby increasing government's share of transactions services; extension of the scope of trade increased producer demand for government trade restrictions; with the increased participation of married women in the labour force the structure of families is altered to externalize to government some of its functions, especially of the social security and welfare type; increased specialization dramatically increases the number of special-interest groups via the increasing specificity of possible issues. On the supply side the increasing extractive power of government is emphasized. Specialization meant that sales and income taxes became major sources of revenue whose direct (assessment and collection) costs are borne by the traders and employers. This increasing efficiency of government taxation is clearly not unlike the tax handle argument.

4.6   A MARXIAN RATIONALE

A final general approach comes from the Marxists. Their explanations of the increasing role of the public sector receive scant attention in the popular texts on public finance and the economics of the public sector. Nevertheless, they put forward an explanation of the operation of Wagner's Law that deserves consideration. One contribution is discussed here by way of illustration. O'Connor (1973) begins by outlining the two often contradictory functions of the state in the capitalist world. The first is to maintain conditions which make profitable capital accumulation possible (remember for Marx the state encompassed more than simply government and was the coercive instrument of the ruling class). The second function is a legitimating one. The state has to create and maintain conditions for social harmony. These functions are often contradictory because if the state uses its power to help one class at the expense of another, then it is clearly in danger of losing legitimacy. On the other hand, if it does not make capital accumulation profitable, the source of its power (the tax on the surplus value produced) is endangered. Given this dilemma, the state must tread a difficult path, mystifying its activities wherever possible. (This is similar to the literature on special-interest effects with majority voting.)

Corresponding to the state's two functions are two types of expenditures for the provision of social capital and social expenses. The former are expenditures required for profitable accumulation and comprise social investment and social consumption. Social investment consists of projects and services that increase the productivity of a given amount of labour power and *ceteris paribus* increase the rate of profit. Social consumption consists of projects and services that lower the reproduction costs of labour and *ceteris paribus* increase the rate of profit. Social expenses consist of those projects and services which are required to maintain social harmony. O'Connor argues that nearly every state agency is involved in both functions, and goes on to present two basic theses. First, that growth of the state sector and state spending is functioning increasingly as the basis for the growth of the monopoly sector and total production. Simultaneously, it is argued that the growth of state spending is the result of growth of the monopoly sector. In short, the growth of the (American) state is both the cause and effect of the expansion of monopoly capital. Second, accumulation and social capital and social expenses is a contradictory process which creates tendencies towards crises of all forms. Particularizing this argument, health care expenses, for example, are viewed as social consumption, the 'socialization' of which (via Medicare and Medicaid) is favoured by monopoly capital and labour: the former because of the burden of expansion of medical insurance plans won by unions through collective bargaining, and the latter because this way they meet membership demands for comprehensive and better medical care. It is also possible to view vast and rapidly increasing expenditures of Medicare and Medicaid as social expenses designed to 'buy off' the poor and the unemployed.

Although interesting, broad explanations of public expenditure growth do not readily provide falsifiable predictions. For those wedded to the 'positive' approach, the Marxist approach in particular seems to be over-protected (in Popper's terms) yielding no refutable hypotheses. Foley (1978), in an alternative Marxist discussion of government expenditures, appears to come close to actually stating this when he writes: 'The exact mechanism by which capitalists as a class exercise pervasive power over state policy differ depending on historic and institutional realities' (Foley, 1978, p. 224).

4.7   LIMITS TO PUBLIC EXPENDITURE GROWTH

A natural question to ask concerns the limits to the public expenditure growth process implied by the various mechanisms in the literature. Beeton (1985) considers six, in his view complementary, 'global' theories of public sector expansion and suggests that they contain the seeds of their own limitations. The six theories associated with Wagner (1883, see Musgrave and Peacock, 1958), Baumol (1967), Peacock and Wiseman (1961), Busch and Denzau (1977) and Meltzer and Richard (1981) are reduced to four causal forces:

1   Wagner's Law and Baumol's productivity lag argument relate to *technical progress*;
2   Wagner's Law and Baumol's congestion costs[2] argument relate to *urbanization*;
3   Wagner's Law, Peacock and Wiseman's displacement hypothesis, Busch and Denzau's bureaucratic voting model and Meltzer and Richard's median voter model relate increasing demand for government sector output to the *extension of the franchise*;
4   Wagner, and Meltzer and Richard, associate economic development with public sector growth via *cultural change*.

As regards (1) Beeton suggests that the opportunities for large-scale technical advance are decreasing, and therefore the relative price of government activity should rise less quickly. Additionally he draws on Birch and Cramer (1968), who show that as the general government sector share in total employment rises, government sector wages fall further and further behind private sector wages. As for (2) urbanization (and hence congestion costs) should be on the wane as in the UK the percentage of the population living in metropolitan areas fell by over 13 per cent, 1963 to 1983.

Extension of the franchise is seen as a consequence of economic development for Peacock and Wiseman, and the source of permanent pressure that allows demand for government expenditure to rise in excess of government revenue *only* until the franchise is complete (which has occurred). Busch and Denzau's bureaucratic voting model is seen as self-limiting because extending the size of the low-productivity government sector reduces total output of the economy. Eventually bureaucrats have to face the fact that a larger share of a smaller pie will be less than a smaller share of a larger pie, and therefore they will self-interestedly desist from pushing for a larger public sector share. In the Meltzer and Richard model the median voter (with a lower income than the mean) triggers transfers from the minority to the majority. However the disincentive effects of taxation again suggest a pie-reducing constraint to the process. The final cultural change argument (4) is countered by the claim that cultural development, resulting in the introduction and growth of the welfare state, seems to be shifting emphasis away from this root towards private, rather than the collective provision, of welfare state activities. Hence Beeton suggests an upper limit to the size of the government sector and offers some evidence consistent with this limit having been reached. However a more detailed quantification of the upper limit has yet to be furnished.

4.8   SUMMARY AND CONCLUSIONS

The objective of this chapter has been to acquaint the reader with a broad selection of the wide variety of explanations which have been advanced in order to explain the growth of the public sector. It is the case that in some instances the public sector may be perceived to have grown according to the wishes of the community, and in response to advances in technology. In this respect it would be wrong to equate a growth of the public sector with the appearance of Leviathan. Leviathan exists when the growth of the public sector is 'excessive'; growth *per se* should not be equated with a threat to individuals and, indeed, may be perceived as a fulfilment of their wishes.

Some evidence and arguments consistent with a limited public sector have also been discussed. For many commentators, however, this is not sufficient to modify their view of the threatening Leviathan state.

It is then to areas where a threat appears to have presented itself that we now turn. We hope to reconsider whether Leviathan is real or a figment of a fertile imagination. Has growth of the public sector itself instilled paranoia?

4.1A   APPENDIX: EMPIRICAL WORK AND PUBLIC EXPENDITURE GROWTH

Econometric work on public expenditure has taken two forms. The first, which is outlined here, deals with isolating the determinants of public expenditure, whilst the second concentrates on the impact of the public sector on indicators of macro-economic performance (see chapter 9). The broad background of the work that has been done can be, to some extent, deduced from the discussion above, and is highlighted in Thompson (1979). There are a large number of sometimes competing, sometimes complementary, *a priori* explanations, not all of which involve variables that lend themselves to easy expression in regression analysis. This, combined with the fact that by and large different individuals have contributed to the theoretical and empirical debates, has made the econometric work somewhat *ad hoc*. A second theme is that there are strong political overtones to the results obtained, even if these are not central to the work of some of the researchers themselves. Finally because the work uses data from national income accounts it holds out possibilities of cross-section, time-series and pooled work for a myriad of possible definitions and categorizations of the statistics (see chapter 3). This to a large extent makes each piece of work unique.

As regards the main question asked, most of the earlier work was devoted to 'testing' Wagner's Law (viewed as a steadily increasing public sector share in GNP) and the Peacock and Wiseman hypothesis of displacement effects (involving discrete shifts away from a steady growth path). More recent work has been set out in a broader context involving political and other variables. Two contributions that typify those strands in the empirical work are Abizadeh and Gray (1985) and Solano (1983). These are discussed here as illustrations of the two genres. Abizadeh and Gray note that empirical work on Wagner's Law offers conflicting results. They are critical of the methodology that typically measures the elasticity of the ratio of government expenditures to GDP per capita (i.e. a single independent variable) in an indiscriminate sample of countries that includes those that are developed, developing, as well as those still in a pre-development stage. They cite the original works of Wagner (1883) and Bird (1971) as indications that the 'law' should apply to developing countries only, be applied in a time-series context, and involve more than a single development indicator. Hence their study involves the division of 53 countries into three roughly equal groups classified on the basis of the physical quality of life indicator[3] into poor, developing and developed countries. The data covered the period 1963–79 and were pooled within country groupings. The basic model was:

$$ER = \alpha_0 + \beta_1(T) + \beta_2(YRP)_{it} - \beta_3(AR)_{it}$$
$$+ \beta_4(ENP)_{it} + \beta_5(OP)_{it} - \beta_6(FI)_{it} + u$$

where i = countries 1, 2, ... n (number of countries);

t = years 1, 2, ... , m (number of years);

ER   = government expenditure ratio: total government expenditure in year t divided by GDP in year t, both in current value terms;

T   = time;

YRP = real per capita GDP in US dollars;

AR   = agricultural ratio: the proportion of GDP generated in the agricultural sector;

ENP = total commercial energy consumption per capita (coal equivalent in kilograms);

OP   = openness: (exports + imports) divided by GDP, both in current value terms;

FI   = financial intermediaries: currency outside banks divided by money supply, based on IMF definitions (approximately M_2) both in current value terms.

T was designed to capture the pace of development; YRP the level and trend of economic development; ENP the level and trend of industrialization; OP the development and diversification of the economy; AR is an additional variable used to measure both diversification and industrialization; FI is intended to capture the extent of financial sector development (the extent of reliance on cash transaction). The hypothesized signs are as in the equation, which was estimated using the ordinary least-square method (OLS). On the basis of the estimated coefficient, F value and R^2 the author concluded Wagner's Law did not apply to poor countries, did apply to developing countries and applied in *reverse* to developed countries (a declining ER being implied).

Solano's (1983) work relates to a cross-section of 18 highly developed (income per capita $1000 and over) democracies for the fiscal year 1968/69, and is distinctive because it considers: disaggregated budgets for defence, education and social security (health and welfare) as well as aggregate expenditures; central and non-central government spending as well as national outlays and institutional variables among the independent variables. The systematic variables were: economic development (PCI = per capita income in US dollars); federal or unitary form of government (FED, coded 1 for federation and zero for unitary countries); tax centralization (CTAX = proportion of national tax revenues collected by central government). For national and central expenditures variables relating to leftist parties (LEFT), coalition governments (COAL) and legislative decision rules (DEC) were tested. Demographic factors as captured by the dependent population (DEMO), the young (YOUTH) and country size (POP) were also employed in OLS coefficient estimation.

As Solano's study is partly concerned with disaggregated analysis, variables do not appear significant in all cases; however variables that were significant in a number of equations were: economic development (+); federal countries (−); tax centralization (+); legislative decision rules (+ where only one house has veto power over the central government budget); coalition government (+); demographic influences (YOUTH, POP but not DEMO). Interestingly, leftist parties did not appear to have a particular influence on public spending. The main conclusion Solano draws is that disaggregation is needed to identify the forces determining public expenditure.

Abizadeh and Gray offer some comfort for those arguing an anti-Leviathan line (the purpose of part II) suggesting there is a negative Wagner's Law for developed countries. Solano's evidence for coalition governments, tax centralization, federal and unitary systems and central legislative decision rules as significant variables in public expenditure determination, offers comfort for the public choice economists.

NOTES

1　Le Grand's own position has been misrepresented in some places. It is true that he highlights the lack of significant redistribution in Britain's welfare state, but this is with a view to increasing redistribution with the welfare state, rather than disbanding it.

2　Baumol (1967) argues that relative demand for public sector output will increase with the square of the urban population. This is because the greater the number of people, the more negative externalities are generated and the greater the number of people, the more affected parties there are for each externality.

3　The physical quality of life index uses combined information on life expectancy at age one, the reciprocal of infant mortality and literacy rates.

REFERENCES

Abizadeh, S. and Gray, J. (1985), Wagner's Law: A pooled time-series, cross-section comparison, *National Tax Journal*, vol. 38, no. 2, pp. 209–18.

Alt, J. E. and Chrystal, K. A. (1983), *Political Economics*, Brighton: Wheatsheaf.

Bacon, R. and Eltis, W. (1976), *Britain's Economic Problem: Too Few Producers*, London: Macmillan.

Baumol, W. J. (1967), The macroeconomics of unbalanced growth, *American Economic Review*, vol. 57, no. 3 (June), pp. 415–26.

Becker, G. S. (1985), Public policies, pressure groups, and dead weight costs, *Journal of Public Economics*, vol. 28, no. 3 (December), pp. 329–47.

Beeton, D. J. (1985), Is the growth of government inevitable? A critical assessment of the 'global' theories of public expenditure. Department of Economics, Queen Mary College, University of London, Paper no. 142.

Bergstrom, T. C. and Goodman, R. P. (1973), Private demands for public goods, *American Economic Review*, vol. 63, no. 3 (June), pp. 280–96.

Birch, J. W. and Cramer, C. A. (1968), Macroeconomics of unbalanced growth: comment, *American Economic Review*, vol. 58, no. 4 (September), pp. 893–6.

Bird, R. M. (1970), *The Growth of Government Spending in Canada*, Toronto: Canadian Tax Foundation.

Bird, R. M. (1971), Wagner's Law of expanding state activity, *Public Finance/ Finances Publiques*, vol. 26, no. 1, pp. 1–26.

Bird R. M. (1972), 'The displacement effect': a critical note, *Finanz Archiv*, N.F., Band 30, pp. 434–63.

Borcherding, T. E. (1985), The causes of government expenditure growth: a survey of the U.S. evidence, *Journal of Public Economics*, vol. 28, no. 3 (December), pp. 359–82.

Borcherding, T. E. and Deacon, R. T. (1972), The demand for services of non-federal governments, *American Economic Review*, vol. 62, no. 3 (December), pp. 891–901.

Brown, C. V. and Jackson, P. M. (1986), *Public Sector Economics*, 3rd edn, Oxford: Martin Robertson.

Buchanan, J. M. (1958), *Public Principles of Public Debt*, Homewood, Illinois: Richard D. Irwin.

Buchanan, J. M. and Wagner, R. E. (1978), *Fiscal Responsibility in Constitutional Democracy*, Leiden, Boston: Martinus Nijhoff.

Burton, J. (1985), *Why No Cuts?* Hobart Paper no. 104, London: Institute of Economic Affairs.

Busch, W. C. and Denzau, A. T. (1977), The voting behaviour of bureaucrats and public sector growth, pp. 90–9 in Borcherding, T. E. (ed.), *Budgets and Bureaucrats: The Sources of Government Growth*, Durham NC: Duke University Press.

Clarke, C. (1945), Public finance and changes in the value of money, *Economic Journal*, vol. 55, no. 220 (December), pp. 371–89.

Clarke, C. (1977), The scope for and limits of taxation, pp. 19–28 in Prest, A. R. *et al.* (eds), *The State of Taxation*, London: Institute of Economics Affairs.

Cooper, M. H. and Culyer, A. J. (1968), *The Price of Blood: An Economic*

Study of the Charitable and Commercial Principle, Hobart Paper no. 41, London: Institute of Economic Affairs.

Davis, O. A., Dempster, M. A. H. and Wildavsky, A. (1966), On the process of budgeting: an empirical study of congressional appropriation, *Public Choice*, vol. 1 (Fall), pp. 63–132.

Downs, A. (1957), *An Economic Theory of Democracy*, New York: Harper & Row.

Foley, D. K. (1978), State expenditure from a Marxist perspective, *Journal of Public Economics*, vol. 9, no. 2 (April), pp. 221–38.

Friedman, M. (1957), *A Theory of the Consumption Function*, Cambridge, Mass: National Bureau of Economic Research.

Galbraith J. K. (1962), *The Affluent Society*, Harmondsworth: Penguin.

Heald, D. (1983), *Public Expenditure*, Oxford: Martin Robertson.

Klein, R. E. (1976), The politics of public expenditure: American theory and British practice, *British Journal of Political Studies*, vol. 6, pt. 4 (October), pp. 401–32.

Le Grand, J. (1982), *The Strategy of Equality*, London: Allen & Unwin.

Lewis, A. (1979a), An empirical assessment of tax mentality, *Public Finance/ Finances Publiques*, vol. 34, no. 2, pp. 245–57.

Lewis, A. (1979b), Public awareness of the fiscal connection. Paper at a Symposium on the Control of Public Expenditure, University of Bath (mimeo).

Linbeck, A. (1985), Redistribution policy and the expansion of the public sector, *Journal of Public Economics*, vol. 28, no. 3 (December), pp. 309–28.

Meltzer, A. H. and Richard, S. F. (1981), A rational theory of the size of government, *Journal of Political Economy*, vol. 89, no. 5 (October), pp. 914–25.

Mueller, D. C. and Murrell, P. (1986), Interest groups and the size of government, *Public Choice*, vol. 48, no. 2, pp. 125–45.

Musgrave, R. A. (1969), *Fiscal Systems*, New Haven and London: Yale University Press.

Musgrave, R. A. (1985), Excess bias and the nature of government growth, *Journal of Public Economics*, vol. 28, no. 3 (December), pp. 287–308.

Musgrave, R. A. and Musgrave, P. B. (1976), *Public Finance in Theory and Practice*, New York: McGraw-Hill.

Myhrman, J. (1985), Introduction: reflections on the growth of government, *Journal of Public Economics*, vol. 28, no. 3 (December), pp. 275–85.

Niskanen, W. A. (1968), The peculiar economics of bureaucracy, *American Economic Review*, Papers and Proceedings, vol. 58, no. 2 (May), pp. 293–305.

Niskanen, W. A. (1971), *Bureaucracy and Representative Government*, New York: Aldine–Atherton.

North, D. C. (1985), The growth of government in the United States: an economic historian's perspective, *Journal of Public Economics*, vol. 28, no. 3 (December), pp. 383–99.

O'Connor, J. (1973), *The Fiscal Crisis of the State*, New York: St Martin's Press.

Peacock, A. T. and Wiseman, J. (1961), *The Growth of Public Expenditure in the United Kingdom*, London: Oxford University Press.

Peacock, A. T. and Wiseman, J. (1979), Approaches to the analysis of government expenditure growth, *Public Finance Quarterly*, vol. 7, no. 1 (January), pp. 3–23.

Pryor, F. L. (1968), *Public Expenditure in Communist and Capitalist Nations*, London: Allen & Unwin.

Sandford, C. T. (1979), *Control of Public Expenditure*, Bath University, Centre for Fiscal Studies.

Solano, P. L. (1983), Institutional explanations of public expenditures among high income democracies, *Public Finance/Finances Publiques*, vol. 38, no. 3, pp. 440–57.

Smith, D. (1982), Transfer payments and public expenditure, pp. 3–40 in Maunder, P. (ed.), *Case Studies in Public Sector Economics*, London: Heinemann.

Thompson, G. (1979), *The Growth of the Government Sector*, Milton Keynes: The Open University Press.

Titmuss, R. M. (1970), *The Gift Relationship – from Human Blood to Social Policy*, London: Allen & Unwin.

Wagner, A. (1883), Three extracts on public finance, pp. 1–15 in Musgrave, R. A. and Peacock, A. T. (eds) (1958), *Classics in the Theory of Public Finance*, London: Macmillan.

Weisbrod, B. A. (1975), Toward a theory of the voluntary non-profit sector in a three-sector economy, pp. 171–95, in Phelps, E. S. (ed.), *Altruism, Morality and Economic Theory*, New York: Russell Sage Foundation.

Wolf, C. Jnr (1979), A theory of non-market failure: framework of implementation analysis, *Journal of Law and Economics*, vol. 22, no. 1 (April), pp. 107–40.

Wildavsky, A. (1964), *The Politics of the Budgetary Process*, Boston: Little, Brown.

Wildavsky, A. (1975), *Budgeting: A Comparative Theory of Budgetary Processes*, Boston: Little, Brown.

Wildavsky, A. (1985), A cultural theory of expenditure growth and (un) balanced budgets, *Journal of Public Economics*, vol. 28, no. 3 (December), pp. 349–57.

Williamson, O. E. (1967), A rational theory of the federal budgetary process, *Public Choice*, vol. 2 (Spring), pp. 71–89.

Part II

Perhaps, after all, Leviathan is a mythical beast.

Oates, 1985, p. 756

As I see it, a realistic appraisal does not sustain the hypothesis that distortions in the fiscal process have been the primary cause of budget growth; nor does it sustain the proposition that bias must necessarily be towards excess. Quite possibly the public, by and large and subject to correction over time, gets what it wants.

Musgrave, 1981, p. 306

5

Constitutional Bias and Fiscal Illusion

We got to Oxford in little over an hour. The M40 is a very good road. So is the M4, come to think of it. I found myself wondering why we've got two really good roads to Oxford before we got any to Southampton, or Dover or Felixstowe or any of the ports.

Bernard explained that nearly all of our Permanent Secretaries were at Oxford. And most Oxford colleges give you a good dinner.

This seemed incredible – and yet it has the ring of truth about it. 'But did the Cabinet let them get away with this?' I asked.

'Oh no,' Bernard explained. 'They put their foot down. They said there'd be no motorway to take civil servants to dinners in Oxford unless there was a motorway to take Cabinet Ministers hunting in the Shires. That's why when the M1 was built in the fifties it stopped in the middle of Leicestershire.'

There seemed one flaw in this argument. I pointed out that the M11 has only just been completed. 'Don't Cambridge colleges give you a good dinner?'

'Of course,' said Bernard, 'but it's years and years since the Department of Transport had a Permanent Secretary from Cambridge.'

Lynn, J. and Jay, A. (eds) (1982), Yes Minister, vol. 2, p. 53, London: British Broadcasting Corporation.

Humphrey is wrong, wrong, wrong! In my view the country *does* care if the money is mis-spent, and I'm there as the country's representative, to see that it isn't.

'With respect, Minister,' began Humphrey, one of his favourite insults in his varied repertoire, 'people merely care that the money is not *seen* to be mis-spent.'

Lynn, J. and Jay, A. (eds) (1982), Yes Minister, vol. 2, p. 29, London: British Broadcasting Corporation.

5.1   INTRODUCTION

In chapter 2 and chapter 4 it has been explained how the political process of representative democracy can generate public sector growth to such an extent that the size of the public sector might be deemed 'excessive'. There are a number of different arguments concerning the political process, all of which generate this same conclusion. One main line of approach concentrates on the process of simple majority voting (50 per cent +1). A second looks not to the constitutional rule but to the lack of understanding, information and exit possibilities on the part of voters who enact the process of representative democracy. It is readily appreciated that there is nothing inherently 'optimal' about the simple majority voting rule (Buchanan and Tullock, 1969). Here, however, we focus on those defects which expand public sector activity, either in terms of redistributive (transfer) expenditure, or the provision of public services (exhaustive expenditure).

An analysis of the impact of majority voting and redistribution has led to an acceptance of 'the tyranny of the majority'. It may be probable, it is alleged, that a majority of voters will approve redistributive schemes which transfer the assets and income from the minority to the majority. Brennan argues that 'to leave any net wealth or income in the hands of the minority groups that the majority could obtain would be irrational' (Brennan, 1984, p. 66). It is not inherently obvious how the majority coalition will form, e.g. they may constitute the wealthy who redistribute from the poor, or vice-versa (Mueller, 1979). Yet in so far as there are more spoils to be had from redistributing from the rich than from the poor, the median voter is more likely to join the poor (Tullock, 1973). Subtle amendments to the voting rule (e.g. a qualified majority or log-rolling arrangements) will not adequately restrain the final tyranny (Sugden, 1981). As such, this result forms an impressive basis for the call for a fiscal constitution. It is argued that tax policy should not be the outcome of the tax process, but should restrain the tax process. The necessity to tax on the basis of horizontal equity, for example, may restrain discriminatory treatment of the poor (Brennan and Buchanan, 1977).

This general line of argument has a long and distinguished heritage. De Tocqueville (1835) directly linked the extension of suffrage to the poor with the rise in income redistribution from the rich to the poor. Yet, while the potential for such tyranny has been manifestly explained, many modern commentators have been puzzled by the limited degree of redistribution invoked by the public sector. In the case of the UK, this absence of extensive redistribution is widely documented (e.g. Le Grand, 1982). The problem then becomes that of the reconciliation of this observation with the powerful predictions of theory. The answer would appear to lie in a plethora of safeguards which, in point of fact, will limit the role of the public sector as a redistributive agency.

In considering demands by the poor for redistribution from the rich, higher-income people may be viewed as 'suppliers' of redistribution and lower-income people as 'demanders'. Reasons can be presented to explain both considerable supplier resistance and weakened demander incentives. On the supply side, high-income people have political power disproportionate to their numbers. As a class they have greater incentives to take part in politics simply because they have more to lose. Similarly, their greater wealth affords the purchase of information and influence (party contributions, etc.). Additionally, a feature of representative democracy is that the representatives are drawn predominantly from the higher income groups creating a natural coincidence of concerns. Indeed, one argument for redistribution is to offset the disproportionate political power the well-off would wield. On the demand side, there is a further list of modifying points to be considered. First, the initiation of redistributive schemes may be believed to create a disincentive on the part of the high-income individuals to work, save or invest. The blind pursuit of redistribution by one sector of the community may in the long run reduce the total available for transfer. Second, individuals in low income ranges may expect to do better at a later time, so that they will refrain from excessive damage to their expected income position. Third, exit options may exist for the minority which restrain the redistributive goals of the majority. Recently, perhaps the most obvious example of this is found in the decline of urban areas as the wealthy evade high rates by movement to the suburbs. Fourth, on both the demand and supply sides, the whole theory is premised on the view of individuals as both rational and selfish. They are neither benevolent nor malevolent, and simply concerned with their own welfare. By contrast, it may be that individuals behave in a Kantian fashion and consider it appropriate that some standard of income exist for all. Alternatively, a consensus ethic as to the entitlement of individuals to earnings may restrain redistribution. Such explanations are associated with a quite broad spectrum of literature (e.g. Musgrave, 1981; Culyer, 1980; Meltzer and Richard, 1981). We note them here as essential mitigating factors to the prediction of Leviathan invoked by majority *redistributive* goals.

An alternative, though related, version of the tyranny of the majority exists, however, with respect to the provision of public services. It concentrates on the impact which majority voting creates on the apparent price of public services. Tullock (1959) sets up the basic argument. With unanimity voting being the system that safeguards Pareto improvements, any deviation from this decision rule may generate inefficiencies. In particular, a majority decision rule with, say, equal tax prices for a given collective activity,[1] is open to abuse in that the majority (half $N + 1$, where N is the electorate) can force the whole electorate to pay for a collective activity, effectively reducing its price from (1/half $N + 1$) to $1/N$ times the cost of the collective activity. The result is that majority voting produces what appears to be partial 'free lunches' cooked with the resources of the whole community which thereby encourages overeating. The overeating results from the 'price effect' contingent on having 'forced riders'. Given many collective decisions and a changing composition of the majority coalition, the average individual may expect to be part of a winning coalition as many times as he is a 'forced rider'. While the income effects will tend to disappear the same is not true of the price effects, and hence the general prediction towards overexpansion of the public sector is established.

Musgrave (1981) finds this argument unconvincing. He questions that such goods should be provided by a centralized public source. If, for example, they are private access roads, ought they to be considered more appropriately provided privately or by local authorities encompassing the beneficiaries? The fault in this sense lies not with majority voting but with the inappropriate referral of this issue to centralized government. Perhaps more importantly, he questions the response of the forced riders. Why would they not bribe a member of the majority coalition in order to establish a new winning majority of non-spenders? In the long run, surely forced riders will bring some electoral influence to bear.

The argument between Tullock and Musgrave is clearly important to the Leviathan debate. It misses, however, one crucial ingredient of the electoral process – uncertainty. When issues are won or lost by interested parties for either side the process typically involves campaign or pressure group activity costs. If majorities are to be formed to support issues, interested parties invariably will be asked to incur costs of contribution to such campaigns, as well as the costs of actually voting. These costs are incurred with no guarantee that the outcome will be successful, and the issue may be lost at the vote. It is precisely this observation which leads economists to be sceptical as to the motivation for individuals who participate politically. As each individual plays such an insignificant role in determining the electoral outcome, it is doubtful that the expected value of participation can exceed the costs involved (Downs, 1957). Yet despite this insight, it is clear that individuals do participate, given the risks involved. As in the literature on public good provision, it would appear that individuals do attach some importance to their own actions (Bohm, 1972). On the one hand, if voters are motivated by factors other than self-interest – e.g. duty, social responsibility – it is questionable that the tyranny of the majority literature carries through. On the other hand, if voters are motivated by self-interest, it implies that the net expected value of contributing to electoral causes (either in campaign contributions and/or time and trouble of voting) is positive.

Pursuing this latter framework, we ask whether or not a pro-spending lobby can cause a majority decision to support their proposals. We question their strength relative to that of the anti-spending lobby. For the Leviathan literature to carry through, the former must be dominant. Two issues then arise. First, how does the uncertainty associated with simple democracy affect individuals? Second, is the bias still with public expenditure growth?

5.2   VOTING BIAS: A REAPPRAISAL

As stated above, the impact of uncertainty provokes careful consideration for the voter who chooses to participate in the democratic process. In figure 5.1 the implicit assumption is that of a risk-averse individual.[2] Under conditions of certainty he has an income of YA, but he is assumed to be subject to a public sector decision which will either provide a public service at reduced cost or cause him to become a 'forced rider' and to contribute to a public service of no value to him. The former outcome increases his income to YW and the latter reduces it to YL. It is assumed that the vote has an equal chance of going either way, so that his expected income is YA. Clearly, if risk-averse, he would prefer to have no uncertainty. If offered YC as certain income he would willingly trade off YA expected income for such an outcome, yet this option is not open. The question, therefore, becomes whether he will fight harder for issues which may increase public spending and possibly make him better off, or fight harder to prevent those spending programmes which would leave him worse off.

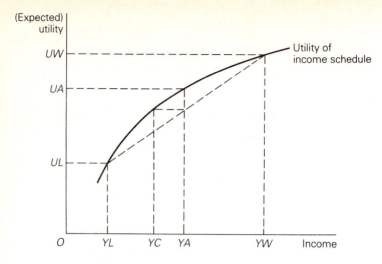

Figure 5.1   The costs of uncertainty

If the assumption of risk-aversion is retained, the relative incentive to secure positive net benefits as opposed to avoiding net losses in the presence of political participation costs challenges the Leviathan orthodoxy. Figure 5.2 illustrates a utility of income schedule for a representative individual. It is assumed for any spending programme the individual knows that the legislation is potentially favourable or unfavourable to him. Further, because the voting bias argument is about the 'tyranny' of simple majority voting, it is assumed that there is a 50–50 chance that any piece of legislation will be accepted or rejected.

First, suppose the individual is at YA facing a 50–50 chance of a piece of legislation that he expects to be favourable to the tune of YA YW if enacted. However, assume that to try and secure such legislation will involve campaign contributions, pressure group activity, time and trouble, costs of voting, etc., to the extent of YT YA. Hence, by acting to support the favourable legislation the individual has expected income YE (where YT YA = $YW'YW$). The figure, for purposes of reference, has been so constructed that a 50 per cent chance of a YA YW gain in the presence of transactions costs leaves the individual indifferent to accepting the certain reference income YA and acting to secure favourable legislation with expected income YE (both have identical associated utility levels Uf).

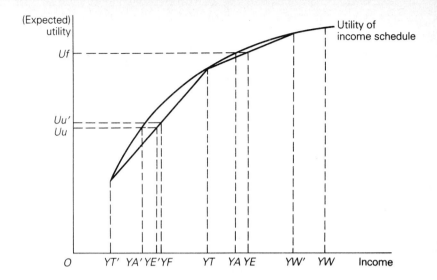

Figure 5.2   Opposing an expected loss *v* supporting an expected gain

By contrast, suppose the individual is faced with a piece of unfavourable legislation with an identical possible loss $YA'YA$ to the potential gain $YA\ YW$. In this threat-type situation the income a risk-averse individual would regard as 'safe' is YA', and we take this as his reference position. Assuming the same political participation costs, $YT'YA'\ (=YT\ YA)$, the individual confronts YA' or, if he attempts to oppose the unfavourable legislation, a 50–50 chance of YT' or YT whose expected value is YF. Clearly the opposition strategy is attractive with higher expected utility $Uu' > Uu$. The inference is that, *ceteris paribus*, the individual is more likely to oppose unfavourable legislation than to support favourable legislation. This asymmetry arises because of the assumption of diminishing marginal utility of income (risk-aversion).

The overall result can be read in two ways. For given political participation costs those opposed to legislation will lend actions to their feelings with a lower probability of success. In the illustration YE' has the same associated utility as YA' (that is Uu), but involves a less than the 50–50 gamble needed to put the individual on the margin of decision for a favourable piece of legislation at YE. Alternatively, for any given probability of success those opposed to legislation will incur greater participation costs than those favouring the legislation. The upshot of this argument is that, other things equal, on any issue those expecting to be losers should be more likely to take opposing action than expected gainers taking supporting action. This result suggests that it may not be as easy as previously thought to establish a bias towards spending programmes that stems from the voting mechanism. Losers will provide more forceful opposition to 'net' taxation than gainers press for 'net' expenditure programmes.

5.3 INFORMATION AND COMPETITIVE BIAS: A RECONSIDERATION OF EVIDENCE

Above, a theoretical case is made offering a reason for doubting the power of Leviathan. However, there have been other more empirically based literatures that need to be recognized. In particular three propositions have emerged that have in common a bias in the fiscal system that results in 'too much' government expenditure. The first proposition is that governments having tax structures that induce differentially greater revenues as a result of inflation or real income growth will have the highest levels of tax paid and expenditure. The mechanism through which this effect is alleged to work is an informational one. Tax revenue increases that arise in an automatic, unlegislated 'fiscal drag' manner have low visibility, and hence little CV resistance can be predicted for expenditure covered in this manner. That an income-elastic tax system fosters Leviathan is an hypothesis examined by Oates (1975), who found some support for it especially at the US local level. However Oates questions the causality indicating that a tax-elastic revenue structure may simply indicate that consumer voters prefer higher taxes and expenditures rather than their being 'fiscally illuded'. Di Lorenzo (1982), however, found opposing empirical evidence on the elasticity hypothesis at the US local level indicating a negative relationship between the income tax elasticity of the tax system and the level and growth of local expenditures. In contrast, at the state level Craig and Heins (1980) provide evidence favouring the elasticity proposition. Clearly the evidence and interpretation are somewhat mixed.

A second proposition is one associated with the works of Brennan and Buchanan (1977 and 1980), and has been recently tested by Oates (1985). Here Leviathan is argued to be present in a more extensive form where exit is impossible and the forces of competition completely muted. In terms of a federal structure, like America's, it is at the local level that CVs have the option of voting with their feet and 'exiting' a jurisdiction; hence Leviathan can be expected to be in chains. More succinctly, *ceteris paribus*, public sector size should vary inversely with the extent of fiscal decentralization. Oates, using regression analysis of data on 43 countries and 48 contiguous US states, suggests that 'there does not exist a strong, systematic relationship between the size of government and the degree of centralisation of the public sector' (Oates, 1985, p. 756). A third proposition that relates to fiscal bias also involves informational considerations as in the elasticity proposition, and it is to this that the next two subsections are devoted.

Visibility and Tax/Expenditure Complexity

That the majority rule *per se* does not always imply increased public spending is clear when uncertainty of outcome is considered. In practice, however, the uncertainty associated with a positive or negative outcome is far from the only uncertainty associated with political participation. In figure 5.1 it was assumed that individuals knew the range of influence of government activity (YW to YL) but were uncertain only as to the direction in which majority voting would move them. That such is the case is, however, also in dispute. For some writers (e.g. Puviani, 1903; Goetz, 1977), there is a distinct bias by which individuals incorrectly estimate the effect of government activity towards YW, i.e. they have 'optimistic fiscal illusions'. The argument is that voters systematically underestimate the cost (taxes) of public sector activity and, with the help of political rhetoric, overestimate the benefits of government expenditures. For any particular programme of government expenditure the costs are borne across all taxpayers, but the benefits are concentrated in favour of a small number. Benefits are hence more observable and costs less visible. Bureaucrats who wish to maximize their budget size will concentrate on activities the benefits of which are more visible (Lindsay, 1976). Vote-maximizing governments will be at pains not to emphasize the costs of their proposals. In so far as individuals thereby overestimate the benefits of government activity, they will choose 'excessive' government. The overestimated marginal benefits of government programmes will be equated with an underestimated notion of marginal costs.

Once again, however, this is by no means the only interpretation that need be placed upon fiscal illusion. An alternative school of thought points to pessimistic fiscal illusions? Downs (1960) predicted that the public sector would be underexpanded because the benefits of

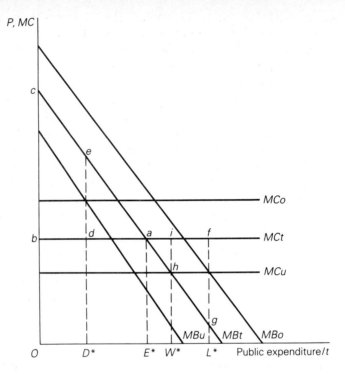

Figure 5.3   Welfare costs and fiscal illusions

government expenditures are less visible than the 'sacrifice' of taxes. Benefits are alleged to be long-term and in many instances diffuse (e.g. expenditure on overseas aid). Galbraith (1962) is associated with this same school of 'public poverty'. He argues that private goods are generally more vigorously advertised and marketed than are public sector goods.

What is at stake here can be illustrated by reference to figure 5.3. The 'true' marginal benefit and cost of public sector activities are assumed to be *MBt* and *MCt* respectively, offering a consumer surplus triangle gain *abc* at the efficient level of output OE^*. The Downs–Galbraith equilibrium can be envisaged as OD^*, where marginal benefits are underestimated at *MBu* and marginal costs are overestimated at *MCo*. By reference to the true valuations, the welfare cost of an inefficiently small budget is triangle *ade*. The Leviathan equilibrium is OL^*, where marginal benefits are overestimated at *MBo* and marginal costs underestimated at *MCu*. Here the welfare loss triangle by reference to true valuations is triangle *afg*. The figure has been drawn symmetrically to avoid presentational bias. Any deviation from *OE** involves a welfare loss, but the question is as to the source of the loss.

In a recent conference on the anatomy of government deficiencies, Downs and Galbraith were contrasted with Leviathan economists who perceived 'excess supply' from the public sector. It was noted that while 'only empirical investigations can prove which of these is closer to the truth ... we know much too little about this issue' (Hanusch, 1983, p. 5). Until the past decade arguments presented were more speculative than empirical. R. E. Wagner (1976) is one of the initiators of the newer literature which has contributions in a similar vein from Pommerehne and Schneider (1978), Baker (1983) and Breeden and Hunter (1985). Wagner draws special attention to the role of tax structure in fiscal illusions. In particular he considers revenue raising and postulates that: 'The accuracy of a person's perception of the cost of government will vary inversely with the complexity of the revenue structure' (Wagner, 1976, p. 52). The underlying argument is that taxpayers systematically underestimate their tax burden and that this underestimation is more significant the more complex the tax system.[3] (In terms of figure 5.3 the equilibrium would be a position like *OW** with a welfare loss triangle from overprovision of *aih*). If the argument, which finds econometric support, can be carried on to expenditures, an assumption made here, then the following proposition emerges: other things equal, overall 'pessimistic' or 'optimistic' fiscal illusions will arise depending on whether the tax structure is less complex than the expenditure structure. There is no necessary *a priori* prediction one way or the other; the outcome will depend on the fiscal structure under study and therefore be an essentially empirical matter (see Cullis and Jones, 1987).

Wagner associates complexity with spatial, temporal and obtrusive aspects of taxes. A single direct tax source used once per time period on a non-withholding basis approximates simplicity. Since complexity has no natural units of measurement, Wagner uses as an empirical proxy for complexity the Herfindahl index, familiar as a measure of concentration in industrial economics. The Herfindahl index (*H*) is defined as

$$H = \sum_{i=1}^{n} P_i^2$$

where *n* is the number of major sources of revenue (four in Wagner's work) and P_i is the share of *i*th major tax item in total taxes. Wagner tested his theorizing against a regression model of public expenditure for the 50 largest US cities using data for 1967 and 1970.

Two major points can be made in relation to Wagner's study. First his regression equation ignored the 'simplicity of the city's expenditure structure' as a variable, which would seem to be a significant omission in a budgetary choice model. Second, his empirical work does not use direct evidence (see Lewis, 1982) but rather involves an indirect 'testing' of individual tax perceptions and infers from a significant (negative) coefficient on the variable 'simplicity of the city's revenue structure' that his postulate quoted above applied. Though Wagner's approach has been pursued by other researchers (Baker, 1983; Breeden and Hunter, 1985), the asymmetric treatment of taxation and expenditure remains a weakness.

A suitable complement to Wagner's empirical method is followed here and involves two stages. First, an *a priori* prediction about the relative visibility of taxes and benefits is made on the basis of the complexity of the tax and revenue structure (of the UK public sector), and second this prediction is compared with direct survey evidence on individual fiscal perceptions. For 1979/80, using data as presented in the Government Statistical Service's *Social Trends* (1981 edition), relevant H values are 0.17 for central government revenue raising, and 0.15 for general expenditure disbursement, indicating a simpler tax than expenditure structure. Hence, the overall prediction if anything favours somewhat greater tax than expenditure visibility on behalf of individuals.

It must be recognized that there are two elements of arbitrariness involved in this application. A first relates to the appropriateness of the Herfindahl index as a measure of complexity. It was adopted here to provide a measure of consistency with Wagner's empirical work and it is not suggested that it is the only, or necessarily the best measure of complexity. Secondly, it is clear that the value of the index is not independent of the nature of the accounts on which it is based. The Herfindahl index is sensitive to the number of taxes and expenditure benefits, and to their classification. It is not in the least improbable that for other specifications to be found in government statistics the value of the Herfindahl index changes. Also government statistics are themselves open to interpretation. Revenue accrues to different levels of government and between different levels of government. Above, for example, the role of local taxes, such as rates, is omitted in the comparison. In dealing with this issue the question arises as to whether or not revenues and expenditures ought to be assigned to a specific level of government. If so, taxonomies are affected, and the Herfindahl indexes alter.[4] The difficulties in pursuing this line of approach therefore can hardly be overestimated.

In the light of these problems it is difficult to make predictions based on Wagner's approach. Our intention then is simply to stress that, if estimates are presented at all, those for expenditures cannot be arbitrarily neglected. The estimates above suggest little awareness both of taxes and benefits, but it would be heroic to suggest that one would expect a strong bias either way between awareness of taxes and expenditure. As it is difficult to resolve this debate by using the proxy suggested by Wagner, we move to a more direct test independent of the problems above.

Survey Data

The survey carried out by Marplan Ltd (report dated May 1981 and made available to researchers at Strathclyde University) was designed to study the public's comprehension of UK economic affairs. It was based on a quota sample of people aged over 18 with controls for age and social class. In total there were 900 respondents: 467 females and 433 males, 93 aged 18–24; 388 aged 25–44; 259 aged 45–64 and 160 aged 65 and over. 168 were classified in social class AB, 199 C1, 288 C2 and 245 DE. The two questions asked that are reported here are:

> All governments spend money on a variety of different things. What are the main things that government spend their money on?

and

> Do you know where governments get the money to pay for services?

To both questions respondents were allowed a free response, and were then probed but not prompted, after mentioning one or more sources, to think of others. To determine *visibility*, such an approach was clearly essential. Table 5.1 presents respondents' beliefs about the origins and destinies of government revenue. Because of the nature of the question, the number of mentions far exceeds the numbers of respondents (i.e. each respondent could mention an open-ended number of items). As a result, the figures which appear in the table are not discrete, and unfortunately, statistical analysis would be spurious. This limitation is compensated for by the fact that the data relate *directly* to accounts of fiscal illusion, being the sample individuals' unprompted awareness of

Table 5.1 Some evidence on fiscal knowledge

Revenue items	Overall (N = 900)		Expenditure items
Income tax	93% (834)	51% (460)	Hospitals and the health service
Tax on goods	56% (500)	13% (120)	Police and the law courts
Tax on vehicles	38% (343)	16% (148)	Pensioners and help for the old
Tax on tobacco	35% (316)	44% (400)	Schools and education
Tax on petrol	36% (324)	53% (473)	Defence and the armed forces
Tax on alcohol	34% (303)	21% (188)	Roads
Rates	21% (190)	17% (151)	Housing
Customs and excise	11% (101)	12% (111)	Assistance to industry
National Insurance contributions	15% (138)	26% (236)	Social security
Revenue from nationalized industries	7% (60)	19% (173)	The nationalized industries
International Monetary Fund (IMF)	4% (36)	19% (169)	Unemployment benefits/ redundancies
Revenue from banks	3% (24)	14% (126)	Local government
Revenue from government investments	8% (71)	11% (99)	Foreign aid
Overseas earnings	6% (50)	5% (44)	Common Market
Common Market (EEC)	3% (26)	17% (156)	Other
North Sea oil	13% (115)	6% (50)	NI
Others	19% (171)		
DK/NI*	1% (9)		
Total responses	3602	3054	
Average responses per person	4.0	3.4	
Average responses per category	212	204	

* DK = Don't know; NI = not included (these data excluded from the summary statistics).
Source: Cullis and Jones (1987).

taxes and spending. To this extent they may offer greater reliability than the proxy in Wagner's test.

As regards the sources of government finance, respondents mentioned overwhelmingly income tax, confirming the view that it is direct taxation that has high visibility. Marginally, over half the total sample mentioned goods taxes, whereas all other (relatively minor) sources of finance were mentioned by only a minority of respondents. Approximately a third pointed to taxes on vehicles, petrol, tobacco and alcohol. One in five people answering the questions mentioned rates as a source of revenue, which, given that their level is often an issue of considerable local controversy, is surprising.

Turning to the 'main things that governments spend money on', there is no obvious evidence of greater awareness of the benefits side of the budget. If the standard of comparison is the fact that over 90 per cent of respondents could list the source (income tax) of well over a quarter of the government's revenue, then people are less aware on the expenditure side. Social security accounted for a very similar proportion of total expenditures as personal income taxes did of total government revenue at the time of the survey, yet only 26 per cent mentioned it. The fact that just over half of the sample stated the two largest items of exhaustive (or real) expenditure, namely health care and defence, redresses the balance somewhat. Additionally, 44 per cent of respondents mentioned schools and education, the third largest real expenditure item at the time of questioning. However, on the most directly comparable items of revenue and expenditure, namely rates and local government, 21 per cent mentioned the former and only 14 per cent the latter.[5] The summary statistics provided at the base of the table favour revenue as opposed to expenditure visibility with the total responses, average responses per person and average responses per category, all being higher on the revenue side.

Down's account of tax and spending visibility would suggest significant differential visibility favouring taxes. This is not evident in these data. Despite other deficiencies, our broad estimates of Wagner's tax structure considerations would, given the complexity of the UK tax system, predict widespread revenue ignorance. This is evident in these data. However, what matters for the Leviathan literature is tax illusions relative to spending illusions, and here these data put a curse on both their houses, suggesting a thick but fairly evenly spread layer of ignorance over the public sector. There is, on this evidence, no clear-cut support for the dominance of overall optimistic or pessimistic tax illusions. The general lack of knowledge supports only the argument that rational voters will not invest time and effort in the accumulation of information (Downs, 1957) that will have little value to them.

5.4 SUMMARY AND CONCLUSIONS

The purpose of this chapter has been to reconsider the models of representative democracy outlined in chapter 2. As they were presented there, the prediction of 'excessive' government appeared predetermined by the framework in which they are set. The question remained of how robust such a prediction was. Here we have initiated a reconsideration of the arguments in the context of uncertainty faced by risk-averse individuals. If such individuals are faced with an uncertain political market, it is not evident that the bias for excessive government need always follow. First, if voters participate in activities, either to promote government spending or to contain the growth of government spending, a decision based upon net expected income may generate greater 'defensive' activity than 'promotional' activity. With decreasing marginal utility of income, voters will exert more effort to avoid income loss as a result of Leviathan than they will to generate income gain through Leviathan. Only if they were risk-neutral would they regard equivalent gains and losses identically. If they are risk-averse they have greater incentive to avoid the income loss result.

Second, voters may certainly underestimate the costs associated with government growth. However, the issue of whether or not they overestimate or underestimate the real costs of government is an empirical one. Some survey data presented here suggest uncertainty and lack of information on the part of consumer voters, but no clear and unequivocal bias either way. Borcherding (1985) seems to agree writing (p. 375) 'no one has yet made a tight case for a biased and growing fiscal illusion'.

These developments are offered not to disprove the proposition that representative democracy can generate Leviathan, but to resist the acceptance of this proposition as dogma. There remain issues still to be addressed. For example, if costs of government growth fall over larger groups than apparent benefits, then public good problems of organizing 'defensive' pressure groups may remain. However, there is more cause to weigh the evidence than to presume the onset of Leviathan.

NOTES

1 Here, the phrase collective activity simply denoted a common decision being established for a group of individuals, not that the activity is a public good.
2 This assumption, common in economics, implies that the second derivative of the utility function is negative.
3 Against a background of 'rational ignorance', Wagner argues individuals will, in the process of abstraction, ignore some taxes and treat others as insignificant. However, for the subset they treat as significant, they will have reasonably accurate information. Such a process, if borne out, establishes optimistic tax illusions.
4 Using data in *Social Trends* it is possible to compare the two Herfindahl indexes for central government revenue and expenditure with those for all local government revenue and expenditure. For 1980 this comparison would be 0.17 and 0.21 as against 0.24 and 0.25.
5 Clearly there is some confusion here, in that education mentioned by 44 per cent of the sample is predominantly a local authority programme. Such confusion does not contribute to a picture of expenditure awareness.

REFERENCES

Baker, S. H. (1983), The determinants of median voter tax liability: an empirical test of the fiscal illusion hypothesis, *Public Finance Quarterly*, vol. 11, no. 1 (January), pp. 95–108.
Bohm, P. (1972), Estimating demand for public goods: an experiment, *European Economic Review*, vol. 3, no. 2, pp. 111–30.
Borcherding, T. E. (1985), The causes of government expenditure growth: a survey of the U.S. evidence, *Journal of Public Economics*, vol. 62, no. 3 (December), pp. 891–901.
Breeden, C. H. and Hunter, W. J. (1985), Tax revenue and tax structure, *Public Finance Quarterly*, vol. 13, no. 2 (April), pp. 216–24.
Brennan, G. (1984), Elements of a fiscal politics: public choice and public finance, *The Australian Economic Review*, 3rd Quarter, pp. 63–72.
Brennan, G. and Buchanan, J. M. (1977), Towards a tax constitution for Leviathan, *Journal of Public Economics*, vol. 8, no. 3 (December), pp. 255–74.
Brennan, G. and Buchanan, J. M. (1980), *The Power to Tax*, Cambridge: Cambridge University Press.
Buchanan, J. M. and Tullock, G. (1969), *The Calculus of Consent: Logical Foundations of Constitutional Democracy*, Ann Arbor: University of Michigan Press.
Central Statistical Office (various years), *Social Trends*, London: HMSO.

Craig, E. and Heins, A. (1980), The effect of tax elasticity on public spending, *Public Choice*, vol. 35, no. 3, pp. 267–75.

Cullis, J. G. and Jones, P. R. (1987), Fiscal illusions and 'excessive' budgets: some in direct evidence, *Public Finance Quarterly*, vol. 15, no. 2 (April), pp. 219–27.

Culyer, A. J. (1980), *The Political Economy of Social Policy*, Oxford: Martin Robertson.

De Tocqueville, A. (1835), *Democracy in America*, reprint edn., Oxford: Oxford University Press.

Di Lorenzo, T. (1982), Tax elasticity and the growth of local government expenditure, *Public Finance Quarterly*, vol. 10, no. 3, pp. 385–92.

Downs, A. (1957), *An Economic Theory of Democracy*, New York: Harper & Row.

Downs, A. (1960), Why the government is too small in a democracy, *World Politics*, vol. 13 (July), pp. 541–63.

Galbraith, J. K. (1962), *The Affluent Society*, Harmondsworth: Penguin.

Goetz, C. (1977), Fiscal illusion and state and local finance, pp. 176-87 in Borcherding, T. E. (ed.), *Budgets and Bureaucrats – the Sources of Government Growth*, Durham NC: Duke University Press.

Hanusch, H. (1983), *Anatomy of Government Deficiencies*, Berlin: Springer-Verlag.

Le Grand, J. (1982), *The Strategy of Equality*, London: Allen & Unwin.

Lewis, A. (1982), *The Psychology of Taxation*, Oxford: Martin Robertson.

Lindsay, C. M. (1976), A theory of government enterprise, *Journal of Political Economy*, vol. 84, no. 5 (October), pp. 31–7.

Meltzer A. H. and Richard S. F. (1981), A rational theory of the size of government, *Journal of Political Economy*, vol. 89, no. 5 (October) pp. 914–25.

Mueller, D. C. (1979), *Public Choice*, Cambridge: Cambridge University Press.

Musgrave, R. A. (1969), *Fiscal Systems*, New Haven and London: Yale University Press.

Musgrave, R. A. (1981), Leviathan cometh – or does he?, pp. 77–120 in Ladd, H. and Tideman, N. (eds), *Tax and Expenditure Limitations: COUPE papers on Public Economics 5*, Washington: Urban Institute.

Oates, W. E. (1975), Automatic increases in tax revenues – the effect on the size of the public budget, pp. 139–60 in Oates, W. (ed.), *Financing the New Federalism*, Baltimore, MD: Johns Hopkins Press.

Oates, W. E. (1985), Searching for Leviathan, *American Economic Review*, vol. 75, no. 4 (September), pp. 748–57.

Pommerehne, W. W. and Schneider, F. (1978), Fiscal illusion, political institutions and local public spending, *Kyklos*, vol. 31, fasc. 3, pp. 381–408.

Puviani, A. (1903), *Teoria della Illusione Finanziaria*, Palermo: Sandron.

Sugden, R. (1981), *The Political Economy of Public Choice*, Oxford: Martin Robertson.

Tullock, G. (1959), Some problems of majority voting, *Journal of Political Economy*, vol. 67 (December), pp. 571–9.

Tullock, G. (1973), The charity of the uncharitable, pp. 15–32 in Alchian, A. A. *et al.* (eds), *The Economics of Charity*, London: Institute of Economic Affairs.

Tullock, G. (1976), *The Vote Motive*, Hobart Paperback 9, London: IEA.

Wagner, R. E. (1976), Revenue structure, fiscal illusion and budgetary choice, *Public Choice*, vol. 25 (Spring), pp. 45–61.

6

Bureaucratic Inefficiency

'The Civil Service does not make profits or losses, *Ergo*, we measure success by the size of our staff and budget. By definition, a big department is more successful than a small one ... this simple proposition is the basis of our whole system.'

Lynn, J. and Jay, A. (eds) (1981) *Yes Minister*, vol. 1, p. 57, London: British Broadcasting Corporation.

'The function of the DAA is to support and service the administrative work of all government departments.'

'Oh no,' he said, 'that bit's fascinating.'

I asked him how anyone could be fascinated by it.

'Well,' he said, 'if you look back to the first report in 1868, when Gladstone set up this department's predecessor, you find that the first sentence is, 'The Department is responsible for the economic and efficient administration of government.'

'Ah,' I said, 'is that what it was for?'

'Yes,' said Bernard, 'but it proved a tough remit. They were responsible for every bit of waste and inefficiency. I suppose Gladstone meant them to be. So when it got too hot they did the usual.'

'What is "the usual"?', I asked.

It emerged that 'the usual' in Civil Service terms is to secure your budget, staff and premises and then quietly change your remit. In 1906 they changed the first sentence to 'The Department exists to *further* the efficient and economic administration of Government.' This removed the responsibility.

In 1931 they got it down to 'The Department exists to support all government departments in *their* pursuit of economic and efficient administration' which pushed the responsibility on to other departments. And by 1972 they had got rid of the embarrassing notions of economy and efficiency, and since then it has said 'The purpose of the DAA is to support and serve the administrative work of all government departments.'

The last vestige of the department's real purpose removed in a mere one hundred and four years, and the department itself one hundred and six times its original size.

Lynn, J. and Jay, A. (eds) (1982), *Yes Minister*, vol. 2, p. 167, London: British Broadcasting Corporation.

6.1 INTRODUCTION

In chapter 2 an outline of the 'standard' economic theory of bureaucracy was discussed. The now traditional model (associated with Niskanen, 1971 and Tullock, 1976) has presented bureaucrats as capable of expanding the public sector beyond the social optimum described in chapter 1. One objective of this chapter is to reconsider the standard model in what might reasonably be regarded as its most general form. In so doing, we reconsider those very specific circumstances in which the effect of bureaucracy is to expand the public sector to *twice* its socially optimum size. A second objective is to integrate the theory of bureaucracy within alternative public sector growth models outlined in chapter 4.

The economic theory of bureaucracy has been criticized as unrepresentative, particularly of the UK experience.[1] We begin, however, by accepting the basic tenets of the model with a view to reconsidering its micro-economic interpretation. Bureaucrats may be considered as liable to maximize the size of their budget at the expense of the 'public interest' in order to enjoy prestige, power, increased salary and other emoluments. The funding agency (Parliament or Congress) may be at an informational disadvantage and able only to monitor bureaucrats according to the constraint that total cost of government expenditure does not exceed total benefit. To accept this framework is to proceed with a model that accords with the much-publicized allegations of waste in bureaucracy (e.g. Chapman, 1978). Certainly, governments have been greatly influenced by such an analysis, and with reference to Niskanen's model Goodin (1982, p. 23) notes 'His ideas are exerting a direct and powerful influence on policy makers, both in America, where Niskanen himself sits on Reagan's three-man Council of Economic Advisors, and in Britain where Sir Keith Joseph assigns one of his tracts (Niskanen, 1973) as required reading for his own civil servants.'

In the light of this widespread concern provoked by the economic theory of bureaucracy, we ask, how great a threat is *this* Leviathan.

6.2 ALLOCATIVE INEFFICIENCY: A 'BALANCED' VIEW

An appropriate starting point for an analysis of the economic theory of bureaucracy is Niskanen (1968). In considering the later development of the literature on this model it is interesting to observe that the original work by Niskanen does not imply an over-expansion of the public sector to the extent now typically accepted. McKenzie and Tullock (1981, p. 186) conclude that 'bureaucracies are large – indeed, roughly twice as large as they should be'. The view is echoed in Breton and Wintrobe (1975); Jackson (1982); and Frey (1983). The negative connotations associated with bureaucracy are emphasized and dramatized by such a conclusion. The shock impact is guaranteed. But what of the original analysis?

In figure 6.1, an attempt is made to illustrate Niskanen's model. The total cost function is:

$$TC = cQ + dQ^2 \tag{6.1}$$

where Q = the output of the bureau per period
TC = minimum total cost of the bureau so that

$$MC = c + 2dQ \tag{6.2}$$

MC = minimum marginal cost to the bureau

In figure 6.1(a) the marginal cost function relates to the total cost function TC^0 of figure 6.1(b).

Niskanen (1968) defines the marginal benefit function as:

$$V = a - bQ \tag{6.3}$$

where V = marginal value to consumers.

In figure 6.1(a) the marginal benefit function is the demand function of the median voter (i.e. $D = MB$). In so far as this demand function can be viewed as instrumental in determining output, it is interesting to make a comparison with outcomes which would arise if the good were provided in the private sector and this were the market demand curve. If such were the case, it would, of course, reflect average revenue for producers (therefore, $D = AR = MB$)[2]. Niskanen's model uses the following expression for total benefit:

$$TB = aQ - b/2Q^2 \tag{6.4}$$

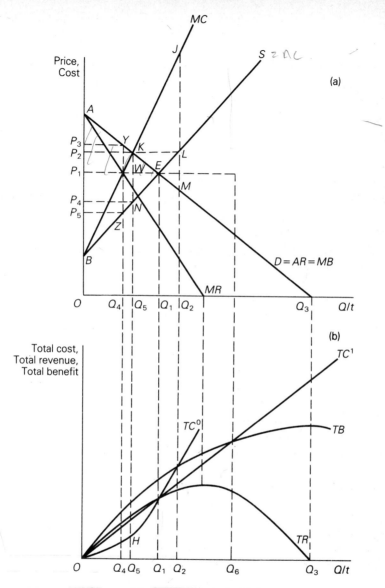

Figure 6.1 Bureaucratic inefficiency

The relationship is seen in figure 6.1, i.e. the total benefit curve (*TB*) in figure 6.1(b) is the integral from the origin to specific levels of output under the demand function in figure 6.1(a), (at output

$$Q_X, \text{TB} = \int_0^{Q_X} P(Q)dQ).$$ Within these parameters the behaviour of the

bureaucrat is precisely predicted by Niskanen (1968). When the bureau is budget-constrained it is the case that total cost must not exceed total benefit. From expressions (6.1) and (6.4), this constraint means that total cost can, at a maximum, be equal to total benefit:

$$cQ + dQ^2 = a - b/2\ Q^2 \qquad (6.5)$$

hence
$$Q = \frac{2(a - c)}{b + 2d} \qquad (6.6)$$

This is the predicted output level for a constrained bureaucrat.[3] If he were not cost-constrained and were able to increase output, provided simply that marginal benefit were positive, then from expression (6.3):

$$dTB/dQ \quad = V = a - bQ = 0 \qquad (6.7)$$

so that

$$Q \quad = a/b \qquad (6.8)$$

This latter expression obviously implies a greater output level.[4] In figure 6.1, for the demand and cost conditions illustrated, this latter level is depicted at OQ_3 and the more usual budget constrained output[5] is OQ_2. The results of the economic theory of bureaucracy may now be related to the outcome of a perfectly competitive market. In such a market, consumer and producer surplus would (as explained in chapter 1) be maximized at output OQ_1. The relevant comparison is then between the constrained output under bureaucracy (OQ_2) and the social optimum (OQ_1). It is clear that the former is not twice the latter.

One aspect of bureaucracy which has received too little attention is the role that the bureaucrat plays as a monopsonist purchaser for consumers. Mueller (1979, p. 157) correctly notes: 'That the buyer of a bureau's output would be a monopsonist follows almost from the nature of the good sold.' He adds (p. 157): 'The usual reason for granting a bureau a monopoly or the provision of a given service is to avoid wasteful duplication.' This means that the cost function facing the bureaucrat is not the same cost function as that which applies under conditions of perfect competition. It is not the case that the price to the bureau is such that it may buy as much as it requires at a constant price. Instead, as the bureau is the sole buyer, it is aware that the effect of increasing purchases is to drive up the price of the good. If the bureau could purchase as much as it likes at a constant price, the total cost curve would be TC^1 in figure 6.1(b) and the constrained output for the monopsonist would be OQ_6 (i.e. $TC=TB$) which is twice OQ_1. But this outcome cannot arise if the supply function (BS in figure 6.1(a)) is upward-sloping, indicating that the bureau must pay higher prices to call forth greater output.

The supply function in figure 6.1(a) is in point of fact the average cost function for the bureaucrat. At output level OQ_2 total cost for him is OP_2LQ_2 in figure 6.1(a) and this is equal to total benefit $OAMQ_2$ (i.e. triangle P_2AK = triangle KLM). The average cost per unit of output is OP_2. The relevant marginal cost is MC, which is above the supply function, indicating that in purchasing one extra unit the cost increases not only by the cost of the additional unit (p) but also by the additional cost for all the existing units ((q) dp/dq) that are to be purchased ($q\ dp/dq$). If marginal cost to a sole purchaser is expressed in this way then:

$$MC = p + q\ dp/dq \qquad (6.9)$$

or

$$MC = p(1 + 1/\eta) \qquad (6.10)$$

Where η is the elasticity of the supply curve. As such, if $\eta > 0$, then for the bureaucrat the marginal cost schedule lies above the supply function. The result is that bureaucrats do not increase output by a factor of twice the social optimum.

It should be noted that a private monopsonist would equate marginal benefit with marginal cost (i.e. at K in figure 6.1(a)), thereby reducing output (to OQ_5) and purchasing at a per unit price of P_4. This is harmful in terms of social welfare as it is associated with dead-weight losses of triangle KEN. For the buyer it is optimal as P_1WNP_4 exceeds triangle KEW, but not for society.

When it is realized that a bureau acts as a monopsonist, it must be appreciated that there is a *countervailing tendency* inherent in this organization which offsets the desire to expand expenditure. As a single buyer with the constraint of covering total costs, the bureau must internalize the same external effect. Thus the bureau can expand to OQ_2. This is twice the output level of the private monopsonist. At the social optimum level the consumer surplus that would have been enjoyed (i.e. triangle P_1AE) is no longer available as consumers pay the maximum they are willing to pay (i.e. triangle P_2AK = triangle KLM or triangle BAK = triangle KJM). Whilst consumer surplus has fallen by triangle P_1AE, producer surplus or factoral surplus has increased by P_1P_2LE. The dead-weight loss associated with a bureaucracy is then triangle ELM. In fact it may be noted that, whilst not optimal, a bureaucrat has lower dead-weight losses than a private monopsonist in the conditions depicted. If anything, the tendency to expand output has ameliorated the usual tendency of a private monopsonist purchaser to reduce output.

Most of what has been said, whilst developed somewhat differently, is broadly compatible in spirit with the conclusion of Niskanen (1968). We have, however, sought to emphasize that the monopsony element in bureaux is a mitigating factor in the discussion of allocative inefficiency, and this will assume ever greater importance later. Certainly there remains allocative inefficiency associated with bureaucracy, but the social optimum is not 'half the output of the maximum equilibrium budget' (Jackson, 1982, p. 142). Similarly, care has to be advised in interpreting the expansion factor associated with Frey's (1984) analysis. There are two conditions in which the output of a budget-maximizing bureaucrat is twice the social optimum. The first is when the supply function in figure 6.1(a) is infinitely elastic, i.e. where there is no monopsony power and marginal cost is equated with the supply function for the bureau (McKenzie and Tullock, 1981) and second, when the bureau acts as a discriminating monopsonist, i.e. pays at the margin the minimum acceptable for additional output, i.e. removing completely factoral surplus (Niskanen, 1968). This would be an extremely strong assumption and a considerable power to be added to the authority of bureaucrats. In such circumstances the supply function again becomes the marginal cost curve.

Once these circumstances are stressed it would be unwise to assume that an expansion by the bureau of twice the social optimum is likely; indeed, the less elastic the supply curve, the more the monopsony influence and the closer the bureau equilibrium accords with the social optimum.

6.3 ALLOCATIVE INEFFICIENCY AND X-EFFICIENCY: A TRADE-OFF

An early criticism of the Niskanen model was that the obsessive use of budget funds to promote the expansion of larger budgets could prove inconsistent with a range of goals which bureaucrats may typically whish to pursue (Migué and Bélanger (1974)). These goals include 'on-the-job leisure' and 'fringe benefits'. Such activity generates X-inefficiency and inflates the cost of provision of public service. However, to the extent that it can be achieved, it is only as a result of a reduction in the expansion of output. To the extent that X-inefficiency is pursued the bureaucrat is interested in net revenue, and the output level may fall. It is important to consider the implications of this trade-off between X-inefficiency and increased output. Here we proceed with the assumption that the bureaucrat wishes first and foremost to maximize budget size but thereafter to enjoy X-inefficiency.

Figure 6.2 is an amended version of figure 6.1 with the only change (for the sake of simplicity) being the substitution of increasing costs of production by constant costs of production. The bureaucrat may try to ensure that the size of the budget is expanded to a theoretical limit at OQ_B with an 'all-or-nothing offer' to government. Total benefit ($OAQ_X - Q_XQ_BG$) and total cost (OP_CEQ_B) in figure 6.2 are equated at output OQ_B. In this instance, however, individuals are actually faced with units of the good which generate marginal disutility (e.g. 'too much' defence). Net total benefit is not negative and gross total benefit is not exceeded by total cost. Of course, 'forced riders' (i.e. those with negative marginal utility) may complain. If such a protest might influence the funding agency the bureaucrat would be unlikely to push output above OQ_X (the budget in this case being OP_CKQ_X). In either event the implication is greater levels of output for public monopolists than either for competitors or private monopolists.

What is unusual about this presentation is the fact that the given environment dictates that the bureaucratic monopolist is operating on an inelastic section of the demand curve, in violation of the received wisdom on monopolists. This inconsistency is resolved once the possibility of X-inefficiency is allowed for. In the illustrated circum-stances the bureau which really wishes to maximize its budget or total cost will foster X-inefficiency to the degree that $LRAC_0 = LRMC_0$ shifts to $LRAC_1 = LRMC_1$. The attraction of this is most readily seen in figure 6.2(b). Here TC_0 and TC_1 are the total curves relevant to the appropriate subscripted average and marginal curves in part (a), and TB is the total willingness to pay.

By adopting X-inefficiency and shifting TC_0 to TC_1, the bureaucratic monopoly achieves a budget increase from OB_0 to OB_1, which is as large a budget as the demand constraining condition will allow. Instead of attempting to attain a budget of OP_CEQ_B (i.e. OB_0) or settling for

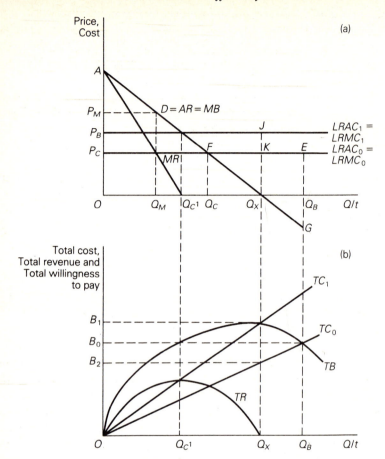

Figure 6.2   The bureaucratic model: allocative and x-inefficiency

a budget of $OP_C KQ_X$ (i.e. OB_2) the inflation of costs permits the attainment of a larger budget (i.e. OB_1). As this point X-inefficiency is measured by the distance B_1–B_2. Although strictly speaking the equilibrium at OQ_X is associated with unitary price elasticity, the bureaucrat is making use of inelasticity with reference to the average revenue and marginal benefit (MB).

   Hence the argument is that any bureaucratic equilibrium involving the negative section of the demand curve, and therefore the falling part of TB, will be eradicated by the bureau adopting X-inefficient practices, thereby maximizing their total budget. It is conventionally argued that bureaus are helped in this respect by having only vaguely specified duties, and by the difficulties involved in enforcing and policing any activities that are specified. The budget-maximizing bureaucratic monopolist should content himself with allocative inefficiency only in those conditions where the competitive price is on the price-elastic range of the demand function.

Allowing *any* X-inefficiency can serve only to decrease the total budget. This result is quite general to the extent that even if the linear marginal cost function displayed increasing costs of production, the bureaucrat would not reveal X-inefficiency where price-elasticity exceeded one at least marginal cost.

The above discussion predicts that bureaucrats will tend to be both allocative and X-inefficient when the price elasticity of demand is less than one, and that they will be allocatively inefficient but X-efficient when the price elasticity of demand exceeds one. The bureaucrat may not, of course, operate precisely where price elasticity of demand is unitary (as in the final outcome in figure 6.2). Clearly, if least cost was in excess of $LRAC_1$, they would be constrained, and also it is accepted that other complications may occur which have not been captured in the above simplified demonstration. It is, however, the case that the tendency to promote X-inefficiency will be greater the lower the price elasticity of demand.

The arguments of the bureaucrats' utility function and the constraints under which they operate are central to this prediction. Implicit is the assumption that, within the utility function, the bureaucrat will not wish to reduce the total budget even if this implies X-inefficiency. Following Jackson (1982) it is possible that leisure is an important argument such that, rather than accrue the power and prestige from a maximum budget size, the bureaucrat inflates costs and forgoes the total possible revenue. This activity, said to be more consistent with UK bureaucrats than bureaucrats in the USA, will of course generate a tendency to X-inefficiency along the elastic range of the demand function. Peacock (1983) noted the distinction between European bureaucracies and US bureaucracies. He specified a utility function for bureaucrats as follows:

$$\text{Max } U = U(N, L, S) \tag{6.11}$$

where N = number of administrative grade officials under a senior bureaucrat's command;
L = 'on-the-job' leisure;
S = fiscal residuum over and above payments to administrative-grade officials.

The bureaucrat is constrained by a budget (B) from which salaries are paid and the surplus enjoyed (i.e. $B = \overline{W}N + S$, where $\overline{W}$ is the salary for administrators). He is also constrained in so far as leisure is reduced with more administrative-grade officials to consider $(L = L(N)$ where $L_n < 0)$. The result is that maximizing with respect to the constraints may 'make it possible for the output level to be below the output produced by the profit maximizing firm producing under conditions of pure competition' (p. 130).

6.4   THE ECONOMIC THEORY OF BUREAUCRACY WITHIN ALTERNATIVE MODELS OF PUBLIC SECTOR GROWTH

While the economic theory of bureaucracy has been appended to explanations of public sector growth, it has not generally been interrelated with existing alternative explanations. Here an exploratory discussion following Cullis and Jones (1984) is offered, with a view to investigating the impact of integrating the economic theory of bureaucracy. The objective throughout is, of course, to highlight the implications for Leviathan. In particular, will the economic theory of bureaucracy complement or prove competitive with existing theories of public sector growth? When placed in the context of traditional models, does the economic theory of bureaucracy augment or mitigate public sector growth?

Baumol's Relative Price Effect

Baumol (1967) provides the prediction that the relative price of public sector outputs will rise over time (see chapter 4). Public services are labour-intensive and technological growth may reduce the relative productivity of public employees to private sector employees. If wages rise in the public sector in line with the private sector, the relative price of public services rises. Given a price elasticity of less than unity, this analysis leads to a rising share of the public sector. This is the initial response of a sequence of events associated with what is known as Baumol's Law. The question now arises as to the effect of this on X-inefficiency in bureaucracy.

The discussion above suggests that, for an unfettered bureaucracy, demand is unlikely to be price-inelastic at the implicit 'tax price' in the bureaucrat's budget. Whilst this tax price may be inflated by X-inefficiency, the relative price effect transfers an economic rent from bureaucrats to other costs of public provision. In the context of the analysis of the preceding section, when the bureau operates at a price elasticity of one the size of public expenditures remains constant, but the relative price effect drives out bureaucratic X-inefficiency.[6]

However, this initial effect ignores the fact that the technological change also increases income, and given positive income elasticity, shifts demand to the right (at all points relevant to the analysis). What ensues depends on how the price elasticity of demand on the new curve is affected by the rightward shift. Three outcomes for linear demand functions are possible:

Case I The price elasticity of demand is unchanged. The rightward shift of the demand curve takes the form of a 'swivel' with the curve anchored at its vertical intercept.[7] If this is the case then the result of the relative price effect is again to drive out bureaucratic X-inefficiency. The new equilibrium involves greater allocative inefficiency but there is no cause for bureaux to adopt X-inefficiency as a response to the shift.

Case II The price elasticity has increased. Here the new demand curve must have an intercept on the vertical axis below the initial one. The predictions for X-inefficiency are as for case I, i.e. the relative price effect should drive it out.

Case III The price elasticity has decreased. Here the new demand curve must have an intercept on the vertical axis above the initial one. The prediction is that bureaux may have an incentive to further X-inefficiency and countervail the impact of the relative price effect. This outcome is analyzed below and placed in the context of Wagner's Law.

The analysis of this chapter points therefore to countervailing tendencies within different theories of public sector expansion. In cases I and II, for example, it is not possible for both bureaucracies and other inputs in the provision of public services to be both generating and enjoying X-inefficiency simultaneously.

Wagner's Law

In chapter 4 it was explained how for Wagner's 'law of rising public expenditures' an important variable is income elasticity and demand for public sector activities. If the *only* driving force for the growth of the public sector is the growth of income per capita, then the economic theory of bureaucracy complements Wagner's Law. It is possible that the share of public expenditures can grow even when quantity of public services demanded has an income elasticity of less than one.

Musgrave (1969), and Musgrave and Musgrave (1976), look to the growth of per capita income and the income elasticity of both consumer goods and services and capital goods to explain the rising share of the public sector. For consumer goods provided in the public sector, 'the basic question is whether the income elasticity of demand for public consumer goods is in excess of unity' (Musgrave, 1969, p. 78). To this question, arguments suggest a rising public to private consumption ratio over the early stages of growth. In later stages this hypothesis is dependent to a degree on complementarity of public services with private consumption. In all, however, there is no 'clear-cut' answer. For capital goods 'one would expect the public share in capital formation to decline over time', though there are 'countervailing trends' (Musgrave and Musgrave, 1976, p. 141).

The theory of bureaucracy advanced above explains why it is possible, when the quantity demanded of a public service is of unitary income elasticity, for 'second round effects' of bureaucracy to result in public expenditures appearing of greater than unitary income elasticity. (Indeed, when the quantity demanded is of less than unitary income elasticity, the relative size of the public sector may yet expand.) In figure 6.3 the example is set for a good provided in the public sector which increases in demand proportionally to a change in income. The objective is to show that public expenditure increases more than proportionally because of bureaucratic X-inefficiency. The initial demand is D_1D_1 and the least costs of provision are $LRAC_0 = LRMC_0$. The bureau maximizes the size of the budget by providing an output of OQ_1 at a total budget cost of OP_1KQ_1. Income is assumed to double and, at the implicit 'tax price' P_1, the demand for this good doubles; the demand function shifts to D_2D_2. To double his budget at least cost, the bureaucrat would demand OP_1JQ_2 (and clearly run the risk that excess capacity would be noted). Far simpler, and possibly safer, would be to inflate costs to the implicit 'tax price' P_2 (i.e. $LRAC_1 = LRMC_1$); output would increase to OQ_3 and the bureaucrat would enjoy an even larger budget of OP_2HQ_3.

The 'second round effect' of cost inflation by the bureau has meant that public expenditures have increased by a greater proportion than income. Since OP_2LQ_4 is $1/2(OP_2HQ_3)$ and given that price elasticity is less than one on the demand function below point L,

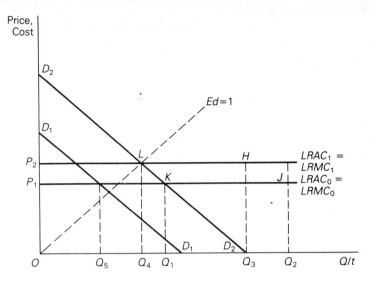

Figure 6.3   The bureau and Wagner's Law

$OP_2LQ_4 > OP_1KQ_1$. That is to say 1/2 times the new government budget is in excess of the old budget for the bureau. Public expenditures then appear to exhibit an income elasticity greater than one, and the share of the public sector in GNP increases (note that in a perfectly competitive market unitary income elasticity of quantity demanded yields unitary income elasticity of expenditure, i.e. output increases from OQ_5 to OQ_1 and no cost inflation occurs).

The impact of bureaucracy can give the impression that the demand for goods provided in the public sector is elastic with respect to income, when in point of fact it is the increase in the implicit 'tax price' that creates a more than proportionate increase in public expenditure. As such it would appear a comment consistent with the evidence of Morris Beck (1976). Beck argued that over time income elasticities of demand for public services exceeded one (e.g. UK, France, West Germany between 1950 and 1974). However, on constant price data the income elasticities were less than one. The question is raised as to why the deflator for price changes is greater in the public sector and the answer, in part, may be in the 'second round' effect of bureaucrats. Such was the conclusion of Buchanan and Tullock (1977), who pointed to a 'disproportionate' increase in the salaries of civil servants and to the 'transfer' that is thereby effected. It is an inference, however, which is not proven beyond doubt, and which is disputed by Beck (1985). It may not always be the case that such 'second round' bureaucratic effects are possible. In the example above, shifts in demand may not be sufficient to change price elasticity from greater than one to less than one; hence no X-inefficiency is promoted. Furthermore, when the slope of the demand schedule changes with an increase in income (i.e. non-separable demand functions), the taxonomy above limits the possibilities of induced bureaucratic X-inefficiency.

The above discussion is an attempt to interrelate the theory of bureaucracy with those explanatory variables pointed to as supporting Wagner's Law. In so doing it explains why the share of public expenditures can grow even when quantity demanded has an income elasticity of less than one. Also, it explains that the relative price effect is a cause of relative growth in the public sector because price inelasticity is promoted by positive income elasticity. It is in this way that price inelasticity invokes growth of the public sector.[8]

6.5 SUMMARY AND CONCLUSIONS

The objective of this chapter was two-fold. First, to set the standard economic theory of bureaucracy into context. Its popular presentation is one whereby government activity reaches 'twice' the social optimum. This is an extreme position and portrays the outcome in terms of allocative inefficiency at its worse. Once the monopsonistic element within the standard model is emphasized, allocative inefficiencies will typically not reach this extent. Moreover, if X-inefficiency is also said to dominate bureaucracies, the excesses of allocative inefficiency are further reduced to the extent that the price elasticity of demand for the good is less than one. That is to say, the bureaucrat cannot indulge costlessly in *all* abuses to the extent typically implied. Certainly Leviathan is present, but rather more constrained than generally implied. It should be emphasized that in arriving at these conclusions the tenets of the standard model have been applied. Bureaucrats have faced only the constraint that total benefit equal total cost. Some authors have suggested that techniques such as cost-effectiveness analysis may constrain the bureau even further (Jackson, 1982).

Second, when the theory of bureaucracy is considered more broadly, there are further checks to its excesses. It has already been noted that the median voter outcome of majority voting may lead to a non-optimal outcome. If preferences were distributed in a way similar to income, the mean would exceed the median (see chapter 2, figure 2.4), and majority voting would result in too small an output of the public good (Boadway and Wildasin, 1985). In this framework the excesses of bureaucracy may in part compensate for the inadequacies of the political market. The discussion of bureaucracy within the other models of public sector growth (e.g. Baumol's relative price effect) by contrast suggests competition limits the ability of any input to indulge in excesses. The rents of other inputs into the public sector can be met only at the cost of the excesses of bureaucrats. Though it has been recognized that in relation to other theories of public sector growth (e.g. Wagner's Law) bureaucracies can appear as an augmenting force.

Sufficient has been said to alert the reader to a broader consideration of the standard bureaucratic model. In the light of this re-appraisal, caution must be advised in considering the typical measures recommended to stem bureaucratic indulgences. The quest for competition between bureaus may not be cost-free (Faith, 1980), and the drive for privatization may not always be appropriate. It is to such matters that we now turn attention.

NOTES

1 For a critique, see Jackson (1982).

2 If
$$D = AR = a - bQ$$

then
$$TB = \int a - bQ \, dQ$$

$$= aQ - \frac{bQ^2}{2}$$

and
$$MB = \frac{dTB}{dQ} = a - bQ = D = AR$$

3 The condition $Q = [2(a - c)/(b + 2a)]$ applies for those values of $a < 2bc/(b - 2d)$. If a (the intercept of the demand function) exceeded this value, the constraint is ineffectual.

4 The condition $Q = a/b$ would surely apply for those values of $a \geqslant 2bc/(b - 2d)$. In such circumstances the constraint that marginal benefit is always positive is operative before the budget constraint.

5 In the diagram even though the budget constraint bites at OQ_2 if the constraint were simply that marginal benefit be positive, then output OQ_3 could be attained.

6 If, however, the bureaucrat had faced closer scrutiny than discussed above, price inelasticity would be predicted along with public expenditure growth.

If not then there is some comfort in the initial effects of the relative price effect.

7   If

$$p = a - bq \tag{1}$$

$$q = \frac{a}{b} - \frac{p}{b} \tag{2}$$

$$\frac{dq}{dp} = \frac{1}{b} \tag{3}$$

now

$$Ed = -\frac{dq}{dp} \cdot \frac{p}{q} \quad \text{substituting for } dq/dp \text{ from (3)}$$

$$Ed = -\frac{1}{b} \cdot \frac{p}{q}$$

Using (2) $\dfrac{p}{q} = \dfrac{p}{\dfrac{a}{b} - \dfrac{p}{b}} = \dfrac{pb}{a - p}$

then

$$Ed = -1 \frac{(pb)}{b(a-p)}$$

$$= -\frac{p}{a - p}$$

i.e. if the demand curve shifts such that $a_1 >, =, < a_0$ then the price elasticity at any p will be lower, unchanged, or raised respectively.

8   When income elasticity is zero, the relative price argument simply drives out bureaucratic X-inefficiency.

REFERENCES

Baumol, W. J. (1967), Macro-economics of unbalanced growth: the anatomy of urban crisis, *American Economic Review*, vol. 57, no. 3 (June), pp. 415–26.

Beck, M. (1976), The expanding public sector: some contrary evidence, *National Tax Journal*, vol. 29, no. 1 (March), pp. 51–21 (see Peacock, 1979, p. 13).

Beck, M. (1982), Toward a theory of public sector growth, *Public Finance/Finances Publiques*, vol. 37, no. 2, pp. 163–77.

Beck, M. (1985), Public expenditure, relative prices and resource allocation, *Public Finance/Finances Publiques*, vol. 40, no. 1, pp. 17–34.

Bird, R. M. (1971), Wagner's 'Law' of expanding state activity, *Public Finance/Finances Publiques*, vol. 26, no. 1, pp. 1–26.

Boadway, R. W. and Wildasin, D. E. (1984), *Public Sector Economics*, 2nd edn, Boston: Little, Brown.

Breton, A. and Wintrobe, R. (1975), The equilibrium size of a budget-maximising bureau, *Journal of Political Economy*, vol. 83, no. 1 (February), pp. 195–207.

Buchanan, J. (1977), Why does government grow?, pp. 3–18 in Borcherding, T. E. (ed.), *Budgets and Bureaucrats: the Sources of Public Sector Growth*, Durham, NC: Duke University Press.

Buchanan, J. and Tullock, G. (1977), The expanding public sector: Wagner squared, *Public Choice*, vol. 15, pp. 147–50.

Chapman, L. (1978), *Your Disobedient Servant*, London: Chatto & Windus.

Cullis, J. G. and Jones, P. R. (1984), The economic theory of bureaucracy, X-inefficiency and Wagner's Law: a note, *Public Finance/Finances Publiques*, vol. 39, no. 2, pp. 191–201.

Faith, R. L. (1980), Rent-seeking aspects of bureaucratic competition, pp. 332–43 in Buchanan, J. M., Tollison, R. D. and Tullock, G. (eds), *Toward a Theory of a Rent-Seeking Society*, College Station: Texas A and M University Press.

Frey, B. S. (1983), *Democratic Economic Policy*, Oxford: Martin Robertson.

Goodin, R. (1982), Rational politicians and rational bureaucrats in Washington and Whitehall, *Public Administration*, vol. 60, no. 1 (Spring), pp. 23–41.

Jackson, P. M. (1982), *The Political Economy of Bureaucracy*, Oxford: Philip Allan.

McKenzie, R. B. and Tullock, G. (1981), *The New World of Economics*, Homewood, Illinois: Irwin.

Migué, J. and Bélanger, G. (1974), Toward a general theory of managerial discretion, *Public Choice*, vol. 12 (Spring), pp. 27–47.

Mueller, D. C. (1979), *Public Choice*, London: Cambridge University Press.

Musgrave, R. A. (1969), *Fiscal System*, New Haven and London: Yale University Press.

Musgrave, R. A. and Musgrave, P. B. (1976), *Public Finance in Theory and Practice*, New York: McGraw-Hill.

Niskanen, W. A. (1968), Non-market decision making: the peculiar economics of bureaucracy, *American Economic Review*, vol. 58, no. 2(May), pp. 293–305.

Niskanen, W. A. (1971), *Bureaucracy and Representative Government*, Chicago: Aidine.

Niskanen, W. A. (1973), *Bureaucracy: Servant or Master?*, Hobart Paperback 5, London: IEA.

Peacock, A. T. (1979), *The Economic Analysis of Government and Related Themes*, Oxford: Martin Robertson.

Peacock, A. T. (1983), Public x-inefficiency: informational and institutional constraints, pp. 125–138 in Hanusch H. (ed.), *Anatomy of Government Deficiencies*, Berlin: Springer-Verlag.

Tullock, G. (1976), *The Vote Motive*, Hobart Paperback 9, London: IEA.

7

Private Responses to Public Expenditure Decisions

7.1 INTRODUCTION

The term 'crowding out' has become fashionable in recent years, but is ambiguous to the extent that it applies to a variety of arguments. The linking thread in all of them is that they describe offsetting responses to government policy action. Two distinct literatures can be identified. The first, associated with macro-economic policy, concerns the efficacy of government fiscal policy when the rate of interest, price level and wealth effects consequent on increasing government expenditure are fully incorporated in a macro-policy analysis. Some discussion of the first of these can be found in chapter 9. The second crowding out literature is much more micro-economic in orientation, dealing as it does with individual responses to government provisions as in, say, a welfare state. The concern here is this second micro-economic literature.

When, for example, education is made more available within the public sector, demand for this service in the private sector is reduced (e.g. see Peltzman, 1973; West, 1975). As the state takes greater responsibility for the provision of welfare, private charitable contributions become less important (e.g. Abrams and Schmitz, 1978; Roberts, 1984). In such a fashion individuals adjust to government activities by their own private expenditures. The existence of the private sector enables individuals to augment consumption of certain goods when public expenditure is inadequate, and to reduce their private expenditures when public provision increases.

Within the literature which identifies Leviathan, there is considerable emphasis upon the difficulties individuals experience in resisting the growth of government activity. The transactions costs in mobilizing large groups to 'voice' opposition are well known. However, following Hirschman (1970), when 'voice' involves high transactions costs, 'exit' may be a preferred mode of response. 'Exit' refers to the adjustment an individual may make in response to a threat to his real income. Provided that this option is open, the tendency to invoke a collective response is muted. If a market exists, then individuals respond to the price increase of one good by substituting an alternative. It is only when markets are an inadequate defence that individuals will be perceived collectively to make a fuss and stage opposition.

7.2 PRIVATE SECTOR ADJUSTMENT MECHANISMS

In chapter 1 an efficient level of provision of a good or service involved equating marginal social benefit (the vertical sum of marginal private benefit and marginal external benefit, if any) with marginal social cost (the vertical sum of the marginal private cost and marginal external cost if any). In chapter 2 an economic account of how actual decisions on public sector provisions are made was reviewed. It was evident that there was no necessary coincidence between the normative prescriptions of chapter 1 and the essentially positive prediction of chapter 2.

In summary, the outcome of chapter 2 was a level of provision of public sector goods and services that could not be predicted to completely please many. For example, in figure 2.1 in chapter 2, with equal tax prices and majority voting, the median voter choice is selected and this leaves all except CV3 dissatisfied with the collective decision. CVs 1 and 2 want a smaller quantity and CVs 4 and 5 a greater one. Such dissatisfaction is likely to be the spur for individual adjustments which may allow individuals to increase their welfare.[1] In some measure the problem may arise because the collective decision is being made at the wrong level in the fiscal constitution. Ideally, the benefits and costs of a collective decision would be well defined over a group of given size, and this would tend to minimize the number and extent of dissatisfied CVs.

Altering a collective decision to a different fiscal jurisdiction presupposes the formation of a pressure group. The problems associated with this response have been noted above. Leaving aside the more dramatic and discrete response associated with revolution, because this also requires coalition formation on some scale, it is individual adjustments that are most likely to be observed. Internal and external migration are possible avenues of adjustment. External migration is a much-discussed topic especially associated with the 'brain drain'. Internal fiscally induced migration has been long recognized (Tiebout, 1956) and explored (see for example, Aronson, 1974). Aronson has a model in which individuals respond to their imputed fiscal transfer in any location (the difference between per capita expenditures in their community and taxes paid). Empirical work relating to Harrisburg in the USA and Leeds and Manchester in England leads him to conclude that fiscal factors affect the distribution of population. The model performed rather better for the US data, which may be accounted for by the greater fiscal differences encountered in the USA. Hence incurring relocation costs was more likely to be a welfare-increasing strategy. Locational adjustment mechanisms are adopted only at considerable cost. However, the remainder of this chapter explores the extent to which a private–public mix, mentioned in the Introduction, provides individuals with a more easily employed safety mechanism against Leviathan. How will it reduce the welfare costs they may otherwise experience? If such a mechanism exists, upon what factors does it depend?

7.3 MARKET CORRECTION AND GOVERNMENT GROWTH

When private expenditures are reduced in response to the growth of public expenditures, the public sector is said to have 'crowded out' the private sector. In order to explore the analytics of this form of direct 'crowding out' (also see chapter 9) we look to the provision of a typical welfare service W (e.g. education, health care). The private market expenditures (Q_W) on such a good would be expected to vary negatively with market price (P_W). However, in the light of the 'crowding out' literature it will also respond negatively to government provision[2] (G_W). The substitution response in the private sector will depend on the degree (θ) to which public sector provision is considered comparable to that supplied within the market sector. If both goods possess identical attributes (Lancaster, 1966), then one might expect a corresponding decrease in private market demand in response to an increase in public output (i.e. $\theta = 1$). This follows, of course, provided public provision is 'direct' and 'zero-priced', which is generally typical for the goods considered here (Brennan and Pincus, 1983).

The question of how the public output is financed is also relevant in another way. To the extent that recipients of these goods and services perceive them as zero-priced (and do not consider the full tax price), recipients appear to experience an increase in their real income. If T_W reflects the tax price, then recipients of governmental expenditure receive an income of (G_W-T_W) according to their underestimate of T_W. While for society these sums may be equal in terms of production cost (i.e. there are 'no free lunches'), for the affected sections or for the fiscally illuded, this expression may appear positive. Thus, if α is the marginal propensity to consume W with respect to income, the consumption of W in the market may increase as a result of an 'income effect' $(\alpha(G_W-T_W))$ consequent upon public sector provision. This 'income effect' will to some extent offset the 'substitution' effect (θG_W) which occurs when public provision is available.

Drawing these arguments together, it is possible to express the private sector demand for $W(Q_W^M)$ as a function of certain variables:

$$Q_W^M = \lambda - \beta P_W - \theta G_W + \alpha(G_W-T_W) \qquad (7.1)$$

where λ is a constant and β the degree of demand sensitivity to price.

The interdependency with public provision then becomes apparent. Assume that government considers the market to 'underprovide' good W. It may be that positive external effects are, or are thought to be, associated with the consumption of the good (e.g. education), or that the government perceives the good as a merit good (e.g. certain forms of medical care). The motive, however, is initially assumed genuinely to accord with government behaving in a socially responsible manner, and not in response to government failure. If Q_W^S is the social target for the provision of W and if Q_W^M is the existing market provision, then government provision (G_W) initially will be:

$$G_W = Q_W^S - Q_W^M \qquad (7.2)$$

The need to augment provision of W appears clear to government; it simply adjusts to market failure. The consequences determined by 'crowding out', however, would appear to cast government in an altogether different light.

In figure 7.1 the relationship between current market output and the socially optimum output is illustrated on the horizontal axis $(Q_W^S > Q_W^M)$. $R_G R_G$ depicts a reaction function, by which government must increase its output as the market output falls further below the

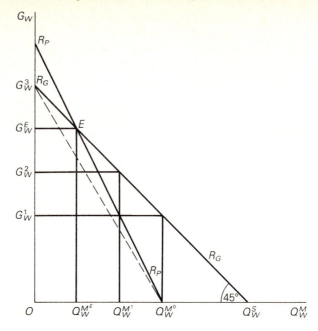

Figure 7.1   Private and public sector interdependence

socially desired output Q_W^S. The slope of this function has a value equal
to (minus) one, depicting a corresponding increasing role for government as market output falls (i.e. from equation (7.2), dG_W/dQ_W^M is
negative and equal to one when $Q_W^S > Q_W^M$). By contrast, the function
of R_PR_P depicts the 'crowding out' response in the private sector.

The slope of this function (when $\theta = 1$) is easily determined by
rewriting (7.1):

$$G_W = \frac{\lambda - \beta P_W - \alpha T_W - Q_W^M}{1 - \alpha} \qquad (7.3)$$

So that:

$$dG_W/dQ_W^M = \frac{-1}{1-\alpha} \qquad (7.4)$$

and it is clear that, provided $\alpha > 0$, the slope of R_PR_P exceeds that of
R_GR_G.

In figure 7.1 $Q_W^S > Q_W^{M^0}$ and initially the government seeks to make
good the deficit by supplying G_W $(= Q_W^S - Q_W^{M^0})$. The simple action

of market correction generates a series of responses on the part of private and public sectors. Decision-makers are assumed to adjust in a Cournot fashion, i.e. they ignore the consequent response to their action of changes in the other sector.

At a public sector output of G_W^1, it is clear that there is 'crowding out' on the part of the private sector; the size of which falls to $Q_W^{M^1}$ (on the reaction function $R_P R_P$). The public sector is thereby forced to expand provision of W if Q_W^S is to be attained. Public sector provision increases to G_W^2. The sequence of events outlined will continue until an equilibrium position E is attained. The *ratio* of public to private activity has altered dramatically from $G_W^1/Q_W^{M^1}$ to G_W^E/Q_W^{ME}. However, the total provision of the good is equal only to the social optimum Q_W^S.

There are a number of implications of the analysis which bear upon the allegation that public sector growth is 'excessive'.

First, when government intervention is socially responsible, and *not* the illegitimate product of bureaucrats, pressure groups or politicians, *public sector growth* is required for market correction. Such growth. *per se*, can be equated with the appearance but not the reality of a Leviathan state.

Second, when government failure arises from the processes within the Leviathan literature, the private sector can act as a constraint on excessive provision. In figure 7.1 the smaller the existing market provision and/or the smaller the value of α the more likely the private sector reaction function will intersect the vertical axis below, or at G_W^3. In such a circumstance the public sector cannot be 'excessive' unless the private sector has been totally eliminated and public sector provision exceeds G_W^3. That the private sector must be removed to infer public sector provision appears a demanding constraint, and it has been noted elsewhere (Cullis and Jones, 1983; Roberts, 1984). Clearly, it all depends upon the situation in hand, but how large, for example, can α possibly be?

7.4 THE DETERMINANTS OF 'CROWDING OUT'

The above example is an extreme one, and has been designed to emphasize the 'exit' potential of the private sector. This safeguard is influenced by: the value of θ (which above is assumed equal to one); the value of α the value of $(G_W - T_W)$ and the relative size of the private sector.

Table 7.1   Summary of government 'crowding out' effects for an increase[a] in government provision

Substitution effect	Income effect		Government 'crowding out'
	α-value	$(G_w^1 - \dot{T}_w)^b$	
-1	$\alpha \lessgtr 0$	0	1 for 1
-1	$\alpha = 0$	1	1 for 1
-1	$\alpha > 0 < 1$	1	<1 for 1
-1	$\alpha = 1$	1	Zero
-1	$\alpha > 1$	1	Negative ('crowding in')

[a]   Decreases in government units of provision would reverse the substitution effect and generally result in 'crowding in'; however, given the nature of the arguments for bureaucratic and government imperfections this process is not pursued here.

[b]   For values of $(G_w^1 - T_w) > 0 < 1$ as long as $\alpha \leqslant 1$ then 'crowding out' occurs.

Source: Cullis and Jones (1983).

In table 7.1 we continue initially with the assumption that $\theta = 1$ and consider the crowding out effect of an additional unit of government provision for alternative values of α and $(G_W - T_W)$. If $(G_W - T_W)$ equals zero, for example, there can be no 'income effect' and full crowding out occurs. Alternatively, if $(G_W - T_W)$ is positive, the degree of crowding out will vary according to the value of α; the smaller the value of α the greater the degree of crowding out.

The greater the degree of 'crowding out', the more important is the safeguard against 'excessive' public provision. Here, however, the smaller the value of θ, the less 'crowding out' can be expected. The less publicly provided goods are perceived as substitutes for privately produced goods, the less 'crowding out' will occur. That public or private (not-for-profit) provision of welfare services is not a perfect substitute for private good provision, because the latter provides a greater element of individual control, has been advanced by Weisbrod (1975). The question of the elasticity of substitution between public and private units of provision becomes essential. To the extent that the private good is different, the existence of the private sector is more likely in the event of over-provision. In figure 7.1 the slope of $R_P R_P$ is equal to $(-\theta)/(1-\alpha)$, and the lower is θ the greater the slope will be. When $R_P R_P$ has a higher slope then, for any initial private sector, the likelihood that the private sector will be totally eliminated before excess provision (i.e. greater than Q_W^S) occurs is diminished. The test of the existence of the private sector as an indicator that government excesses cannot be significant is less appropriate.

The question of whether the private sector may mitigate the abuses of Leviathan, therefore, becomes an empirical issue. How might the evidence be interpreted? The value of α, *ceteris paribus*, needs to be low if crowding out is significant. With respect to the demand for health care, Newhouse (1981) reports low income elasticities, noting (p. 92) that 'estimated income elasticities have varied from near zero to approximately 1.0'. Similarly, to the extent that government welfare services crowd out private charitable activity, Feldstein (1975) reports the income elasticity of charitable activity to be about 0.8 between 1948 and 1968. Income elasticities are not the same as α, the marginal propensity to consume with respect to income. However, they imply low values of α. Since they refer to *expenditure* the elasticity is $dQ/dY \cdot Y/Q$, and as Y/Q is likely to be greater than 1 (and probably considerably greater than 1), then with the elasticity < 1 and $Y/Q > 1$, dQ/dY must be less than 1.

Income elasticities raise the expectation that the income effect of government provision will not cancel the substitution effect and crowding out will result. Some studies support this. Abrams and Schmitz (1978) studied the interrelationship between government transfers and voluntary charitable activity in the USA. They assumed that voluntary charitable activity was a function of the individual's income, the price of giving and the amount of transfers being made by the government. The price of giving is equal to the cost of giving one dollar to a charity. Given tax expenditures, this cost is equal to one dollar less the marginal income tax rate. The results of this study refer to the period 1948–72 and, with different specifications of government activity, a statistically significant negative relationship is found. Alternative specifications of government transfers were : per capita federal expenditures on health, hospitals, education and welfare; per capita state, local and federal expenditure on health, hospitals, education and welfare and social security transfers. In all cases, significant 'crowding out' was reported.

With respect to education, Peltzman (1973) identifies 'crowding out' in the USA. By making the units of observation the states of the USA, he applied two-stage least-squares regression to determine whether government education expenditure influences the demand for private education. By postulating that educational expenditure per capita of private-owned institutions of higher education in each state was dependent on: personal income per capita, the proportion of population of student age; the ratio of median income of college graduates to high school graduates; and the educational expenditures per capita by government, he confirmed the negative 'crowding out' impact of the public sector. Between 50 and 75 cents of every dollar spent by institutions providing government subsidies in-kind replace private expenditures. While this test considered cross-section data. West (1975) has looked historically to the interdependence of private and public sectors in education in England. He similarly noted 'crowding out' in the provision of education. Indeed, he finds it difficult to conclude that the institution of widespread government provision of in-kind subsidies increased the total output of elementary education substantially.

These studies relating to health, private charity and education are illustrative rather than exhaustive. The debate in each case may be continued. For example, with respect to private charity, compare the observation of 'crowding out' by Roberts (1984) with the insignificant element of 'crowding out' in studies reviewed by Sugden (1982). The debate may continue, but it seems very unlikely that it will become possible to dismiss completely the 'exit' potential of the private sector. A safety value does exist by which consumer voters may adjust to governmental failure and 'exit' may be less costly than 'voice'. 'Exit' can restrain any actual or potential excesses of Leviathan.

7.5   PRIVATE OR PUBLIC PROVISION: IS THERE A POPULAR ISSUE?

If the existence of 'exit' (or 'crowding out') permits the individual to use the private sector to respond to government provision, then the question is raised, as in Brennan and Pincus (1983), as to whether or not government spending *per se* has any significant resource allocation effects.[3] If significant welfare costs were experienced (because private adjustment to government provision were constrained) then, following Hirschman (1970), it seems probable that 'voice' would play a more prominent role. Failure to privately adjust would prove a spur for public outcry against the encroachment of the state. A collective expression of discontent, of course, may itself involve those transaction costs associated with mobilizing public opinion.[4] It is therefore possible that the costs of government intervention would have to exceed the costs of 'voice' for such a protest to become evident. Yet while there may be an absence of obvious and active engagement in protest, individuals, *when asked* as to their opinion of government, would indicate their feelings were they subjected to the indulgences of Leviathan. It seems reasonable to predict when exit is inadequate that either individuals will mobilize to protest or, failing this, will express discontent in public surveys. In this way failure to adjust privately would be obvious in a popular expression of discontent with government interference.

That such a protest does exist is the claim of commentators on both sides of the Atlantic. In the USA the various fiscal initiatives of the late 1970s appeared to be attempts at the state/local level to reverse the growth of the public sector by cutting taxes. The evidence in the USA, which is offered as an expression of disenchantment with government, emerges from fiscal referenda. The much-publicized passage of the Californian Proposition 13 suggested that individuals, far from being neutral, did object to at least some element of public provision. In 1978 the Jarvis–Gann Amendment was passed by a majority of two to one and restricted Californian property tax to 1 per cent of assessed values. In addition the measure adjusted property assessments to 1975–76 market values and constrained the annual growth of the assessed values of properties not sold to 2 per cent.

Although some have seen this as the beginning of resistance to the growth of the public sector (see for example Davis and Meyer, 1983), the case of California and other subsequent events offer a different perspective. In particular Levy (1979) offers a 'micro' analysis of Proposition 13. Against a background of tax reform attempts dating from 1965, it is argued that California voters had as a major concern the high and rapidly increasing property taxes (especially for single-family homes). Also it must be noted that Proposition 13 was passed when California had a budget surplus (although of uncertain size). Levy (1979) notes that the vote was described by some commentators, especially Howard Javis, 'as an attack against inflation, large and arrogant government and taxes of all kinds'. He observes, however, that 'This interpretation was soon adopted by the media, but existing evidence suggests it is hyperbolic' (p. 85).

Although it is true that other states followed where California led, details of the initiatives varied considerably. Levy (1979) points out that most state electorates voted on tax shifts or future limits to expenditure growth as opposed to cuts in current expenditure. Of the 17 states with one or more fiscal initiatives on the ballot paper in November, only four voted on actual expenditure cuts. Only Idaho passed the cuts in a straightforward fashion. Nevada passed the cuts with a second confirmatory vote to take place in 1980 before any action occurred. In Oregon and Michigan the expenditure cuts were defeated. By 1981 Ranney could write on the basis of the November 1980 referenda that 'For one thing, it is evident that "Proposition 13 fever" has largely subsided: six states had measures putting limits on property taxes, and they lost in five states' (p. 40).

The interpretation of discontent with government in general may prove less than obvious in the USA. In the UK such an interpretation has similarly been associated with public opinion survey evidence of the Institute of Economic Affairs. Yet once again it is important to look more closely at this apparent impression. Lewis (1982) poses the question 'why is it that Ralph Harris and Arthur Seldon (1971) of the Institute of Economic Affairs in London have repeatedly shown, and have argued cogently, that there is a growing desire among the general public to shift welfare services from the state to the private sector' (p. 45). Is it correct that apparent public response to questionnaires is accurately reflected in these studies? Seldon (1977) places much reliance on the 'priced' nature of their questions. That is, the tax elements of the fiscal connection is given prominence. However Lewis (1982) criticizes Harris and Seldon (1971) who found that 58 per cent of their British sample favoured contracting out of the National Health Service and agreed that 'The state should continue the present service but allow people to contract out, pay less contributions and so on and use the money to pay for their own service.' He points out that only 20 per cent supported the option of fewer taxes and decreased services, and poses the question. 'But who wants to pay more tax for better services when the present service could continue as it is, even with fewer people contributing the full amount? It is indeed a bargain not to be missed, and it seems to reflect a desire not for change or increased contracting out but for services to be maintained at their present level' (p. 47). In the table reported in Seldon (1977) the questions were of the form: 'If (instead of "free" state education) the government gave you £75 a year for each child aged 11 or more which could only be spent on education – and you have to pay another £150 yourself to make up the fees – would you accept this offer or not?' (p. 207). The question was also asked with the monetary sums reversed. A similar question was asked in relation to a health insurance premium. Although the results are described as a fascinating glimpse into suppressed preferences, only one of the socioeconomic groups (the highest) for one of the questions (£150 education voucher and £75 in cash) attracted majority support (52 per cent). Of the other 15 minority percentages only two are above 40 per cent. This may be 'fascinating' but it is not great support for a radical deviation from the status quo even when there is a 'you put £1 in and the state will put £2 in' element to the question.

It is not our intention here to say that the much-quoted referenda results and questionnaire data are not capable of other interpretations. After all, such evidence interpretation is notoriously difficult. Rather it is our intention to suggest that these results, on closer inspection, are not quite what they are often thought to be.[5] They are not easily accepted as evidence of the existence of 'voice' and therefore of the failure of 'exit'. Whilst government may be criticized within this evidence, it does seem possible to overestimate the degree of dissatisfaction. Close examination of apparent fiscal protest may indicate a greater degree of satisfaction than typically supposed.

That 'voice' is not so prevalent may itself be explained by the endogeneity of preferences. Preferences may alter as a result of involvement within different institutional arrangements and, as such, individuals may come to prefer the status quo. The recognition of this point suggests there is a neglected aspect to the Leviathan debate. In mainstream economics preferences are taken as a given, and the incorporation of endogenous preferences has received scant attention. Although this omission is not rectified here, this is not to deny the issue is an important one, worthy of considerable attention. *A priori* it is not clear which way the argument would go. For some, the very words 'collective provision' conjure up the notion of fostering concern and altruism among individuals. For others, public sector provision via the coercive powers of taxation reduces individual responsibility and concern for the fate of others, thereby encouraging isolationist and selfish individuals. The fact that individuals may perceive public provision in different lights adds a dimension to the debate over and above questions of allocative or X-efficiency. An example of this is the debate between Titmuss (1970) and various economists, e.g. Cooper and Culyer (1968) on blood donation. Cooper and Culyer concern themselves with alternative mechanisms that might secure sufficient quantities of blood for transfusion; Titmuss had something more fundamental in mind. In part Titmuss seems to argue for the endogeneity of preferences so that different forms of institutions not only modify human behaviour by altering the cost–benefit framework in which individuals find themselves, they also alter the nature of individuals themselves. In short some institutions, it could be argued, foster those values in people that make for the 'good' society.

Endogeneity of preferences questions the standard welfare comparison of public *v.* private provision. To many, endogeneity of preferences is central. Gintis (1974) makes this clear: 'The Marxist observation, translated into neo-classical terminology, holds that individual preference structures are products and change according to variables *endogenous* to the economic model: prices, quantities, and availabilities of consumption goods, jobs and the social institutions conditioning the supply of labour' (p. 415). Here we raise the issue as a basis for further consideration.

7.6 SUMMARY AND CONCLUSIONS

The existence of the private sector provides the private individual with a defence mechanism against some of the allocative ineffiencies which stem from governmental failures. In the first instance, if 'excessive' provision stems from government, 'crowding out' of private expenditures mitigates welfare losses. In certain conditions it would, in fact, be difficult to imagine that total provision of the good (private and public) were excessive by reference to individuals' preferences, until the private sector were virtually eliminated. Preoccupation with *government growth* without reference to private sector adjustment would certainly be inadequate to substantiate gross over-provision.

Individuals respond to different constraints to maximize welfare. *Within* the public sector individuals may move from one locality to another to ensure they reside in a local authority jurisdiction with local tax and expenditure patterns that accord to their preferences (Tiebout, 1956). Similarly, individuals adjust *outside* the public sector to relate consumption of services to their preferences. Indeed to the extent that there is an *increase* in private sector provision of health, education, social security, etc., there is reason to be sceptical of excess government provision. Of course, privately provided goods may not be perfect substitutes for publicly provided goods. This we accept but, without evidence on the degree of substitutability, growth of private provision may represent supplementation of inadequate public supply. (Criticism that relates to under-provision by government is discussed in Appendix 7.1A, below.)

In the final section of this chapter evidence on individuals' views on the public sector as represented in referenda and questionnaires was discussed. Inspection of much-quoted results did not seem to accord with a picture of widespread unhappiness with public expenditure. It was also noted that a missing element in the Leviathan debate was the endogeneity of preferences. Does more or less public provision foster the 'right' preferences in people?

In this chapter the emphasis has been upon allocative inefficiency, i.e. 'too much' of the good being provided. We now turn to evidence of X-inefficiency, i.e. units of the good being provided at 'too high' a cost in the public sector. Does this occur? Does a return to the market-place offer substantial gains in this respect?

7.1A   APPENDIX: HOW TO CRITICIZE PUBLIC PROVISION

The central theme of this book is an evaluation of the allegation that the public sector has become a Leviathan; that it has grown to monster proportions and that it thereby imposes intolerable costs upon the individual. Yet the public sector has simultaneously been accused of 'under-providing' goods and services. In the UK the existence of waiting lists for publicly provided services (e.g. medical care, housing) is offered as evidence of this failure.[6] In effect the public economy stands accused of both being 'too large' and of providing 'too small' a level of service (reminiscent of the Woody Allen line that a restaurant's food was awful and such small portions were offered!) Of course, critics will argue that if costs of provision in the public sector are particularly high this result is compatible with 'excessive' public *expenditure* and 'inadequate' levels of *service*. The issue of productivity in the public sector will be addressed in chapter 8. Here our intention is to explore the possibility that output of the public sector may be 'too small' or 'too large' when X-inefficiency is absent in the public sector. The objective is to indicate that *both* 'under-provision' and 'over-provision' is possible by reference to a private market allocation. Further we wish to argue that the private sector stands as a 'safety-valve' for *both* over- and under-provision. (Over-provision is dealt with in the main body of the chapter.)

In figure 7.A1 the horizontal axis measures the provision of a government sector good or service (G). Provision is assumed to take place in an X-efficient manner, represented by *LRMC*. A private market outcome is represented by quantity OQ_m and price OP. Assume that a decision is made to replace private provision with public provision. The level of public provision may turn out to be less than OQ_m at OQ_u. This may arise for several reasons; e.g. because of the impact of voting (e.g. median voter model with or without pessimistic fiscal illusion) or government correcting a perceived negative externality. This level of provision, *coupled with zero user charges*, leads individual consumer voters, whose views are effectively captured in the market

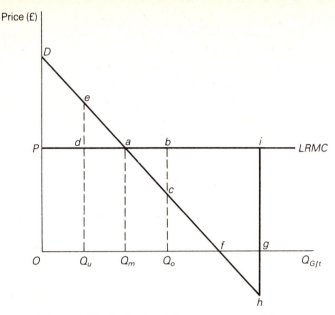

Figure 7.A1   Stylized public economy provision

demand curve D, to sense under-provision (witnessed by excess demand (some recorded as waiting lists) $Q_u f$ and welfare loss triangle *dea*). If government provides OQ_o a quantity greater than the market outcome (either because of the impact of voting, bureaucratic pressures or government correcting a perceived positive externality), again the consumer voter is dissatisfied. Those who realize the 'tax price' of G sense the welfare loss triangle *abc* generated by over-provision and, as zero user costs apply, witness excess demand $Q_o f$. Those who equate zero user charges with 'free' provision note under-provision as indicated by the *apparent* welfare loss triangle $Q_o cf$. They also witness excess demand (a proportion of which may form a waiting list) $Q_o f$.

All this assumes that those who receive G under government provision are the ones who would receive G in a market; namely, those with the highest marginal valuations as represented by the demand curve D. However, in many instances the purpose of public production is deliberately to engineer a *non*-market allocation, so that either OQ_u or OQ_o is allocated to consumer voters along the whole length of D. Such allocations, whether justified on other grounds (needs, positive discrimination, etc.), or not, inevitably look like an arbitrary decision attracting criticism from those who do not receive G. In addition, they will always look allocatively inefficient against a market test. Furthermore, if allowance is not made for producers' (or agents') decisions replacing consumer voter decisions over-provision (by reference to the consumer voters' uninfluenced demand curve) to the extent of causing disbenefit can be envisaged. If D is now viewed as the producer-uninfluenced demand curve of a given individual, a level of provision, Og, causes *disbenefit* to the extent of triangle *fgh* (this corresponds to Illich's (1976) case against health care providers), as well as being inefficient to the extent of triangle *aih* against a market test.

If the starting point of any public provision analysis is an equilibrium private market outcome, it is evident that cause for concern can be easily generated with respect to: under-provision and waiting lists; over-provision and waiting lists; arbitrary (bureaucratic) and unfair allocation and generating disbenefit (actually making people worse off). Although *this is deliberately offered as a caricature* of treatments of public provision, it is not far from the picture presented in first-year economics of social policy/public issues texts. Two points are apparent. First that straightforward market comparisons may be the reference point of general debate against public provision, but that this must be supplemented by more careful analysis of market failure. Second, that a traditional market framework may be ill-suited to the analysis of public policy in the first place. Market displacement may, in some instances, be the object of the exercise. Criticisms that 'this would not happen in a market', are then actually flattering. Having said this, we emphasize that this is not to imply that all criticisms of public provision are more apparent than real. Rather our purpose is to counsel more careful argument and appreciation of other perspectives.

Moving to the second objective of this appendix, it is necessary to explore the operation of the private sector when individuals consider that there is under-provision by the public sector. As is evident from figure 7.A1 the public sector can be accused of under-provision by reference to a market outcome when this is correct (i.e. public output OQ_u) and incorrect (output OQ_o). The reason is that individuals may not be aware of the 'tax price'; certainly grievances are made as to the existence of waiting lists. The question that is rarely asked, however, is what is the 'optimal' length of the waiting list? In the case of the National Health Service (NHS) is it reasonable to suppose that facilities should stand ready to supply medical care for *all* complaints at the moment at which they are required? A market system would obviously apply a rationing device (i.e. price) so that many who appear on the waiting list of the NHS would not reveal their demand when provision is left to the market. Given the resource implications it seems unlikely that, despite the criticism which has arisen, informed consumer voters would regard the optimum waiting list for the NHS as zero. The issue of '*optimum*' waiting time in this way should become the focus of concern (see Cullis and Jones, 1985).

By reference to market provision the criticism of waiting lists in the NHS would seem more apposite in terms of those individuals waiting whose marginal valuations of medical care exceed price. To the extent that these individuals consider that they have paid the 'tax price' of medical care, the need to wait becomes a source of complaint. Whether their tax payments have entitled them to instant medical care or to a place on the waiting list is a moot point. However, given that they must wait, how costly can this be? Cullis and Jones (1986) argue that if the private sector exists, within which there is access to medical care, the costs of waiting can never exceed the price of access to that sector. When individuals are placed on waiting lists they have the choice of opting for private medical care (their tax payments must be made irrespective of their decision). If individuals suffer from perceived 'under-provision' in the public sector the private sector exists as a safety valve. If individuals suffer from waiting, then it is unlikely that they suffer more than the costs of immediate treatment in the private sector. For 1981 Cullis and Jones estimate the costs of waiting for treatment in the NHS as falling between £1205.2 million and £2155.1 million.[8] Whilst for any individual these costs may be high, in aggregate they represent 9.1 per cent and 16.2 per cent respectively of government expenditure on the NHS in 1981–2. It is therefore quite reasonable to find that in surveys *of patients* in the NHS waiting is not a major cause of complaint (Halpern, 1985). Again 'voice' may not be so important when analyzed closely.

To conclude this section we would stress that we are not arguing that waiting for publicly provided services is not a problem. Rather we are arguing that the current perception of this problem may be exaggerated. This, of course, will only be resolved when the issue of optimum waiting for public provision is defined. It seems reasonable at this stage to suppose that this need not be zero. If the costs of waiting are less than the resource cost implications of removing the need to wait, the simple observation that there are costs of waiting is not by itself an adequate criticism of public provision. For individuals who wait the costs of waiting are bounded by the price of access to the market sector. 'Exit' again mitigates the worst fears of the public sector.

NOTES

1 Weisbrod (1975) introduces the so-called three-sector economy in this way. He postulates that those under-satisfied by government provision will supplement that provision via the private market (where the good is an individual (private) one) and the voluntary non-profit (charity) sector (where the good is a collective (public) one).

2 It must be recognized that the room for manoeuvre is constrained somewhat by the inability to opt out of the tax system. Additionally, it may well be the case that the public and market provision are non-separable, so that recourse to the market must be an alternative rather than a supplemental activity.

3 The reader will note that at this stage we are precluding the issue of productivity, distortionary taxes and freedom, which will be dealt with later.

4 Olson (1971) notes the difficulties of mobilizing collective action, and these are relevant here.

5 Stiglitz (1986) similarly raises questions with reference to surveys which indicate an apparent general impression of government inefficiency. He compares them with specific surveys of those parties who had non-routine dealings with a federal government agency. These specific surveys indicate high satisfaction levels. Those with regular dealings with government were less inclined to subscribe to the generally held view.

6 Under-provision is a charge that might also be levelled at the public sector when there is failure to 'take up' benefits provided within the public sector. Individuals who are entitled to claim benefits fail to come forward. This result seems inconsistent with a budget-maximizing bureaucracy when it is claimed that the bureaucracy itself causes such under-provision by the complexity it creates in claiming benefit.

7 The claim that agents replace consumers in demanding services is often levelled at the role of doctors in generating demand for patients.

8 It should be noted that the estimation of the costs of waiting has been based upon the particular approach to waiting lists explored by Lindsay (1980) and Lindsay and Feigenbaum (1984).

REFERENCES

Abrams, B. A. and Schmitz, M. D. (1978), The 'crowding out' effect of government transfers on private charitable contributions, *Public Choice*, vol. 33, no. 1, pp. 29–39.

Aronson, J. R. (1974), Financing public goods and the distribution of population in metropolitan areas: an analysis of fiscal migration in the United States and England, pp. 313–42 in Culyer A. J. (ed.), *Economic Policies and Social Goals*, London: Martin Robertson.

Brennan, G. and Pincus, J. M. (1983), Government expenditure growth and resource allocation: the nebulous connection, *Oxford Economic Papers*, vol. 35, no. 3 (November), pp. 351–65.

Cooper, M. H. and Culyer, A. J. (1968), *The Price of Blood: an Economic Study of the Charitable and Commercial Principle*, Hobart Paper no. 41, London: Institute of Economic Affairs.

Cullis, J. G. and Jones, P. R. (1983), The welfare state and private alternatives towards an existence proof, *Scottish Journal of Political Economy*, vol. 30, no. 2 (June), pp. 97–113.

Cullis, J. G. and Jones, P. R. (1985), National Health Service waiting lists: a discussion of competing explanations and a policy proposal, *Journal of Health Economics*, vol. 4, no. 2 (June), pp. 119–35.

Cullis, J. G. and Jones, P. R. (1986), Rationing by waiting lists: an implication, *American Economic Review*, vol. 76, no. 1 (March), pp. 250–6.

Davis, J. R. and Meyer, C. W. (1983), *Principles of Public Finance*, Englewood Cliffs, NJ: Prentice Hall.

Feldstein, M. A. (1975), The income tax and charitable contributors: Part I – aggregate and distributional effects. *National Tax Journal*, vol. 28, no. 1 (March), pp. 81–100.

Gintis, H. (1974), Welfare criteria with endogenous preferences: the economics of education, *International Economic Review*, vol. 15, no. 2 (June) pp. 415–30.

Halpern, S. (1985), What the public thinks of the NHS, *Health and Social Service Journal*, vol. 94 (June), pp. 702–4.

Harris, R. and Seldon, A. (1971), *Choice in Welfare 1963, 1965, 1970*, London: Institute of Economic Affairs.

Hirschman, A. O. (1970), *Exit, Voice and Loyalty*, Cambridge, Mass.: Harvard University Press.

Illich, I. (1976), *Limits to Medicine*, London: Boyars.

Lancaster, K. (1966), A new approach to consumer theory, *Journal of Political Economy*, vol. 74, no. 2 (April), pp. 137–57.

Levy, F. (1979), On understanding proposition 13, *The Public Interest*, no. 56 (Summer), pp. 66–89.

Lewis, A. (1982), *The Psychology of Taxation*, Oxford: Martin Robertson.

Lindsay, C. M. (1980), *National Health Issues: the British Experience*, Nutley, NJ: Hoffman-LaRoche.

Lindsay, C. M. and Feigenbaum, B. (1984), Rationing by waiting lists, *American Economic Review*, vol. 74, no. 3 (June), pp. 405–17.

Newhouse, J. P. (1981), The demand for medical care services: a retrospect and prospect, pp. 85–103 in Van der Gaag, J. and Perlman, M. (eds), *Health, Economics and Health Economics*, Amsterdam: North Holland.

Olson, M. (1971), *The Logic of Collective Action*, Cambridge, Mass.: Harvard University Press.

Peltzman, S. (1973), The effect of government subsidies in kind on private expenditures: the case of higher education, *Journal of Political Economy*, vol. 81, no. 1 (January/February), pp. 1–27.

Ranney, A. (1981), Referendums, 1980 style, *Public Opinion*, (February/March), pp. 40–1.

Roberts, R. D. (1984), A positive model of private charity and public transfers, *Journal of Political Economy*, vol. 92, no. 1 (February), pp. 136–48.

Seldon, A. (1977), *Charge*, London: Temple Smith.

Stiglitz, J. E. (1986), *Economics of the Public Sector*, New York and London: Norton.

Sugden, R. (1982), On the economics of philanthropy, *Economic Journal*, vol. 92, no. 366 (June), pp. 341–50.

Tiebout, C. M. (1956), A pure theory of local expenditures, *Journal of Political Economy*, vol. 64, no. 5 (October), pp. 416–24.

Titmuss, R. M. (1970), *The Gift Relationship – from Human Blood to Social Policy*, London: Allen & Unwin.

Weisbrod, B. A. (1975), Towards a theory of the voluntary non-profit sector in a three-sector economy, pp. 171–95 in Phelps, E. S. (ed.), *Altruism, Morality and Economic Theory*, New York: Russell Sage Foundaton.

West, E. G. (1975), Educational slow-down and public interventions in 19th century England: a study in the economics of bureaucracy, *Explorations in Economic History*, vol. 12, pp. 61–87.

8

Privatization

The minutes of the last meeting went through on the nod. Then we came
to Matters Arising. The first was *Accommodation*. Sir Humphrey pre-
empted the Assistant Secretary who usually spoke on this matter. As
the young man opened his mouth to reply, I heard Humphrey's voice:
'I'm happy to say that we have found a five per cent cut by selling an
old office block in High Wycombe.'

Lynn, J. and Jay, A. (eds) (1982), *Yes Minister*, vol. 2, p. 59,
London: British Broadcasting Corporation. (p. 59)

8.1 INTRODUCTION

In recent years one response to the growth of the Leviathan literature
has been the strength with which 'privatization' has been advocated.
'Privatization' is a word which was invented by politicians and widely
used by political journalists.[1]. Here it is used as a general description,
applicable to many government policies all of which possess the common
aim of strengthening the market at the expense of state provision. The
theme of our discussion has been the difficulties inherent in comparing
market and governmental failures. Here we illustrate these problems
by questioning the cost-effectiveness of private and of public provision.
As such, the case for 'privatization' will rarely be obvious.

A highly over-simplified taxonomy is frequently applied in the
analysis of privatization. Chart 8.1 outlines the possibilities that exist
as between the financing and production of services. Category four is
the polar case of government production. Movements from this extreme
may take many forms. For example, contracting out the production of
services may be considered as a movement to cell 3. The introduction
of charges and pricing is a step towards cell 2. The complete sale of
assets of nationalized corporations is a more direct movement to cell 1.

Advocates of privatization appear to condone *any* movement away

Chart 8.1 The public–private mix: a taxonomy

	Private production	Private production
Private finance	1	2
Public finance	3	4

from cell 4. For example, with reference to a movement towards cell 3, Pirie (1982, p. 84) writes 'the approach is *undoubtedly* better than no movement at all towards the private sector' (our emphasis). Similarly, Heald (1983a) criticizes Seldon for prescribing, without qualification, any movement from cell 4. Such an extreme position is a difficult one to cling to. It would appear more reasonable to consider the advantages of any movement between cells for specific goods and services. Those that take extreme positions appear to base their case on the proof that a decentralized atomistic market will, under well-defined conditions, produce a Pareto optimal allocation of resources (see chapter 1). When the virtues of the market are extolled, the public sector is seen as deficient in the Leviathan literature. The comparison appears automatically to imply the desirability of 'privatization'. But is such a comparison reasonable? Market failures abound (see chapter 1) and the appropriate comparison, often recognized but seldom adhered to, is between provision of goods in an *imperfect market* and by *deficient government*. Theoretically it has been shown that planned economies can ape the final outcome of perfect markets. Reality implies, however, that both mechanisms of provision will be imperfect. The case for public or private provision is then more pragmatically related to the associated transactions costs incurred in dealing with various problems (Arrow, 1970). Blind faith in 'privatization' may be potentially harmful, and it is clear that recommendations concerning movements between cells are generally difficult to make. A recent comment on studies in the health sector emphasizes 'the error implicit in setting up an idealised, perfectly competitive health market as an alternative to the existing NHS,and the opposing error of an idealised public system against the reality of an uncompetitive market system' (Heald, 1983a). Here we accept that both private and public provision will be subject to imperfections, and indeed that part of the problem in estimating costs of provision in either sector relates to these imperfections.

There are clearly two issues in chart 8.1 – finance and production. Services may be privately financed and privately produced in the market or, for example, publicly financed with 'contracting' of private firms to produce the service. The first question that arises is, when will public financing necessarily replace private finance? When the appropriate source of finance is determined, the second issue is which sector should be employed to produce the good? Here we proceed by first looking at the problems of turning to private finance arrangements for goods typically associated with the public sector. Having explored the question of finance, we then address the question of whether private or public firms should be employed to produce the service. In this step-by-step fashion we may move from one cell to the other within the table. Discussion of *suitability* must, of course, rest upon some criteria. Looking at the case of welfare provision, Klein (1984, p. 13) writes with reference to privatization that

> we might argue that the aim should be to maximize individual choice and to minimize centralized bureaucracy; we might maintain that the aim should be to maximize the total amount spent on welfare; we might claim that the aim should be to maximize the efficiency with which welfare is provided or to minimize the burden that falls on the productive sector of the economy; we might urge that the aim should be to maximize the contribution of the family and the community and to minimize the burden falling on the public sector of welfare.

Throughout this discussion we focus simply on the pursuit of allocative and X-efficiency in a Paretian sense. The privatization debate has often involved a wider perspective. Rees (1986) considers the arguments that privatization will: reduce public borrowing; allow greater choice of shareholding; undermine trade union power; stimulate efficiency and innovation; lead to less political intervention; encourage employee co-operation. He is, however, sceptical of the claims that these effects will create significant positive advantages. Indeed, Kay and Thompson (1986, p. 19) perceive these multiple objectives as indicative of the absence of a clear purpose for the policy of privatization so that 'any objective which seems achievable is seized as justification'. Here we lay greater emphasis on the issue of efficient provision and postpone wider issues associated with government financing for a later chapter.

8.2 PRIVATIZATION, PROPERTY RIGHTS AND COMPETITION

Competition is an extremely important ingredient of the privatization argument. Beesley and Littlechild (1983, p. 5) write: 'Competition is the most important mechanism for maximising consumer benefits and for limiting monopoly power. Its essence is rivalry and freedom to enter a market. What counts is the existence of competitive threats, from potential, as well as existing competitors.' The degree of competition then becomes an indicator of successful 'privatization'. Empirical evidence, to the extent that it is at all helpful, would suggest that, whether output stems from either the private *or* the public sector, *competition* is the ingredient which reduces costs per unit (Millward and Parker, 1983).

For private goods and services, where consumers have adequate information, competition may thrive. It is our submission, however, that the kinds of goods and services typically financed in the public sector do not often easily lend themselves to a competitive environment. It is an issue of property rights that explains the existence of public sector finance. When the private sector is modified to enable it to cope with the problems of provision of such goods, it is competition that is often sacrificed in the endeavour.

Take, as an extreme example, the provision of public goods. Even the classic example, lighthouse facilities (Samuelson, 1954) can in practice be financed and produced by private entrepreneurs. The evidence is that they can, and have, been privately provided (Coase, 1974; Peacock, 1979). While philanthropy has been characterized as a public good (Collard, 1978), private charities exist. Such goods as these were thought unlikely to flourish in the private sector because consumers did not possess property rights in the good produced. Non-exclusion was a characteristic that suggested preferences would not be revealed. How then can the divorce of theory and practice be explained?

An answer is that the inherent property rights failure has been met by the conferment of property rights on producers themselves. By this means private finance is generated for the provision of goods with a public good element. Thus, lighthouses flourished in nineteenth-century England because lighthouse-owners were given the right to levy a charge on shipping in neighbourhood ports. In effect, spatial monopolies were created. Similarly, charities frequently occupy a market which is imperfect (Cullis, Jones and Thanassoulas, 1984). Flag days may (justifiably) be organized between charities to maximize joint revenue, but such a cartel arrangement has little to do with competition. Indeed it is argued that unfettered competition would completely reduce the fund-raising potential of charities (Rose-Ackerman, 1982). In such a fashion markets may deal with the problems of public goods only if they are so structured as to make *competition* inoperative in the normal sense. Non-exclusion problems are simply tackled by the appropriation by fund-raising bodies of 'coercive' and/or non-competitive authority.

Thus, referring back to our taxonomy, we can argue that public goods, financed by taxation, could be moved into another cell, but it must be recognized that the private sector position will not, of necessity, be *truly competitive*. Lighthouse provision can move from cell 4 to 1, charity provision can move from cell 4 to a hybrid of 1 and 3 (with tax concessions) but it is short-sighted in the extreme to imagine that the final outcome will or can be necessarily competitive.

The discussion has concentrated on goods with an important public good element. It implies that *financing* could not easily be shifted to the private sector except by muting the forces of competition in the private sector. Of course, for strictly private goods this may not be the case, as preference revelation is not a problem in the same way. Movement of the provision of private goods from the public to the private sector may be possible without damaging the prospects of competition within the private sector. However, it is another argument again that implies that moving the provision of goods from cell 4 to cell 1 *automatically* increases the forces of competition. Private goods produced in the public sector may already compete with private goods produced in the private sector. Why then will a change in ownership (a large private firm replacing a large public firm) automatically increase competition. For example, the current policy of privatizaion for the British Gas Corporation (BNOC) includes measures to move the production of this product between sectors, e.g. November 1982, 51 per cent of share capital in Britoil (a subsidiary of BNOC) offered for sale; October 1981, BGC instructed to sell its on-shore oil interests in Dorset. Yet analysis of such actions has drawn the criticism that 'it is difficult to see why the privatization measures so far announced will increase competition' (Webb, 1984, p. 3). The analysis of such strategy is simply in terms of a public sector firm being replaced by a private sector firm. It is important, then, to distinguish between such a transference of ownership and an increase in competition. Certainly, one can suggest policies that will increase competition, e.g. removal of restrictions on coal imports (Rees, 1983). Yet these are not inherently associated with a transference from cell 4 to cell 1.

The theory of contestable markets has drawn attention to the argument that, even when markets are characterized by a small number of firms, competition may be present, provided there is ease of entry and of exit for potential customers (Baumol, 1982). Firms, however large and apparently powerful, are led to behave in a competitive fashion if this potential exists. Thus, it is tempting to argue that the sale of large public firms to the private sector need not be equated with the transference of a public monopoly into a private monopoly. But the argument is inappropriate. It is not *ownership per se* that ensures appropriate response, but the *potential of competition*. Davies and Davies (1984, p. 51) note that 'although in general the new theory (of contestable markets) gives a green light to market forces, it gives a cautionary amber to privatisation – indeed, to some forms it authoritatively offers a glaring red'. They conclude:

> on the simple question of whether a state monopoly should be privatized or not, the theory is discreetly neutral, its concern being not about structure or ownership but rather on the need to keep open access to information and competition in either case. On the other hand, the red light begins to flash with regard to durable public infrastructural investment, where the risks and uncertainties associated with heavy, sunk or irrecoverable costs may well frighten off private funding.

The same reservation is made by Rees (1986, p. 22), who questions the possibility of competitive potential as 'the markets with which we are chiefly concerned do not seem contestable – such costs would be huge in all of them'. Of course, even if it is not possible to generate competition in terms of the product, then it may be possible to create competition by franchising. In this instance, an auction of rights to a monopoly would create an incentive to minimize costs per unit of output as well as possibly aiding income distributional problems. However, it does not deal with the allocative inefficiencies of monopoly prices, and the problems of organizing an efficient bidding system are formidable (Kay and Thompson, 1986).

While the theory of contestable markets should not be considered a blanket support for the act of selling assets to the private sector, it has reinforced the argument that it is competition (or the possibility of competition) rather than privatization *per se* that is the stimulus to efficiency. For those firms which enjoy a monopoly scenario after ownership is transferred from the public to the private sector, evidence suggests that they will actually be *less* efficient (Thompson, 1986; Kay and Thompson, 1986). It should be noted, therefore, that there is a distinct difference between a policy of privatization which takes as its objective the process of deregulation and competition enhancement, and one which focuses solely on the sale of government-owned industries. Both policies appear to have been employed in the 1980s by the Conservative government in the UK. The former has more validity if economic efficiency is the goal.

While privatization, in terms of the sale of assets, is potentially harmful when unaccompanied by increased competition, the same is true of the policy of contracting out. This much is recognized by proponents of contracting out. For example, Hartley (1984, p. 104) notes: 'For efficiency improvements, privatisation and contracting-out are not sufficient: competition is required.' To the extent that private ownership is supposed to supply more incentives for efficiency (Alchian, 1965) property rights theory suggests that government should remain merely an agency, contracting for all services that government is supposed to provide. However, markets for contracts may themselves suffer market failure and may therefore not provide full information of the cheapest supplier. The view that contracting out is always superior to production within the government has therefore been challenged (Blankart, 1985). Williamson (1975) is sceptical that contracts can be fully specified, and he notes that while competition may exist *before* the contract is made, the supplier and the demander may find themselves in a bilateral monopoly position *after* the contract is signed. The prospect that suppliers may under-cut prices in the short run to gain a monopoly position in the long run cannot be discounted. To preclude this, tenders would have to be invited on a frequent basis and the transaction costs cannot be dismissed. Certainly there is room for doubt that contracting out automatically can be equated with an increase in competition over the lifetime of the project.

In this section we have reflected on problems associated with privatization as simply discussed in terms of movement in the matrix of chart 8.1. We conclude this section with the following observations:

First: with reference to public goods it is difficult to ascertain whether changes in financing arrangements are necessarily efficiency-enhancing. The allocation of property rights will mitigate the problems of non-exclusion but at the same time appears to mute the forces of competition. Moving provision of such goods from cell 4 to cells 1 or 2 may pose difficulties, and the more obvious consideration may be for limited privatization from cell 4 to 3.

Second: with reference to private goods, a typical consideration involves those goods in cell 2 (e.g. the output of 'public economy firms') which are privatized by sale of assets to the private sector (i.e. a movement to cell 1). Here we emphasize that competition is the objective, not the change of ownership *per se*. Thereby we call into question the idea that simple transference of ownership is itself relevant.

Finally, we reflect on those goods which remain in cell 3. Here contracting out is the more limited way that privatization has occurred. We note that, in theory, markets for contracts can be imperfect.

If *a priori* discussion has no overwhelming prediction that privatization *must* promote competition, and thereby efficiency, the response must be a case-by-case analysis of pros and cons. But how are public and private production to be compared?

8.3 PRIVATIZATION: SUITABLE CASES FOR TREATMENT

If, as argued above, privatization can be recommended only on a case-by-case appraisal, it will be important to ensure that criteria for selection are appropriately applied. Assume for example that (following Weisbrod, 1975) the provision of some welfare service is possible in either the market for profit (i.e. private sector); the voluntary not-for-profit (charitable) sector; and the non-market (public) sector. If finance is available from the public sector, which firm (private, charity, public) should be selected to provide the service? How should resources be distributed between sectors? Will it always be appropriate to 'contract out' from public provision? Here the object is to provide an introduction to the problems inherent in this decision (i.e. a choice between cells 3 and 4).

In figure 8.1, $D_T D_T$ represents the economy-wide demand for the given good or service A, whose quantity is recorded on the x-axis. It can be thought of as a combination of horizontal and vertical sums of individual marginal valuation curves. The horizontal addition captures the extent to which A is rival, and vertical addition deals with any non-rival externality or public goods aspects associated with the production and consumption of A (preference revelation problems are ignored). The supply curve, labelled MC, is the horizontal sum of the marginal cost curves, MC_1, MC_2 and MC_3. These curves reflect the marginal cost of producing A in the three sectors: private-for-profit (panel (a)); non-profit voluntary (panel (b)) and public (panel (c)). In these circumstances efficiency would dictate the equalization of the marginal costs of production in each sector and the output allocation in each one would be OQ_1, OQ_2 and OQ_3 respectively. The same diagram can be used to illustrate the allocation of production within each sector with panels (a), (b) and (c) now representing the different units of production within each sector. The guiding principle remains the same:

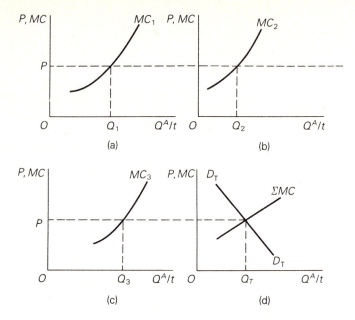

Figure 8.1 Inter- and intra-sector production allocation

the marginal cost of production should everywhere be equalized, i.e. inter- and intra-sector marginal costs would be the same. The actual pattern of production resulting would be a matter of indifference.

While the principle is clear in theory, its enactment in practice is fraught with problems. Here we point to some of the more central qualifications that need to be made in any application of the preceding principle.

Dependence on 'First-order' Conditions

With respect to each sector it is the case that the information presented will correspond to an increment of output in that sector. These marginal costs still require interpretation. What does it mean to say that the marginal costs of producing a good are lower in one sector? What is implied by the fact that marginal costs are downward-sloping (rather than upward-sloping)? In response to this question, it is important to recognize that if there are increasing returns to scale, the logical outcome is to concentrate all output in one sector. However, in these circumstances, information concerning marginal costs will be inadequate in choosing which sector to expand.

Consider figure 8.2. Here the marginal cost functions of two sectors (private and public) are illustrated. They are not perfectly symmetrical; indeed, given their dependence on different past decisions there is no reason why they should be. At Q_1 the economy allocates OQ_1 to production in the private sector and O_1Q_1 to the public sector. A team of economists now report that marginal costs of production are higher in the public sector. An immediate response would be to transfer production of the desired output OO_1 to the private sector, and indeed this response would result in all production being located in the private sector. It would, however, be an inadequate interpretation of the information. The marginal costs depend on the output levels in the two sectors, and it is only that the starting point is OQ_1 for the private sector that such an apparent advantage is recorded. Had the starting point been to the left of the intersection of the marginal cost functions, the outcome on the same rule would be reversed.

If this is accepted, it is clear that marginal costs, however accurately estimated, are insufficient evidence on which to proceed with discrete allocation decisions. Not only the marginal cost, but the marginal cost function, should be considered. As such in figure 8.2 it is clear that total costs (the integral of the marginal cost function) are lower for the

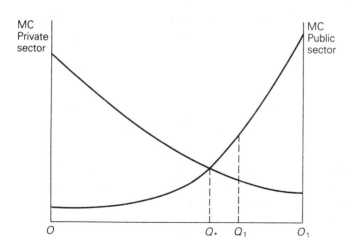

Figure 8.2 Relative cost-effectiveness

public than the private sector, and allocative efficiency demands any insistence on total specialization should be in *this* sector.

Tenders or cost comparisons which consider the costs of incremental adjustment may be insufficient. The second-order condition (or the rate at which these incremental costs are a decreasing function of output) may also be relevant. To further illustrate this argument, figure 8.3 shows that simple adjustment to reported relative costs can lead to more than one outcome. Even though costs are accurately reported, decisions that ignore the nature of the cost function can be suboptimal.

In figure 8.3 it is clear that deciding on the basis of reported costs leads to different outcomes. Here the marginal costs of provision in the private sector are assumed to be U-shaped (i.e. *AHK*) and in the public sector they are *LJ*. If the initial point is Q_2 then the optimal location of activity in the two sectors will appear to be represented by point *E*. This will be attained if public sector activity is 'hived off' to the private sector. Conversely, if the starting point is Q_1 the same rule would lead to complete specialization in the public sector. Which then is the correct split? The answer to this question depends on the relative sizes of *ABJ* and *BHE*. If *ABJ* exceeds *BHE* then specialization in the public sector is recommended. If *ABJ* is less than *BHE* then the split at *E* is to be recommended. Note that equalizing marginal costs is no longer a satisfactory guideline; i.e. it is not appropriate to rely solely on the strategy of expanding that sector which reports the lowest

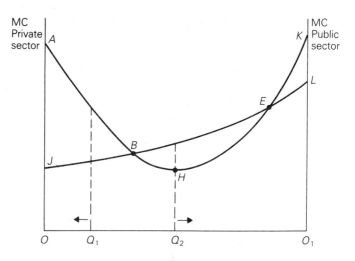

Figure 8.3 Choosing a locational division

incremental costs of output expansion from *existing* levels. In this context the comparative studies on public and private provision should be qualified further before they can operate in a prescriptive fashion (see section 8.4).

The question of long- and short-run costs has already been raised, but in the context of the above discussion it is important to stress that 'adjustment' (e.g. movement from Q_1 or Q_2) will not be costless, as would appear to be implied. Decline in the public sector may leave capital equipment which is not easily moved into the private sector. Though the product is identical, the organization costs in moving capital between sectors may not be zero, so that capital equipment may be written off at an earlier date. These then are some of the costs of the act of privatization, and they should be set against the cost reduction benefits apparent in figures 8.2 and 8.3. Since they may occur at different times, the net benefit of privatization may depend on the social discount rate. Further, if such costs are positive, it poses the question of whether or not a less costly policy to improve efficiency in either sector could not be proposed.

Dynamic Considerations

In the long run there is more to consider than simply the marginal costs of production. In particular there are dynamic arguments that may counsel against the 'marginal' dictates of static efficiency. Dynamic considerations refer to shifts of the marginal cost functions. It has long been recognized that practices which are statically inefficient may be justified as dynamically efficient. For example, giving workers 'tenure' of employment may be important in production processes that rely on one worker teaching or training another, because it removes the fear of being displaced by the trainee (see Thurow, 1976, pp. 194–5). Similarly, today's high-price producers may be the low-cost providers of tomorrow, if the surplus facilitated by high prices goes to research and development that results in the lower future cost structures (this is, of course, one of the classic defences of monopoly). Transaction costs may also be important. Supplying at short-run marginal cost may not be attractive if the organization cannot sustain the position in the longer run. The costs of finding and contracting new supplies may well swamp any short-run gain from simply looking for current least marginal cost. The suggestion is, then, that longer run considerations can be at odds with ones of shorter run.

Social and Private Opportunity Costs

Notwithstanding the need to be mindful of such long-run considerations, it is clear that a comparison of current costs of production in any sector is far from straightforward. The first and obvious point concerning the comparison of tenders from different sectors is that, if inefficiencies are located in each of the sectors, estimates based on market prices will be inappropriate. For example, if within one sector a firm enjoys such monopoly power as to cross-subsidize the costs of producing a good x, then like will not be compared with like when tenders are examined. In effect, it is the opportunity costs in terms of lost resources which should be compared in the decision of where to locate production. To accept unadjusted estimates is to deny all that has been said earlier of the inefficiencies of different sectors.

Strict adherence to the notion of opportunity costs will indicate the manner in which adjustment has to be made. Take, for example, the case of a 'public economy firm' which, already possessing a vacant site suitable for production activity, imputes a zero cost. The tender must, of necessity, be adjusted by a factor which adequately measures the value of the site in its alternative use. Similarly, when considering tenders placed by charities, the question is begged as to whether or not some adjustment is required for uncosted voluntary effort. As it is appreciated that it is social opportunity costs which are relevant, comparisons of tenders based solely on pecuniary costs could be potentially misleading. If the choice of sectoral location of activity may also influence the spatial location of production, it is clear that technological externalities such as pollution, noise, etc., will need to be incorporated fully into the cost estimates. In this sense the costs alluded to in figure 8.1 must be the marginal social opportunity costs.

Output Quality

While the necessity of adjusting tenders arising from different sectors is clear, it should also be explicitly understood that the quality of the good to be produced in each sector must be identical for meaningful comparisons. All that has been said so far will be meaningless unless costs relate to an identical quality (packaging, distribution, after-sales service, etc.). The importance of this consideration is explained below (section 8.4).

8.4 PRIVATIZING SERVICES: SOME OBSERVATIONS

Some of the difficulties of estimating whether or not the private or the public sector performs efficiently are now evident. The continued refinement of cost comparisons has brought with it evidence that belief in the inherent superiority of *one* sector only is misplaced. There are cases where the public sector may 'out-perform' the private or the not-for-profit (charity sector). Moreover, the initial enthusiasm for acts of privatization has more recently been muted on the part of commentators who recognize the attendant costs.

One example of reconsideration of the 'received wisdom' on the deficiencies of the public sector is found in a study by Knapp and Missiakoulis (1982). The private and the voluntary sectors in the UK have always played a prominent part in the provision of day-care services for the elderly. Here the private and voluntary sectors have typically been presented as more efficient than local authority equivalents. Persistent criticism of public sector managerial inefficiency, higher wage levels, higher staff–client ratios, greater overheads and the onslaught of spurious cost comparisons have established a 'social policy mythology' concerning the superiority of the voluntary sector. The study by Knapp and Missiakoulis (1982) estimated the cost function for day centres by regressing average cost (staff and running expenses) per daily attendance on a number of factors which would affect the calls made upon voluntary organizations and area health authorities. Data for 55 day units were analysed, and the resultant cost function is presented in table 8.1. Prior to this analysis, non-standardized cost comparisons of public and voluntary sectors appeared to favour the voluntary sector. However, this study suggested differences between the activities of the two sectors in terms of the services provided for users and the dependency of users. The estimated cost function relates costs to these factors. Once the influences of user dependency and unit treatment are removed, a comparison of the average cost function for both sectors suggested a 'fairer' comparison of the costs of the two sectors. It *appeared* that units with an annual attendance in excess of 360 per week were more cheaply run by local authorities than by voluntary organizations. The confidence interval for predictions on the cost estimates for voluntary and local authority sectors overlapped. Therefore the authors more carefully concluded that, whilst voluntary care is on average more expensive than local authority care when

Table 8.1   Estimated cost function for day centres

The estimated cost function indicates that average cost (staff and running expenses) per daily attendance is equal to:

2.39*	
+ 6.90*	if unit run by an Area Health Authority
− 2.75	if unit run by voluntary organization
− 0.1026	× no. of daily attendances per year (÷ 1000) for local authority units
− 0.3471*	× no. of daily attendances per year (÷ 1000) for Area Health Authority units
+ 0.0577	× no. of daily attendances per year (÷ 1000) for voluntary units
− 0.6724	× no. of times local library visited in previous month
− 1.4709*	× no. of times parks visited in previous month
+ 0.4822*	× no. of times shops visited in previous month
+ 1.5206	× no. of times local exhibitions visited in previous month
− 6.5500*	× proportion of users completely unable to walk, or only with staff assistance
+ 3.3027*	× proportion of users able to walk alone with aids or appliances
+ 2.9540	× proportion of users unable to use toilet (and incontinent) or only with staff assistance
+ 1.2123	× if day unit gives physical treatment to users

Significance levels: *$p < 0.05$ (All other coefficients significant at level < 0.20)
$R^2 = 0.76$; adjusted $R^2 = 0.68$; $n = 55$.
Source: Knapp and Missiakoulis (1982).

provided in larger day units, this difference could possibly be due to errors in prediction.

The study of Knapp (1984) outlines how the apparent 'obvious' superiority of the voluntary sector over local authority provision is called in question when the quality of the service has been standardized.[2] The need to pause and reflect on the alleged efficiency of the private sector is clear. Birch (1985) reassesses areas where a policy of contracting out was ill-advised. With respect to health care, he warns that 'the temptation to contract out THRs [total hip replacements] to the private sector should be resisted'. Studies reviewed by Birch suggested that, in this instance, the finding that length of stay in hospital for NHS total hip replacements is greater than that in the private sector could not be taken to indicate the relative efficiency of the private sector. NHS patients tended to be older on admission. This mix of patients were likely to place greater demand on the NHS. Moreover, recent reviews of contracting out geriatric care to private sector nursing homes have thrown doubt on the notion that this activity was cheaper in the private sector. Further analysis showed that the private sector accepted only certain kinds of NHS patients under such contractual arrangements. The care offered by the private sector was incomplete by comparison to the NHS (e.g. occupational therapy and physiotherapy services were still provided by NHS staff). The private sector required indemnity that, should a patient prove difficult, he or she might be returned to the public sector. Experience has led the NHS to begin withdrawal from some of these contractual agreements.

It is clear that on a wider front, experience with contracting out is less than satisfactory. For example, the House of Commons Select Committee refer to the government's privatization programme for hospital cleaning, laundry and catering as 'hardly a startling success so far'.[3] Considerable effort has been expended on the exercise, with little return. Doubt must be raised as to whether appropriate costings are in effect being employed.

After surveying a wide range of studies of cost comparisons between the private and public sector, Thompson (1986, p. 100) concludes that 'it is far from clear that private enterprise is always better than public enterprise'. In this respect he is not unique – Millward and Parker (1983), as stated earlier, consider that private or public ownership is not the key issue in cost comparison. Stiglitz (1986) concludes that 'not all studies show that government enterprises perform more poorly than private' (p. 164). He quotes studies of the two major rail systems in Canada (one private and one public), as well as government agencies in the USA, to indicate that the private sector will not necessarily out-perform the public sector.[4]

Thompson (1986) detects a specific taxonomy in the studies he reviews. First, public enterprises which face competition in their product market have lower efficiency than private competitors because the consequences for private firms (e.g. the threat of takeover or bankruptcy) are more significant. In such circumstances private provision may appear superior because inefficient private firms are 'weeded out'. Yet for a second category, i.e. industries where competition is generally absent (e.g. electricity supply in the USA), public enterprise performance is superior to private enterprise performance. Thus studies such as Pyke (1982), which focus on the former industries, reflect well on privatization but other studies are less supportive. Public ownership is common when competition is unlikely (e.g. natural monopolies such as gas, water, electricity). The comparison now is between public firms and regulated private firms. Kay and Thompson (1986) refer to studies of American electric utilities and German insurance companies where public firms now appear to perform markedly better than private firms. Regulation arguably reduces incentives to minimize costs. Yet such a defence only underlines the problem that, when looking with hindsight at private and public performance, allowance has to be made for those constraints on public economy firms which of necessity restrain the profit motive. If regional policy, social policy, environmental policy, anti-inflationary policy of government is partly pursued through government enterprise again it appears unfair not to allow for this in cost comparisons. If government interference has been legitimate these factors must be noted. If government interference has been illegitimate these factors must be combated, but not necessarily by privatization. If evidence shows that privatization creates less efficient private regulated monopoly, there may yet remain the need for regulation. It is the case, therefore, that the costs of regulation cannot be ignored. Byatt (1985, p. 206) refers to the need to regulate industries which have been privatized. In the UK British Telecom has been moved into the private sector and the provision of telephone cables approximates the case of a 'natural monopoly'. Byatt notes that 'the rules governing the ability of other telephone operators to interconnect with the BT network and the charges made for such interconnections will be a major element in regulation of a privatised telecommunications system'. Rees (1986, p. 19) comments that:

> The idea that privatisation will subject the major group of enterprises to the 'disciplines of market forces' either in product markets or in the capital market, is largely an illusion – the enterprises will retain far too much monopoly power for that. The use of regulatory agencies, whether already in existence, like the Civil Aviation Authority, or newly created, like OFTEL and OFGAS, reflects the acceptance of this by the Government.

The result, therefore, is that privatization may be harmful.

As more considered calculation replaces rhetoric it is far from clear that privatization should be received as a remedy for all parts of the public sector. Moreover, experience with privatization has emphasized that the *act* of privatization in itself involves costs. Sale of public economy firms is not a simple matter. In the Federal Republic of Germany the share sale of VEBA (chemical and oil industries) involved problems which meant that while the initial share offer was over-subscribed, the government's increase in share supply led to it being forced to buy back part of the shares to stop share prices falling (Blankart, 1985). Similar problems have occurred in the UK when the government failed to set an appropriate share price when Amersham International and Britoil were privatized (Heald, 1983b). Kay and Thompson (1986, p. 28) note that 'the mechanics of privatisation have proved unexpectedly difficult, and in general, the sales proceeds have been less than could have been obtained by tight pricing of the issues concerned and have been less than necessary to maintain the net worth of the public sector'. If public firms are sold at less than market price then the community *as a whole* may not necessarily suffer, but it would be imprudent to ignore the income redistributional effect of privatization and the resource use in administering the act.

What is becoming clear is that privatization is not costless. Indeed, the recent literature on rent-seeking theory (Buchanan, Tollison and Tullock, 1980) appears to bring this point to the fore. The failure of government bureaux (discussed in chapter 6) has led to recommendations for an increase in competition between bureaux. Thus, for example, Hartley (1977, p. 171) writes:

Ministries might cease to have monopoly property rights in specific services. Thus, the Departments of Education, Employment and Industry together with the Manpower Services Commission and the Ministry of Defence might compete to supply the State's requirements for education and training services. Similarly, the Ministry of Defence might be split into separate Army, Navy and Air Force departments competing with each other, as well as with other Ministries, for the supply of defence services.

That such advances in competition *may* be welcome appears almost self-evident, but that the costs involved must be monitored is also essential. Faith (1980, p. 342) notes:

it does not necessarily follow that making the bureaucracy more competitive by introducing several smaller bureaux, each producing an identical line of services, will improve the economic efficiency of the government sector. On the one hand, increasing the number of producers of each output may well reduce the amount of rent seeking by any one bureau, as each bureau has a smaller expected gain at the expense of bureaux producing other products. But the introduction of several producers of each output creates greater substitutability between bureaux, increasing the return to political advertising with respect to a given output. Further, the introduction of several additional producers of each output will increase monitoring and evaluation costs for the various review committees, thereby increasing the ability of bureau managers to divert resources away from the production of authorized output and into demand-increasing activities. The net effect on aggregate bureaucratic rent-seeking cannot be predicted *a priori* (our emphasis).

8.5 THE CASE FOR PUBLIC ECONOMY PRODUCTION AND SOME INEFFICIENCY

A staple question of many a public finance paper relates to the distinction between public finance and public production. Usually students are invited to conclude that the former, if and when justified by 'market failures', does not imply the latter. There are many ways to intervene in the economy that fall short of public economy production. Forte (1984) provides a convenient list that includes vouchers, subsidies to profit and/or not-for-profit producers, conditional grants, compulsory consumption, etc. Despite not adopting a pro-public production position himself, Forte (1967) provides some reasons why public production may be attractive. These cover five arguments: only public sector provision may be the 'right' quality; only public provision may be of sufficiently large scale; private production may confer too much economic power; private production may confer too much political power and finally, activities may be added to public sector activities at low marginal cost because of unexploited economies of scale. Various aspects of military activities can be used to illustrate all these points. A mercenary army may lack the quality of loyalty so that their bravery is in question. Defence systems may be so large that no single private entrepreneur could handle them. Being a very large buyer of certain metals, etc., might give the military monopsony power. Private armies raise the spectre of an anti-democratic military coup. Army disaster relief activities might exemplify the final argument.

There is no doubt that there are always alternatives to public production, but where there are a whole series of complicating factors, such as with defence and say, health care, minimizing transaction costs (contract, search, bargaining, etc.) broadly defined may indicate public production.

The cost of this 'minimizing' policy is the alleged allocative and X-inefficiency that have been the theme of this book. So far the arguments have been mainly in terms of assessing the relative inefficiencies of actual market and public economy production; however, there is a *case for dulling efficiency incentives*. Baumol (1984), whilst not building a formal model of the case for the public economy firms, indicates the foundation on which one can be built. The key element is 'moral hazard', a term from the insurance literature which relates to the way insurance affects the behaviour of the insured. For example, people insured against fire may be careless with matches (altering the probability of the event) and demand more in the way of replacement should fire occur than they would if they were footing the replacement costs themselves (altering the cost of the event). Baumol notes that the incentive effects set up by the market, like those set up by insurance, may not always be attractive. Examples may include unemployed mercenary (private) armies making work for themselves and the actions of 'tax farmers'.

Market incentives are appropriate where quantity of a good or service is constrained by market-place demand. Once suppliers are in positions, like mercenary armies, to alter both the probability and volume of demand for their services, incentives become perverse (in this sense it is a 'principal–agent'[5] problem). Hence dulling the effects of market incentives via salary and/or tenure of employment in the public sector, as with public army finance and production, becomes an attractive option. On this argument, reducing the efficiency incentives of the market, even at the cost of fostering inefficiency in the public sector, may be a welfare-improving policy.[6] There is a close parallel between this general argument and the specific case of paying doctors (see Pauly, 1970). For a case for in-kind public provision based on positive freedom see section 10.5.

8.6 SUMMARY AND CONCLUSIONS

The case for privatization has been adopted in much the same way as an article of faith. The term privatization has been taken as synonymous with competition, and it is not. Certain forms of privatization may be injurious to competition or in effect have no impact either way. The reasoned response to privatization is that sometimes it can be beneficial and at other times it is not. The problem is how to determine those cases in which it is useful. We outline some of the inherent problems that may be associated with even quite sophisticated cross-sectional cost comparisons. What is evident, then, is that, when more penetrating analysis has been applied to cost comparisons, the notion that low-cost provision need be automatically equated with private provision is nothing more than a myth. Cost comparisons must clearly be rigorous, but it is worth noting that even in cases when public provision appears more inefficient this may not be created simply by the location of production. Stiglitz (1986) refers to the losses of nationalized industries in the UK in the following terms: 'these firms are government enterprises because they were running at a loss; they are not running at a loss because they are government enterprises' (p. 165). Costs must be related to the broader objectives which public sector enterprises are asked to pursue.

It will, of course, be argued that convincing evidence can, in certain cases, be offered to show the superiority of the private sector. This we do not necessarily dispute. Our arguments, and the examples outlined above, are chosen to dispel the belief that the public sector is automatically inferior. Considering also the costs associated with the *act* of privatization, faith in the policy may often therefore be misplaced.

It is one of the ironies of public choice literature that privatization itself has not been placed in a governmental failure model. The enactment of the policy, rather than the policy itself, may be open to criticism in the same way as other government actions can be criticized.[7] In a public choice framework it may appear that a vote-maximizing government would have call to rely on the sale of assets to finance tax cuts in the hope of retaining office. If this were the primary objective, then pressure groups resistant to increasing competition as privatization occurred may be more easily appeased. Kay and Thompson (1986) see private monopoly replacing public monopoly in the UK because of the resistance of management of nationalized concerns to the prospect of seeing their corporations broken down in order to introduce competition. Certainly, in the UK the revenue-raising implications of privatization, and the emphasis government places on this aspect, has not gone without comment. Lord Stockton has characterized the policy more in terms of the need 'to sell the family silver' for revenue purposes.[8] Thompson (1986) disputes that the practice of privatization in the UK has accorded with the alleged objective of maximizing competition.

The final section of this chapter has drawn attention to the existence of a positive case for public economy production. In particular, a 'moral hazard' problem on the supplier's side of a market system for some goods and services was emphasized.

NOTES

1 See for example, Donnison (1984).
2 Knapp (1984) produces evidence that some aspects of private (rather than voluntary) provision of care for the elderly were cost-effective. Our objective is not to deny that such may be the case, only that it must be satisfactorily proven.
3 The Sixth Report of the Social Services Committee: House of Commons Paper 339 is quoted (*The Times*, 5 July 1985, p. 28) as reporting: 'This whole exercise, which has now been under way for around four years, has involved a considerable amount of time and effort; has caused disruption and discontent, not exclusively among NHS staff directly employed in these services; and to date has not brought home the bacon.'
4 Stiglitz (1986) notes the studies of Caves and Christensen (1980) and Peltzman (1971).
5 Indeed the privatization issue might be recast in a principal–agent context. As, for example, with health care the location of production – public or private economy – may be of limited significance. What matters is the incentive structures the principals (patients) can construct for the agents (doctors) in the circumstances where:
   (a) agents have better/additional information on the nature of production than do principals;
   (b) agents' actions may be directly unobservable/uncheckable, so that information has to be gleaned from outcomes which are the product of agent action and random events.
   This general approach is emphasized in Rees (1985) and Cowell (1986).
6 Peters (1985) has shown welfare-improving piecemeal policies may require initially increasing public sector inefficiency along the path of adjustment.
7 Brittain (1986) offers an alternative approach to the act of privatization.
8 The *Daily Telegraph* (7 February 1985) reports Harold Macmillan (Lord Stockton) as commenting on current policy: 'First of all the Georgian silver goes, and then all the nice furniture that used to be in the saloon. Then the Canalettos go. In other words, the government are selling to provide for current spending – in a business a sure way to go bankrupt – i.e. selling the family silver to pay the servants wage.' (Harold Macmillan was Britain's Conservative prime minister from 1957 to 1963.)

REFERENCES

Alchian, A. A. (1965), Some economics of property rights, *Il Politico*, vol. 30, pp. 816–29.
Arrow, K. J. (1970), The organisation of economic activity: issues pertinent to the choice of market versus non-market allocation, pp. 59–73 in Haveman,

R. and Margolis, J. (eds), *Public Expenditure and Policy Analysis*, Chicago: Markham.

Baumol, W. J. (1982), Contestable markets: an uprising in the theory of industry structure, *American Economic Review*, vol. 72, no. 1 (March), pp. 1–16.

Baumol, W. J. (1984), Towards a theory of public enterprise, *Atlantic Economic Journal*, vol. XII, no. 1 (March), pp. 13–19.

Beesley, M. and Littlechild, S. (1983), Privatisation: principles, problems and priorities, *Lloyds Bank Review*, no. 149 (July), pp. 1–20.

Birch, S. (1985), Contracting out, tread carefully: private waters, *Health and Social Service Journal*. vol. 95 (June), pp. 710–11.

Blankart, C. (1985), Market and non-market alternatives in the supply of public goods: general issues, pp. 192–203 in Forte, F. and Peacock, A. (eds), *Public Expenditure and Government Growth*. Oxford: Basil Blackwell.

Brittan, S. (1986), Privatisation: a comment on Kay and Thompson, *Economic Journal*, vol. 96, no. 381 (March), pp. 33–8.

Buchanan, J. M., Tollison, R. D. and Tullock, G. (1980), *Towards a Theory of the Rent Seeking Society*, Texas: A and M University Press.

Byatt, I. (1985), Market and non-market alternatives in the public supply of public services: British experience with privatisation, pp. 203–12 in Forte, F. and Peacock, A. (eds), *Public Expenditure and Government Growth*, Oxford: Basil Blackwell.

Caves, D. W. and Christensen, L. R. (1980), The relative efficiency of public and private firms in a competitive environment: the case of Canadian railroads, *Journal of Political Economy*, vol. 88, no. 5 (October), pp. 958–76.

Coase, R. H. (1974), The lighthouse in economics, *Journal of Law and Economics*, vol. 17, (October), pp. 357–76.

Collard, D. (1978), *Altruism and Economy: A Study in Non-Selfish Economics*, Oxford: Martin Robertson.

Cowell, F. A. (1986), *Microeconomic Principles*, Oxford: Philip Allan.

Cullis, J. G., Jones, P. R. and Thanassoulas, C. (1984), Are charities efficient 'firms'? A preliminary test of the UK charitable sector, *Public Choice*, vol. 44, no. 2, pp. 367–73.

Davies, G. and Davies, J. (1984), The revolution in monopoly theory, *Lloyds Bank Review*, no. 153 (July), pp. 38–52.

Donnison, D. (1984), The progressive potential of privatisation, pp. 45–57, in Le Grand, J. and Robinson, R. (eds), *Privatisation and the Welfare State*, London: Allen & Unwin.

Faith, R. L. (1980), Rent-seeking aspects of bureaucratic competition, pp. 332–43 in Buchanan, J. M., Tollison, R. D. and Tullock, G. (eds), *Towards a Theory of the Rent-Seeking Society*, Texas: A and M University press.

Forte, F. (1967), Should public goods be public? *Papers on Non-Market Decision Making*, vol. VIII (Fall), pp. 39–46.

Forte, F. (1984), Controlling the productivity of bureaucratic behaviour, *Atlantic Economic Journal*, vol. XII, no. 1 (March), pp. 32–40.

Hartley, K. (1977), *Problems of Economic Policy*, London: George Allen & Unwin.

Hartley, K. (1984), Why contract out?, pp. 9–15 in *Contracting Out and the Public Sector*, London: Royal Institute of Public Administration.

Heald, D. (1983a), *Public Expenditure*, Oxford: Martin Robertson.

Heald, D. (1983b), Privatisation of public firms: the experience during the Thatcher government, University of Glasgow (mimeo).

Kay, J. A. and Thompson, D. J. (1986), Privatisation: a policy in search of a rationale, *Economic Journal*, vol. 96, no. 381 (March), pp. 18–32.

Klein, R. E. (1984), Privatisation and the welfare state, *Lloyds Bank Review*, no. 151 (January), pp. 12–29.

Knapp, M. R. J. (1984), *The Economics of Social Care*, London: Macmillan.

Knapp, M. R. J. and Missiakoulis, S. (1982), Inter-sectoral cost comparisons: day care for the elderly, *Journal of Social Policy*, vol. 11, pt. 3 (July), pp. 335–54.

Millward, R. and Parker, D. (1983), Public and private enterprise: comparative behaviour and relative efficiency, pp. 199–274 in Millward, R. *et al.* (eds), *Public Sector Economics*, London and New York: Longman.

Pauly, M. V. (1970), Efficiency incentives and reimbursement of health care, *Inquiry*, vol. 8, no. 1 (March), pp. 114–31.

Peacock, A. (1979), *The Economic Analysis of Government and Related Themes*, Oxford: Martin Robertson.

Peltzman, S. (1971), Pricing in public and private enterprises: electric utilities in the United States, *Journal of Law and Economics*, vol. 14 (April), pp. 109–47.

Peters, W. (1985), Can inefficient public production promote welfare? *Journal of Economics*, vol. 45, no. 4, pp. 395–407.

Pirie, M. (1982), *The Logic of Economics – and its Implications for the Public Sector*, London: Adam Smith Institute.

Pryke, R. (1982), The comparative performance of public and private enterprises, *Fiscal Studies*, vol. 3, no. 2 (July), pp. 68–81.

Rees, R. (1983), Energy pricing: eight proposals for a better fuel market, *Public Money*, vol. 2, no. 4 (March), pp. 13–17.

Rees, R. (1985), The theory of principal and agent, Part I and Part II, *Bulletin of Economic Research*, vol. 37, nos. 1 and 2, pp. 3–25 and 75–94.

Rees, R. (1986), Is there an economic case for privatisation? *Public Money*, vol. 5, no. 4, pp. 19–26.

Rose-Ackerman, S. (1982), Charitable giving and excessive fund raising, *Quarterly Journal of Economics*, vol. 97, no. 2 (May), pp. 193–212.

Samuelson, P. (1954), The pure theory of public expenditure, *Review of Economics and Statistics*, vol. 36, no. 4 (November), pp. 387–9.

Shackleton, J. R. (1985), U.K. privatisation–U.S. deregulation, *Politics*, vol.

5, no. 2 (October), pp. 8–16.

Stiglitz, J. E. (1986), *Economics of the Public Sector*, New York and London: Norton.

Thompson, D. (1986), The economics of privatisation, *Economic Review*, vol. 3, no. 3 (January), pp. 9–12.

Thurow, L. C. (1976), *Generating Inequality*, London: Macmillan.

Webb, M. G. (1984), Privatisation and the U.K. energy industries, *Economic Review*, vol. 1, no. 4 (November), pp. 2–5.

Weisbrod, B. A. (1975), Towards a theory of the voluntary non-profit sector in a three sector economy, pp. 171–195 in Phelps, E. S. (ed.), *Altruism, Morality and Economic Theory*, New York: Russell Sage Foundation.

Williamson, O. E. (1975), *Markets and Hierarchies: Analysis and Antitrust Implications, A Study in the Economics of Internal Organisations*, New York: Free Press, and London: Macmillan.

9

The Economic Consequences of Financing the Public Sector

9.1 INTRODUCTION

In order for the government to finance its activities, control over resources has to be diverted from the private sector to the public sector. Basically there are only three methods by which this can be achieved: taxation, borrowing (issuing debt) and increasing the money supply (implicit taxation). All these methods of finance have been identified with 'costs' which exceed the value of the resource transfer. To the extent that a larger public sector requires greater finance, the larger these costs may be. The purpose of this chapter is not to deny that a larger public sector requires greater resources in the public sector, but rather to gauge the importance of attendant costs of achieving this reallocation. Given that the bulk of government revenue is raised by taxation, the bulk of the chapter will be devoted to this topic. However, the other two options are also discussed.

9.2 THE WELFARE COSTS OF GOVERNMENT FINANCE IN A NORMATIVE CONTEXT

Taxation

The expenditure of £1 million on project X in the public sector entails raising £1 million in revenue, and this is described as the direct burden of a tax. Such a burden is inescapable. However, as noted in the Introduction, there are costs over and above this to be considered. These costs, variously known as the indirect burden, excess, welfare or allocative costs, of revenue-raising, arise because in circumstances where the starting point of analysis is a competitive equilibrium intervention will cause choices to be distorted by changing the signals economic actors receive. Although there are instances where there are no welfare costs (allocative distortions), these are thought to be the exception rather than the rule. Illustration of the welfare costs of taxation can be developed at the individual level, the partial equilibrium market level and the general equilibrium level. Additionally, the context can be that of an input or product market. Here we have chosen the example of the input (labour) market and income taxation,[1] because it is the most significant single tax in terms of revenue raising and also it is the most widely discussed example of the '(dis)incentive effects' of taxation. (Dis)incentive effects are interpreted to mean the change in labour market supply associated with income tax. Labour market supply changes directly affect GNP and are important in themselves. However, their welfare consequences are measured in a somewhat different fashion.

In figure 9.1(a) the income leisure (and hence work *hours*) choice of an individual is depicted. The initial no tax equilibrium is at point 1 and it is disturbances from 1 that are the source of problems. A fairly typical so-called degressive tax structure (one with some untaxed initial slice of income and a single tax tax rate beyond) is imposed on the figure. The individual finds equilibrium at 2 and here works slightly more hours, taking less leisure (ΔL). The price effect of the degressive income tax structure has been to induce more market work hours. If this is typical of other individuals, the GNP cake will have been increased in size. This is an incentive effect of the tax. Like all price effects, decomposition into income and substitution effects is possible. In Figure 9.1(a) the income tax revenue raised by the tax is measured by the vertical distance between point 2 and the initial budget constraint, and is equal to T in the figure. If lump-sum taxation (the theoretical non-distortionary benchmark in this type of analysis) could have been used, tax revenue T could have been raised along the dotted budget constraint through point 2. However, with such a budget constraint the individual could adjust to a higher indifference curve at 3, involving less leisure and more work hours in the utility maximizing bundle. Here ΔH–ΔL extra hours of work would be forthcoming under the lump sum as opposed to the income tax, raising the same revenue.

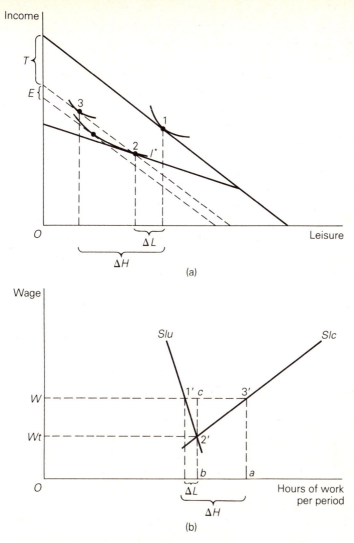

Figure 9.1   Labour supply choices and welfare costs

This corresponds to a Slutsky decomposition[2] with 1 to 3 being the *income effect* of taxes (the unavoidable direct burden) involving fewer work hours because with lower income an individual will buy less of all normal goods including leisure. The movement 3 to 2 is the *substitution effect* of the distortionary income tax involving more leisure–less work in the utility-maximizing bundle as the opportunity cost of leisure (the net of tax wage) falls.

The (dis)incentive (GNP) effects of taxes are measured by reference to the price effect, whereas the welfare costs of taxes are measured by reference to the substitution effect only. The rationale is that the income effect is an unavoidable consequence of deciding to raise revenue. In isolation the income effect means that the cost of £1 of additional taxation is £1. The substitution effect indicates that, once real world distortionary taxes are employed, there is an *excess burden* that needs to be incorporated into the cost of a £1 of tax revenue if efficient public sector decisions are to be made. In figure 9.1(a) this welfare cost can be seen as E. This is the amount of additional tax the government could raise in a lump sum fashion (the additional shift of a parallel budget constraint) and still leave the individual on the same indifference curve that is achieved at point 2, i.e. the individual is indifferent between T raised in a distortionary fashion and $T+E$ raised in a lump sum way.

The welfare cost E can also be seen in figure 9.1(b) where the implied work hours associated with points 1, 2 and 3 in figure 9.1(a) are recorded as 1′, 2′ and 3′. Joining points 1′ and 2′ gives the uncompensated supply of labour curve (Slu) and is here negatively sloped. Joining points 2′ and 3′ yields the compensated supply curve for labour (Slc); compensated in the sense that at both 2′ and 3′ the individual pays T in tax. At 2′ a distortionary effect makes net wage Wt as opposed to the market wage W. At 3′ a non-distortionary lump sum tax means the individual faces the market wave W. Slu is dependent on both the income and substitution effect and can be positively or negatively sloped. Slc relies only on the substitution effect and is always positively sloped. The welfare cost of being at 2′ rather than 3′ can be measured by the difference between lost wages $bc3'a$ and the value of gained leisure $b2'3'a$, i.e. as triangle $2'c3'$. There are well-known formulae for estimating the welfare loss triangles.[3] In this case the relevant one to apply to calculate the excess burden (EB) is:

$$EB = 1/2\ ES\ WLt^2 \qquad (9.1)$$

where

ES = compensated wage elasticity;
W = wage rate;
L = work hours;
t = deductions from wages at the margin (only tax in our example above).

Most economists are agreed on the mechanics of this theory as an estimate of the *total* welfare cost for an individual, but it is evident that what matters for the disincentive effects and welfare costs of an income tax are the empirical evidence on the magnitudes involved. Worked illustrations are provided by Browning and Browning (1979) and Rosen (1985). Rosen has $ES=1.7$, $W = \$6$ per hour, $L = 2000$ hours per year and $t = 0.25$. These figures yield an excess burden of $637 per annum of approximately 20 per cent of revenue raised. Browning and Browning use an elasticity value of 0.2 which if applied to Rosen's figures would yield $75 per annum or approximately 2.5 per cent of revenue raised.

How this translates into the *marginal* cost of public funds has been the subject of recent discussion. Browning (1976) takes t and ES as given, and as applying to all workers. He sums WL over all workers to give total labour income Y. Tax revenue (T) then becomes:

$$T = tY \tag{9.2}$$

If the tax base is unaffected by small changes in t then from (9.1) the additional excess burden is:

$$dEB = EStYdt \tag{9.3}$$

with additional revenue:

$$dT = Ydt \tag{9.4}$$

this yields a marginal welfare cost per £ of revenue as:

$$\frac{dEB}{dT} = ESt \tag{9.5}$$

if this is accepted the marginal welfare cost of taxation is the right-hand term plus unity.

Topham (1984) argues that taking the tax base as unaffected is inappropriate even if the broad evidence of the disincentive effects of taxation are zero (i.e. the income and substitution effects cancel). He argues that the welfare costs of public funds require we ask of the individual the compensating sum he requires to freely accept the tax structure and then deduct the tax paid. In figure 9.2 income and substitution effects are assumed to cancel (point 2 is directly below point 1). If the degressive tax structure is linearized to make the individual have unearned income BY and no tax-exempt earnings, point 2 still represents equilibrium. Topham's compensating sum is now YY' as this allows the individual to reach his no tax utility level on I^*.

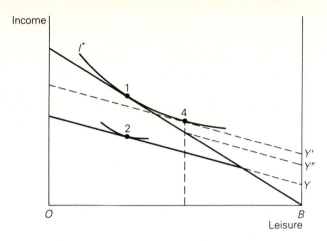

Figure 9.2   The marginal cost of public funds

With hours determined by this hypothetical equilibrium at 4, tax would by YY'' and the welfare cost $Y''Y'$. As for the marginal cost of public funds, the change in the *compensated* tax revenue when t changes is:

$$dT = Y dt + t dY \qquad\qquad (9.6)$$

$$dY = \frac{W \partial L}{\partial W} \cdot \frac{\partial W}{\partial t} \cdot dt \qquad\qquad (9.7)$$

The after-tax wage is $(1-t)W$ and hence $\partial W/\partial t = -W$. Substituting this into equation (9.7) and dividing top and bottom of the right-hand side by L yields:

$$dY = -ESY dt \qquad\qquad (9.8)$$

Substituting (9.8) into (9.6):

$$dT = (1 - tES)Y dt \qquad\qquad (9.9)$$

Dividing (9.3) by (9.9) gives a new expression for the welfare cost of an additional £1 of tax as:

$$\frac{dEB}{dT} = \frac{tES}{(1 - tES)} \qquad\qquad (9.10)$$

and the marginal cost of public funds as unity plus (9.10), that is:

$$1 + \frac{dEB}{dT} = \frac{1}{(1 - tES)} \qquad\qquad (9.11)$$

which must exceed unity as *ES* is positive.

Topham (1984) provides some calculations based on different values of *t* and *ES*. So for example, if *t* = 0.28 and *ES* = 0.61, the Browning estimate yields £1.17 as the marginal cost of £1 of public funds, whereas the Topham formula gives £1.21. Whilst Topham lists a number of reservations about these figures, they are indicative that the welfare cost of £1 of tax finance is approximately 20 pence. For policy purposes the relevance for public expenditure is that the benefits secured must exceed, or be equal to, both the direct and indirect (welfare) costs of taxation if they are to be deemed efficient. The sensitivity of these calculations to the value for *ES* is large. In Browning's original calculation, *ES* = 0.2. If this value is substituted for 0.61 above, the marginal cost of public funds becomes £1.06 both for Browning's formula and Topham's. Much then will depend on both the value of *ES* thought applicable and other reservations discussed in Topham (1984).

The logic developed here in terms of labour is easily transferred to commodity taxation, and once again welfare loss triangles can be calculated (using formulae like 9.1) that vary with the relevant elasticities, tax rates, prices and quantities. Note that the broader the tax base, the lower the tax rate, *t*, can be for any given revenue requirement, and hence the lower the welfare costs. To put this another way, the same *t* will be more harmful as a specific tax, and hence it is reliance on specific rather than general taxes that is likely to generate large welfare costs. Whether governments will employ broad-base taxes is further discussed below. For the moment, the other forms of revenue and their welfare implications are considered.

Government Borrowing

Government borrowing is a controversial topic in two related contexts. The first centres on *who is burdened* by the existence of a large national debt. The second context concerns the *efficacy of fiscal policy* and the 'crowding out' debate. Here emphasis is placed on the 'burden' aspects of the former debate at the expense of the crowding out mechanisms which are dealt with in section 9.5.

The national debt burden involves the contrast of a real resource view of costs with a utility-based view. The real resource school argues that if borrowing takes place to finance a project, and if the project is undertaken, it uses up current real resources. This opportunity cost can never be shifted to future generations. As regards the future servicing and redemption payments for the (internally held) debt, these are simply viewed as financial transfers that can make society neither richer nor poorer. The burden of public debt, therefore, rests with the current and not the future generation. The utility-based school is especially associated with Buchanan (1954). He does not disagree that the real resources are used when a project takes place, but emphasizes that cost is associated with utility. When debt is issued, investors voluntarily take it up and therefore it cannot have imposed a cost on them. By contrast, those taxed in the future to service and redeem the debt are *coerced* by the tax system to do this, and therefore suffer a decrease in utility (the cost has been shifted forward). Debt-holders are simply receiving their expected return for postponing consumption, and cannot be viewed as having their discounted lifetime's command over economic resources enhanced.

The position is debatable as Mishan (1963) pointed out. If government funds were wisely invested in productive assets, the investment might generate such funds as to make future payments to redeem the debt unnecessary. Yet even if the government used the funds wastefully, Mishan argues that Buchanan's conclusion is not warranted. If taxes (to service debt, etc.) are equated with a burden and debt with no burden, then Mishan argues 'we can with more justification obtain exactly the opposite result; namely, that on familiar welfare premises, the community is always better off if the government creates debt to meet its expenditure on some project than if it raises taxes' (Mishan, 1963, p. 533). If debt is repaid by raising funds by further debt issue (rather than taxation) a burden appears to be avoided.

Browning and Browning (1983) argue that the debate on the burden of public debt would be resolved if taxpayers 'capitalize' the knowledge that current debt means future taxation. Hence they internalize the cost of a 'project' financed by borrowing, and it is as if it were financed by taxes (see Barro, 1974). To the extent people do not make the fiscal connection, the cost of a current project appears to be incurred by future taxpayers. This is an aspect of 'fiscal illusion' discussed in chapter 6. It allows an expenditure-maximizing government to gain popularity by giving current consumer voters what may appear as a 'free lunch' if financing stems from borrowing. Hence the interest in constitutional rules calling for balanced budgets annually or over a fixed-period (say 3 years).

The Money Supply and Taxation by Inflation

If the government neither taxes nor borrows to finance its activities, it must resort to increasing the money supply. Finance may now be acquired in the form of an 'inflation' tax. If inflation is unanticipated, individuals holding assets denominated in money terms will suffer a loss in the real value of their assets, and in this sense they will be taxed. However, the analysis of inflation as a tax normally involves individuals who correctly anticipate the actual rate of inflation. Following Dornbusch and Fischer (1978), if the level of real income is fixed, then the quantity of real balances individuals desire is given by $(M/P)^0$ in figure 9.3 (i.e. that quantity demanded when the actual and expected inflation rates are zero). DD' is the demand curve for real balances showing how individuals seek to reduce their holdings of real balances as the inflation rate rises. With real incomes constant, individuals will desire to add to their cash balances in line with the rate of inflation (this is the amount of nominal balances required to make the volume of real balances constant). The real value of an inflation tax Tr is given by:

$$Tr = \frac{\Delta M}{P} \qquad (9.12)$$

where ΔM is the change in nominal balances and P is the price level. Dividing and multiplying the right hand side by M yields

$$Tr = \frac{\Delta M}{M} \cdot \frac{M}{P} \qquad (9.13)$$

with, *ceteris paribus*, $\Delta M/M$ being equal to the rate of inflation ($\dot{P}$). In the short run the inflation tax is equal to $\dot{P}(M/P)$. In figure 9.3, if the actual and expected inflation rates are $\dot{P}e^1$ the desired level of real balances is $(M/P)^1$ and the tax paid equal to the shaded rectangle.

The tax raised in this way is collected by the government buying private sector goods and services with the 'created' volume of nominal balances which individuals wish to add to their money balances to keep the value of real balances constant in each period (that is the shaded rectangle in figure 9.3). Like most taxes this involves a welfare cost. In this case, in the absence of inflation, the additional services of real money balances individuals would demand is represented by triangle $(M/P)^1 A (M/P)^0$ and hence this is the disortion induced by the systematic use of inflation as a tax. Dornbusch and Fischer (1978) note that for

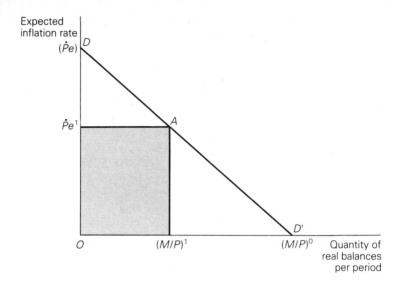

Figure 9.3   The welfare cost of an inflation tax

developed economies there is little recourse to systematic money
creation as a tax-raiser, hence no further emphasis is placed on it here.[4]
   The potential to raise real resources by an inflation tax might be
deemed unconstitutional to the extent that no explicit agreement is
reached as to changes in the rate of tax applied. In this respect,
Leviathan appears unbridled. It should be emphasized, however, that
this problem is not the sole, nor necessarily the main, source of calls
for constitutional constraints on the monetary powers of government.
Leijonhufvud (1985), for example, distinguishes between the impact of
the rate of inflation and the inflation regime. Monetary control is called
for not simply to restrain the tax on real money balances. This would
be to put 'inflation as a social problem in the class of milk subsidies
or sundry excise taxes' (Leijonhufvud, 1985, p. 96). Monetary control
is also required to provide individuals with clear signals upon which
future price levels may be forecast. As such, the potential uncertainty
of random responses by monetary authorities may be mitigated. A
significant improvement may be reaped in terms of the information
created when government's monetary management is constitutionally
constrained.

9.3 THE WELFARE COSTS OF GOVERNMENT FINANCE IN A POSITIVE CONTEXT

In section 9.2 the implicit picture (if there is one at all) is of government as an omniscient benevolent despot seeking to enact financial instruments that minimized the excess burden of taxes. Brennan and Buchanan (1977) highlight and attack this assumption, replacing it with a view of government as a monopoly revenue-maximizer. As such they argue the need to develop a tax constitution that would restrain the use of such powers. Hettich and Winer (1984), in related vein, see governments seeking to minimize the political costs (vote losses) of their tax structure. Here one is reminded that governments periodically have to capture the median voter if they are to remain in power for another term. The question arises as to what tax system would be predicted in such contexts (i.e. a positive question), rather than the prescription of an ideal or optimal tax system (i.e. a normative question). In other words, how would revenue-maximizing or political cost-minimizing governments raise revenue?

There are important considerations in relation to government as a revenue-maximizer. For example, Brennan and Buchanan suggest that government would seek those taxes that most closely approximated lump-sum ones. That is broad-based taxes. To see why this is so, refer back to figure 9.1(a). With a distortionary tax, the government can raise only T in revenue, whilst leaving the individual on utility level I^*. However, if the lump-sum tax is employed $T + E$ can be raised. Hence revenue-maximizers seek approximates of lump-sum taxation. These taxes in turn minimize the welfare costs of taxation, and in this sense, at least, revenue-maximizers follow normative prescriptions. It is important to note, therefore, that pursuit of revenue may not be linked to a growth of welfare costs in the same proportion.

Implicit in the argument of Brennan and Buchanan is the need of a revenue-maximizing government to raise revenue in the way which imposes least excess burden on the voter. An electoral basis for government means that political popularity cannot be ignored. What evidence is there of political manipulation of taxation for electoral purposes?

Hettich and Winer (1984) develop hypotheses concerning the features, rather than composition, of taxes. Broadly these are that this aspect of tax structure will be designed to minimize: the effective rate of those most likely to offer opposition; the extent of 'voice' from organized opposition; the extent of 'exit' to competing jurisdiction and the degree of variability in the tax base (as variability forces planning changes and these are unpopular with voters). The author's econometric work on income tax shares (using proxies for the above factors) in the states of America lends support to their proposition that political costs affect tax structures. Whilst the welfare consequences are not discussed by the author, and indeed not pursued here, it is not *a priori* clear that seeking to avoid offending voters is of necessity, and on balance, welfare-reducing. It is early days for this type of work. R. E. Wagner's (1976) study of the other aspect of tax structure, namely the composition of taxes used, complements this approach and has been discussed above in chapter 5, section 5.3, which deals with fiscal illusion.

Concern with voter popularity links these works with the literature on voting functions and political business cycles. The context of this literature is a positive one, involving a manipulative government attempting to 'manage' its popularity and hence win the periodic elections that will enable the existing government to retain power. Typical of the work favouring this interpretation is Frey and Schneider (1978). Two functions are used to capture the interaction between political status and economic policy. The popularity function relates government popularity to economic performance indicators (unemployment rate, inflation rate, and growth rate of real disposable income). The policy function deals with the government's reaction to its re-election chances. With a buoyant popularity index the government follows policies consistent with its party ideology. A general result is that governments engineer politically inspired economic cycles, especially before elections.

Alt and Chrystal (1985) are authors who are critical of this type of approach and conclude 'no one could read the political business cycle literature without being struck by the lack of supporting evidence' (p. 125). The authors do not deny that political business cycles have occurred, but suggest they are of minor importance compared with other economic fluctuations. Even if it is accepted that governments significantly manipulate economic variables, to improve their chances of continuing power, the empirical evidence has not been very consistent, and the coefficients obtained unstable. The role of taxation in political business cycles is a matter of debate. Not all investigations of political popularity include the tax rate as a variable, but one that does is Pissarides (1980). In this study the dependent variable was government popularity (expressed as a percentage point lead) as measured by the Gallup Poll series on voting intentions. In one of the specifications explored, one of the five economic indicators employed was the ratio of tax revenue (both income and expenditure) to GDP (a sort of overall average tax rate). The results suggest that a high tax revenue to GDP ratio reduces the government's lead. Other studies have not, however, found tax variables significant (e.g. Frey and Schneider, 1980). The evidence on the political importance of tax rate adjustment is clearly open to dispute.

The welfare costs of taxation are clearly influenced by assumptions relating to the objectives of government. To the extent that government's revenue-maximize subject to political constraints total taxation may be 'excessive' but curiously, excess burdens will be minimized. The extent to which governments are constrained is, however, an open question. Evidence is mixed on the question of whether or not government's concern for political popularity has been of over-riding importance in considering their economic policy and performance. A recent discussion (Rose, 1985) would suggest that the inertia found in national tax systems may be attributable to the government's avoidance of making tax reforms, in so far as reforms alarm the electorate. Reluctance to make tax reforms as observed is, of course, not necessarily the same as reluctance to 'exploit' *given* tax systems to maximize revenue. Empirical evidence cannot adequately answer the question of how far political popularity may constrain a revenue-maximizer. Below we consider, therefore, both a revenue-maximizing government which ignores its prospects of re-election, and a revenue-maximizing government which restrains its use of taxation for political reasons.

9.4   GOVERNMENT FINANCE AND SUPPLY-SIDE ECONOMICS

A view of the economy that in recent years has attracted many admirers on both sides of the Atlantic is so-called 'supply-side' economics. The argument is closely associated with Arthur Laffer, and is most often articulated in relation to labour as a factor, although it can be applied elsewhere. The supply of labour, as determined by the price consumption curve between leisure and income is often viewed as backward-bending. In figure 9.4(a) the initial budget constraint allows the individual to find equilibrium at point 1. Now, if large government

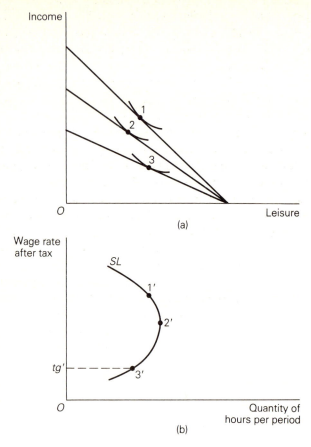

Figure 9.4   Labour supply and increased tax rates

requires successively large tax rates, the individual budget constraint, other things equal, will swivel about its intercept with the *X*-axis offering equilibria at 2 and 3. At 2 the illustrated individual is doing more market work than at any other point on the price consumption curve. Above 2 the individual is working more hours as the tax rate increases, whilst below 2 the reverse is true. In other words, above 2 the income effect of less leisure is dominating the substitution effect of more leisure, and vice-versa below 2. Such an outcome dictates a labour supply curve like the one illustrated as figure 9.4(b).

The tax revenue of government (*T*) is broadly speaking the product of *t* (the tax rate) and *Y* (the national income). Laffer and others argue that, as the tax rate is raised, the total amount of tax revenue will initially increase, but that at high tax rates it will fall because of the disincentive effects on labour supply, showing up as decreased national income. Reinforcing this disincentive effect will be the expansion of the underground or black economy reducing recorded rather than actual national income. Such arguments generate the so-called Laffer curve between t and T illustrated as figure 9.5.[5]

Assume for the moment that government in its revenue-seeking activities has chosen a tax rate like tg' placing our illustrated individual on the positively sloping part of his labour supply curve (tg' in figure 9.4(b)). In addition, assume government in its drive for revenue has also expanded the money supply with inflationary consequences. The scene is now set for the introduction of a supply-side policy of decreasing tax rates, especially on labour, combined with strict money supply control. Once tax rates fall (net-of-tax wages rise) individuals work more hours and national income increases. The lower tax rate makes 'black' activities less attractive and recorded national income rises on this count also. As the tax rate is lowered from tg, the effect on Y initially more than offsets the decrease in t, so that tax revenue actually increases. Now if output increases against a tight money supply, downward pressure must be placed on prices and hence inflation is checked. Furthermore, unemployment has also been reduced by

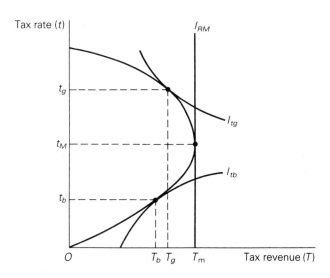

Figure 9.5 Utility maximization and the Laffer curve

offsetting the disincentive effects of high taxation. In summary, a supply-side policy of cutting taxes and a tight money supply checks inflation, raises employment and permits government revenue to rise. There is something for everyone and hence, presumably, its appeal.

Although the logic of this argument is sound, its applicability relies not only on the relevant curves having the shapes illustrated, but also on the starting point being on the crucial segments of the curves. In short, whether the policy will work or not depends on the empirical magnitudes. However, before mentioning some of the evidence, the question must be asked as to how a government would allow the economy to deteriorate into a position where a supply-side policy would be beneficial. If government is a revenue-maximizer without regard to public opinion (or political popularity), then in figure 9.5 it will have an indifference curve like I_{RM} (between tax revenue (T) which government deems good, and the tax rate (t)) to which government is neutral. This would allow the selection of the maximum tax revenue T_m by adopting tax rate t_M. However, such an outcome is inconsistent with supply-side theory, as this requires a tax rate greater than t_M to be operative. Such a rate would be selected only if both the tax rate and tax revenue are 'goods' to the decision-maker as represented in the indifference curve I_{tg}.

The clash between two criticisms of government appears stark. On the one hand, if supply-side economists are correct, there are tax revenues to be gained if tax rates are reduced (i.e. the economy operates on the upper part of the Laffer curve). On the other hand, if government behaves so as to exploit its monopoly position and revenue-maximize then the tax rates will be those that maximize revenues (i.e. the economy operates on the turning point and not on the upper part of the Laffer curve). Yet even at this stage there is further difficulty of consistency with another critique of government – namely, the manipulation by government of economic instruments to ensure re-election. Political business cycles arise if governments which raise tax rates after elections then reduce them prior to election to court political favour. Such literature would suggest that tax rates may not be perceived as neutral by government. Government's indifference curve between tax rates and tax revenue may not be vertical (like I_{RM} in figure 9.5), but convex (like I_{tb} in figure 9.5). Government is criticized when economic management is arranged for the short-sighted goal of political power. However, if such were true, again the question must be raised as to how the economy comes to operate on the upper position of the Laffer curve.

If governments are either revenue-maximizers or preoccupied by political manipulation, how is the Laffer criticism sustained? An ingenious solution to this question provided by Buchanan and Lee (1982) must be acknowledged. They seek to reconcile government revenue-maximization with the supply-side critique. It is explicitly assumed that politicians are concerned only with a time horizon which is bounded by the date of the next election. Individuals, on the other hand, take time to adjust to tax rates. In the short run individuals may be unable to shift out of taxable income. This adjustment generates the possibility of a distinction between a short-run Laffer curve, and a long-run Laffer curve. In figure 9.6 the short-run Laffer curve ($SRLC_0$) assumes a zero tax rate starting point, and lies outside the (heavily drawn) long-run Laffer curve ($LRLC$). This illustrates that an increase in tax rates will increase revenue, more in the short run than in the long run when individuals adjust so as to reduce tax payments at any

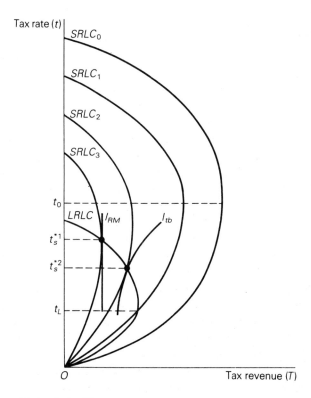

Figure 9.6 The short-run and long-run Laffer curves

tax rate. If, for example, governments initially impose a tax rate of t_0 which by reference to $SRLC_0$ would maximize tax revenues, then in the long run the tax base is eliminated.

The political myopia of governments now explains the apparent paradox. If the government (by chance) were at t_L, the rate which maximized revenue on the long-run Laffer curve, they may be tempted to increase tax rates if their interest lies only in the short run. Moving along $SRLC_1$, an increase in tax rates increases tax revenues in the short run. Yet they will cause tax rates to rise above that for maximum revenue on the long-run Laffer curve. The political equilibrium may occur at t_s^{*1}, where the incentive, even in the short run, to raise tax rates is absent. Buchanan and Lee (1982) present this argument and conclude that 'those who argue that government would never operate on the down slope of the Laffer curve, and adduce evidence in support, are implicitly adopting a short-run perspective' (p. 818). Moreover, they explain how the economy may be locked in a position on the upper part of the long-run Laffer curve. If government cuts taxes, but taxpayers interpret this as a short-run revenue-maximizing measure, government cannot move the economy down the long-run Laffer curve. Taxpayers predict no permanence in reduced tax rates and any adjustment occurs around the short-run Laffer curve. This results in government experiencing less tax revenue (not more) as a result of cutting tax rates. Any benefits in terms of tax revenues, which could arise from cutting tax rates, would only occur when taxpayers' expectations were revised. They would be reaped by future politicians.

The argument of Buchanan and Lee is, of course, based upon the notion of the most extreme political myopia on the government's part. Tax rates maximize revenue in the short run (period one) with no consideration of the forthcoming election and the ensuing period (period two). The political business cycle literature disputes this assumption. It appears, however, that, even if government were constrained by considerations of future political power, the argument of Buchanan and Lee survives. The political equilibrium would simply be t_s^{*2} on $SRLC_2$ in figure 9.6. Such an analysis may yet be queried. First, the evidence that government manipulates tax rates (high in the early post-election years and lower in the pre-election years) surely must have implications for individual taxpayers' perceptions and for movement of the short-run Laffer curve. Why substantially adjust your taxable income only to readjust in a short period of time? What of adjustment costs? In a political business cycle model with adjustments costs for taxpayers, it appears possible that the short-run and long-run Laffer curves are insignificantly different. Second, suppose the government ignored the electorate (and revenue-maximized) and persuaded the electorate that this would be its policy whatever. Surely, while an individual may consider adjustment of his taxable income, he must also assume that the government's intransigence will not soon see it voted out of office and replaced by a new government and tax changes. The individual must feel that there is little chance of change of the tax regime in the long run to make adjustment changes worthwhile for the next period.

The precise significance of the difference (if any) between a short-run and long-run Laffer curve is difficult to test. Certainly Buchanan and Lee have suggested why, when tax rates are cut, no significant supply-side response (in terms of increased tax revenues) may immediately arise. Individuals adjust on the short-run Laffer curve. Therefore evidence of the supply-side argument may be weak. Indeed, *for whatever reason*, it would appear that such evidence is thin. A study of plausible estimates of labour supply in the USA leads Fullerton (1982) to conclude that the US economy is to the left of (below) the turning point of its Laffer curve. Hausman (1981) concludes that a cut in tax rates would reduce tax revenues. Of course evidence can be considered to indicate that, for some economies, the Laffer curve may have relevance (e.g. see the study of Stuart (1981) for Sweden, where effective marginal rates of taxation are about 80 per cent). However, it does not appear easy to generalize that the Laffer curve is operative.

Empirical evidence on labour supply has to date not been very kind in general to the supply-side position. Recall that for tax cuts to increase hours worked significantly supply of labour curves must be positively sloped. Some evidence suggests that there is little sensitivity for males, or that supply curves are negatively sloped, i.e. tax cuts will decrease hours of work. Only for women, it seems, are the supply-siders' hopes likely to be fulfilled. Atkinson and Stiglitz (1980) offer some empirical estimates. For cross-section data for males of normal working age, the supply curve appears to be backward-bending with a low elasticity of between -0.1 and -0.2 (hence the shape of Slu in figure 9.1). Similar results have been obtained for time series. In contrast, women's labour supply curves appear to be forward-sloping (for a survey of this area, see Killingsworth, 1983). This, of course, is not to suggest that these are *the* final estimates of labour supply elasticities, and indeed, some of the more recent research has indicated somewhat greater labour supply sensitivity to wage changes than has hitherto been the case.

As regards the black economy aspects of the 'supply-siders' case, the evidence is as mixed as the estimating methodologies are varied. Dilnot and Morris (1981) survey the position and construct estimates of their own, and clearly do not view the black economy as all that significant at around 3 per cent of UK Gross National Product. Again, whilst not seeking to establish this as *the* measure of the black economy, it is important to note that the evidence does not consistently provide large figures.[6]

Even writers sympathetic to the Leviathian literature cast doubt on the possibilities for supply-side success. Burton (1985) warns that 'supply-side' changes are likely to occur only after long lags when people can adjust to the lower tax rates. In addition he emphasizes that not only must tax cuts be expected to be permanent, they must also not be compensated for by increased borrowing. If individuals treat borrowing as equivalent to future taxation, and internalize it in current decisions, it is as if taxes were not cut and no supply-side gains can be expected.

The connection between government spending and revenue sources has recently been explored by Anderson, Wallace and Warner (1986) and reflects on a number of points made above. They assess three competing hypotheses:

1   the Friedman (1978) view that increases in taxation cause increased expenditure because governments will always spend all revenue received (and more!);
2   the Buchanan and Wagner (1977) view that deficit bond financing causes fiscal illusion and as a consequence government spending growth (see chapter 5);
3   the Barro (1974) view that there is no fiscal illusion even when bond financed expenditures are employed.

The importance of differentiating these views is that (1) implies you cannot reduce government deficits by increasing taxation only by decreasing expenditure. View (2) suggests that financing expenditure by (direct) taxation constrains expenditure because of its invisibility. View (3) suggests that the political system determines expenditure levels and then raises revenue by taxation, borrowing or money creation, none of which affect the level of expenditure, (i.e. there is no fiscal illusion). Econometric evidence in the form of Granger causality tests gave support to view (3), that expenditure causes revenue, and not the reverse as in view (1). The authors found no empirical support for view (2). However this does not give debt finance a complete clean bill of health, as is discussed in the next section.

9.5 PUBLIC SECTOR AND 'CROWDING' EFFECTS

Section 9.2 dealt with the burden associated with debt finance, and ignored the more recent crowding out arguments introduced here. Summaries of macro 'crowding out' invariably begin with the taxonomy provided by Buiter (1977). Buiter pointed out that crowding out can refer to a number of effects, which can be direct or indirect and long- or short-run. Direct crowding out occurs when expansionary government activities are offset wholly or in part by corresponding reductions in private sector activities. At full employment any additional real resources allocated to the public sector must, as in the real resource view above, necessarily decrease resources in the private sector.

The Bacon and Eltis (1976) thesis involves an aspect of this in the sense they viewed government expansion of employment in the UK over the decade since 1966 as being at the expense of manufacturing employment in the private sector. At less than full employment government provision of an activity may simply be offset by a reduction in the level of private provision. This general form of crowding out is discussed in some detail in chapter 7.[7] What has become more important in the macro-economic literature on fiscal policy is indirect crowding out that operates via interest rate changes induced by government borrowing. If the government stimulates the economy then the trans-actions demand for money increases. Other things equal, this leaves less money for speculative balances and hence the rate of interest rises. The interest rate reduces interest-sensitive elements of aggregate demand. Investment is generally thought to be the main victim. Alternatively, the issuing of government bonds can be viewed as displacing some part of the given pool of available funds, decreasing the supply for private corporation borrowing. Either mechanism places upward pressure on interest rates and they are hence thought inimical to the level of private sector investment.

The important relationships in this argument, then, are the connection between public sector deficits and the interest rate, and the response of investment to interest rates. To the extent these functions are significantly positive and negative respectively, future generations will inherit lower levels of capital equipment and a lower potential national income.

As regards the empirical evidence on the 'crowding' arguments, Jackson (1980) makes a number of points relating to the UK. First, he notes that the public sector's claim over real resources was stable over the decade from 1968, and that public sector capital expenditure fell over that period, as did its share in total investment. The Bacon and Eltis argument concerning labour in the public sector displacing manufacturing sector also lacks bite when it is recognized that public sector employment increases have been dominated by part-time married women (see Jackson, 1977), whereas it is men who left manufacturing. Hence Jackson (1980) concludes there is little *prima-facie* evidence for direct crowding out. Other evidence is also consistent with this view. Saunders (1985) tests a number of specific hypotheses concerning the impact of the public sector on economic performance. His empirical work relates to a cross-section of the OECD countries in the past 20 years. The data were broken down into the two sub-periods, 1960–73 and 1975–81 (this reflects the marked break in the series that accompanied the first oil price shock) and then averaged. One strand in Saunders's analysis is a first attempt at measuring the relationship between private sector employment growth and the share of total government expenditure in GDP. Other variables in the regression equation were the average growth rate of real private sector output and the average growth rate of real compensation per employee. With a small sample of ten countries the effect of the government size variable was negative, small and insignificant, offering no clear evidence of a negative impact of government size on private sector employment growth.

Indirect financial crowding out via the interest rate has also been questioned. The theoretical link between real deficits and stocks of public debt and real interest rates is questioned by Barro (1974). Plosser (1982) finds no statistical connection between US government deficits and interest rates between 1954 and 1978. Even if it is accepted that interest rates rise when governments use debt finance the effects on investment may not be very large. First, in good times investment may not be very sensitive to the rate of interest, and in depressed times it is unlikely to be a relevant consideration. Second, to the extent deficit finance stimulates the economy and raises GNP, investment will be induced to meet expanding aggregate demand (crowding in). Overall, in depressed times any crowding out effects may well be dominated by crowding in effects. Given that national debts are expanded considerably during recessions, they can be construed as a 'good thing'. It is conceded that deficits incurred to carry on wars (the other major source of outstanding debt) may depress investment levels; however, an alternative superior form of finance is not obviously available.

A measure of disagreement is offered by Saunders and Klau (1985), who survey some of the evidence on crowding out and conclude 'the general picture which emerges from the econometric or model-based evidence reviewed above, is somewhat conflicting, yet indicative of clear crowding-out effects in most cases, even though they are quite weak in some instances, particularly in the shorter run' (p. 201). The authors add that the models involved are not those suited to picking up the rather more subtle forms of crowding out, and hence the results to date may be prematurely optimistic.

9.6   PUBLIC SECTORS AND ECONOMIC GROWTH

The final major question treated in this chapter is about the relationship between economic growth and public sector size (if any). Two recent studies, coming to different conclusions, concerning this question are Landau (1985) and Saunders (1985) and are illustrative of work in this area. Both Landau and Saunders recognize there are reasons for believing that large public sectors can both stimulate or hinder economic growth, making the question essentially an empirical one. Landau, who has the more econometrically sophisticated approach, recognizes that the evidence will always be open to different interpretations. In this context is it that public sectors have growth consequences or vice-versa? In the absence of fully articulated growth models, which include the effects of government spending, both investigators opt for an unashamedly empirical approach. Landau is specific about his approach. He relates economic growth to levels of physical and human capital and changes in their productivity. One important set of variables affecting the productivity of investment deals with the share of government expenditure in national income. Additional variables employed included a time trend, contraction and expansion year dummies, and the percentage change in the terms of trade. Several specifications of the growth rate and public sector measures were used in the regressions.

The results indicate a detrimental impact on economic growth of government sectors. (The data are a pooled time series over the years 1952–76 involving 16 developed economies including the UK and USA.) A 10 per cent increase in the government share in national income implies in the regression a 0.6–1.6 per cent decline in per capita growth national income. Conclusions drawn by Landau include that both the consumption and investment expenditures by government exhibit a negative correlation with growth, although transfers do not. That transfers may be given a clean bill of health on growth grounds may be significant for the UK where considerable public sector growth can be attributed to transfers.

Saunders (1985), using the data detailed above, considered the impact on economic growth (percentage change in real GDP) of total government outlays as a proportion of GDP, and to allow for other growth influences, the share of gross fixed capital formation in GDP (a constant was also part of the linear regression equation). Although for both periods studied the government share variable is negatively related to economic growth, it is only significant at the conventional level for the early (1960–73) period. The same variables were used in an attempt to explain differences in economic growth between the two periods, but provided no evidence that the post-1973 decline in economic growth bears any systematic relation to public expenditure growth. In addition, the hypothesis that economies with large public sectors were better equipped to withstand the supply-side shocks of the midde 1970s was tested by replacing the government growth variable by the level of the government expenditure share in 1975. The evidence gave some, but not overwhelming, support for the notion that the decline in economic growth after 1975 was slightly less in those countries with larger public expenditure shares.

Saunders reflects that his work, like that of many others, identifies no simple relationships, either adverse or beneficial, between overall economic performance and the size and growth of public sectors. He argues that the way forward is a more disaggregated approach, so that the influences of the structure of different revenue and expenditure policies can be isolated.

9.7   SUMMARY AND CONCLUSIONS

This chapter has dealt with a wide range of themes central to modern public finance economics. In doing so it has been necessary to minimize embellishments, and such empirical estimates that have been discussed are to be viewed as illustrative. Arguments presented do, however, provide a less damning picture of the economic consequences imposed by having to finance a large public sector. Disincentive effects and the welfare costs of taxation are far from settled issues, but to date they have not been estimated at levels consistent with public rhetoric and popular belief. In addition, the 'supply-side' arguments, that combine nearly all that is reputedly bad about having large public sectors, are found to be largely unconvincing. The various 'crowding out' and economic growth arguments, whilst present on most analyses, have again, as yet, to be shown highly significant. It may well be the case that a future consensus will develop around an empirical literature indicating the welfare costs of financing large public sectors as a major concern; however, that consensus has not currently been reached.

NOTES

1 The treatment initially followed here is along the lines of Browning and Browning (1979) and Rosen (1985).
2 There are two measures of income and substitution effects; Hicks/Allen and Slutsky. The reader may wish to examine these in a comprehensive micro-economics text.
3 These formulae are derived in Hyman (1973); also see Collard (1980).
4 This is not to imply that the role of government finances in inflation is not an important and controversial issue, but simply that it is beyond the scope of this book where the emphasis is placed on micro- rather than macro-economics.
5 Fullerton (1982) notes that, 'Ever since Arthur B. Laffer first drew his famous curve on a napkin in a Washington restaurant seven years ago, there has been considerable public debate about the possibility of an inverse relationship between tax rates and government revenue' (p. 3). As he points out, however, the notion of an inverse relationship between tax rates and revenue can be traced back at least as far as Adam Smith in 1776.
6 Estimates of the black economy vary considerably, depending on the method employed in the calculations. Inland Revenue Service estimates for the USA give a figure of approximately 9 per cent of GNP.
7 Social Security programmes are thought to damage investment because of their unfunded nature (see Browning and Browning, 1983, ch. 7).

REFERENCES

Alt, J. E. and Chrystal, A. K. (1983), *Political Economics*, Brighton: Wheatsheaf.

Anderson, W., Wallace, M. S. and Warner, J. T. (1986), Government spending and taxation: what causes what? *Southern Economic Journal*, vol. 52, no. 3 (January), pp. 630–9.

Atkinson, A. B. and Stiglitz, J. E. (1980), *Public Economics*, New York: McGraw-Hill.

Bacon, R. and Eltis, W. (1976), *Britain's Economic Problem: Too Few Producers*, London: Macmillan.

Barro, R. J. (1974), Are government bonds net wealth, *Journal of Political Economy*, vol. 82, no. 6 (November/December), pp. 1095–117.

Brennan, G. and Buchanan, J. M. (1977), Towards a tax constitution for Leviathan, *Journal of Public Economics*, vol. 8, no. 3 (December), pp. 255–74.

Brennan, G. and Buchanan, J. M. (1980), *The Power to Tax: Analytical Foundations of a Fiscal Constitution*, Cambridge: Cambridge University Press.

Browning, E. K. (1976), The marginal cost of public funds, *Journal of Political Economy*, vol. 84, no. 2 (April), pp. 283–98.

Browning, E. K. and Browning, J. M. (1979), *Public Finance and the Price System*, New York: Macmillan.

Buchanan, J. M. (1954), *Public Principles of Public Debt*, Homewood, Illinois: Irwin.

Buchanan, J. M. and Lee, D. R. (1982), Politics, time and the Laffer curve, *Journal of Political Economy*, vol. 90, no. 4 (August), pp. 816–19.

Buchanan, J. M. and Wagner, R. E. (1977), *Democracy in Deficit*, New York: Academic Press.

Buiter, W. H. (1977), 'Crowding out' and the effectiveness of fiscal policy, *Journal of Public Economics*, vol. 7, no. 3 (June), pp. 285–308.

Burton, J. (1985), *Why No Cuts?* Hobart Paper 104, London: Institute of Economic Affairs.

Collard, D. (1980), Excess burden of a tax, *British Journal of Economic Issues*, vol. 2, no. 6 (May), pp. 70–2.

Dilnot, A. and Morris, C. N. (1981), What do we know about the black economy? *Fiscal Studies*, vol. 2, no. 1 (March), pp. 58–73.

Dornbusch, R. and Fischer, S. (1978), *Macro-Economics*, New York: McGraw-Hill.

Frey, B. S. and Schneider, F. (1978), An empirical study of politico-economic interaction in the United States, *Review of Economics and Statistics*, vol. 60, no. 2 (May), pp. 174–83.

Frey, B. S. and Schneider, F. (1980), Popularity functions: the case of the US and West Germany, pp. 47–84 in Whiteley, P. (ed.), *Models of Political Economy*, London and Beverly Hills: Sage.

Friedman, M. (1978), The limitations of tax limitations, *Policy Review*, Summer, pp. 7–14.

Fullerton, D. (1982), On the possibility of an inverse relationship between tax rates and government revenues, *Journal of Public Economics*, vol. 19, no. 1 (October), pp. 3–22.

Hausman, J. A. (1981), Income and payroll tax policy and labor supply, in Meyer, M. H. (ed.), *The Supply-side Effects of Economic Policy*, St. Louis: Centre for the Study of American Business, Washington University.

Hettich, W. and Winer, S. (1984), A positive model of tax structure, *Journal of Public Economics*, vol. 24, no. 1, pp. 67–87.

Hyman, D. N. (1973), *The Economics of Governmental Activity*, New York: Holt, Rinehart & Winston.

Jackson, P. M. (1977), The growth of public sector employment, the case of the U.K., in *Fiscal Policy and Labour Supply*, Institute for Fiscal Studies, Conference Series No. 4.

Jackson, P. M. (1980), The public expenditure cuts: rationale and consequences, *Fiscal Studies*, vol. 1, no. 2 (March), pp. 66–82.

Killingsworth, M. R. (1983), *Labour Supply*, Cambridge: Cambridge University Press.

Landau, D. L. (1985), Government expenditures and economic growth in the developed countries: 1952–76, *Public Choice*, vol. 47, no. 3, pp. 459–78.

Leijonhufvud, A. (1985), Constitutional constraints on the monetary powers of government, pp. 95–109 in McKenzie, R. B. (ed.), *Constitutional Economics: Containing the Economic Powers of Government*, Lexington, Mass.: Lexington Books.

Mishan, E. J. (1963), How to make a burden of the public debt, *Journal of Political Economy*, vol. 71, no. 6 (December), pp. 529–42.

Pissarides, C. A. (1980), British government popularity and economic performance, *Economic Journal*, vol. 90, no. 359 (September), pp. 569–81.

Plosser, C. I. (1982), Government financing decisions and asset returns, *Journal of Monetary Economics*, vol. 9, no. 3 (May), pp. 325–52.

Rose, R. (1985), Maximizing tax revenue while minimizing political costs, *Journal of Public Policy*, vol. 5, no. 3, pp. 289–320.

Rosen, H. S. (1985), *Public Finance*, Homewood, Illinois: Irwin.

Saunders, P. (1985), Public expenditure and economic performance in OECD countries, *Journal of Public Policy*, vol. 5, pt. 1 (February), pp. 1–21.

Saunders, P. and Klau, F. (1985), *The Role of the Public Sector*, OECD Economic Studies No. 4.

Stuart, C. E. (1981), Swedish tax rates, labor supply and tax revenues, *Journal of Political Economy*, vol. 89, no. 5 (October), pp. 1020–38.

Topham, N. (1984), A reappraisal and recalculation of the marginal cost of public funds, *Public Finance/Finance Publiques*, vol. 39, no. 3, pp. 394–405.

Wagner, R. E. (1976), Revenue structure, fiscal illusion and budgetary choice, *Public Choice*, vol. 25 (Spring), pp. 45–61.

10

Freedom and the Public Sector

March 4th
This morning started none too well, either.

Roy [*Hacker's driver, and like all drivers, one of the best-informed men in Whitehall* – Ed.] picked me up as usual, at about eight-thirty. I asked him to drive me to the Ministry, as I was to spend all morning on Health Service administration.

He started needling me right away.

'Chap just been talking about that on the radio,' he said casually. 'Saying the trouble with the health and education and transport services is that all the top people in government go to private hospitals and send their kids to private schools. . .'

I laughed it off, though I sounded a little mirthless, I fear, 'Very good. Comedy programme, was it?'

This egalitarian stuff, though daft, is always a little dangerous if it's not watched very carefully.

'And they go to work in chauffeur-driven cars,' added my chauffeur.

Lynn, J. and Jay, A. (eds) (1982), *Yes Minister*, vol. 2, p. 15,
London: British Broadcasting Corporation.

10.1 INTRODUCTION

In earlier chapters of part II the focus has been on the efficiency aspects of government sector provisions. In this one, however, the focus is changed. Here the emphasis is on the impact of the public sector on individual freedom. Government provision is usually said to be directed at producing an efficient resource allocation and an equitable one. Those policies that are substantially, but by no means exclusively, directed at equity issues are to be found under the heading 'welfare state'. Such policies cover a complex of in-kind provision of goods and services (e.g. health and education) at near-zero user charges as well as transfer payments in the form of social security. The argument of this chapter is not whether such policies have achieved equity or moved individuals in that direction.[1] Instead we ask have any effects, beneficial or otherwise, been bought 'too dear' in the form of lost freedom? The view that individuals take, with regard to the importance of equity, invariably colours the lens through which any loss (or gains) of freedom are assessed. If equity-type policies are unimportant, then any demonstration that they infringe individual freedom is damning. In what follows, an attempt is made to sketch alternative views of the importance of equity with the object of developing a notion of freedoms that may be gained or lost (and to whom they are gained or lost). In short will a significant welfare state prove costly in terms of freedom, and what is the incidence of such costs?

10.2   VIEWS ON EQUITY

It is readily accepted that equity involves making value judgements over and above those embedded in traditional (neo-classical) economic theory[2] and, as such, will always be the cause of controversy. Rather than ask for such value judgements, the question here is why do people disagree on the importance of equity as a goal in the first place? The answer seems to be simply that different people view the world differently. In terms of social policy analysis, people can be said to have different 'assumptive worlds' in which they are operating. Chart 10.1 outlines a taxonomy of some assumptive worlds that rely on two

Chart 10.1   Assumptive worlds

	People have broadly similar abilities	*People have broadly similar tastes*	*Emphasis*
Case 1:	Yes	Yes	Negative freedom
Case 2:	Yes	No	Negative freedom
Case 3:	No	Yes	Positive freedom
Case 4:	No	No	Positive freedom

characteristics which you consider people do, or do not, possess. The first is whether you believe people are broadly similar in their abilities, especially in relation to the market-place. The second is whether you think people have similar tastes or preferences, especially in relation to certain basic commodities.

Case 1 is uninteresting because in a world of broadly similar abilities and tastes there would be little observed inequality, and therefore little need to direct policy towards it.

Case 2 similarly leads to rather little concern about inequality. The different tastes or preferences of people would mean that they would choose different production and consumption patterns. Therefore there would be observed inequality but, given broadly equal abilities, it would be within everyone's grasp to achieve what others around them have. The main purpose of any equality-motivated policies would be towards establishing equality of opportunity.

Case 3 provides grounds for strong welfare state policies, especially those provided in an in-kind form. Unequal abilities would mean considerable inequality being observed in the economy, and would be a rather intractable problem because, for the individuals doing less well, equality of opportunity is not enough; they are fundamentally disadvantaged. However, because tastes or preferences are similar (to the extent, again, that inequality is thought a problem) government in-kind provision is acceptable because there is little efficiency loss where (basic) preferences are not very different.

Case 4 provides similar concern over observed inequality, but suggests that the inefficiency losses from in-kind provision would be large and hence (to the extent inequality is to be tackled) cash transfer payments will invoke less efficiency loss. (Field, 1981, seems to broadly hold this view.)

Cases 2, 3 and 4 all involve observed inequality but, depending on your assumptive world, its significance and the appropriate policy response will vary.

The next question is how, if at all, do different conceptions of freedom relate to this simple taxonomy?

10.3   KINDS OF FREEDOM

'Freedom is a word I rarely use without thinking of the times I like the best' is a sentiment from a song by Donovan, a troubadour of the 1960s. The song goes on to elaborate on those times, but the point here is that freedom is an emotive word and is self-evidently a 'good thing'. Hence any suggestion that the public sector encroaches on freedom is a powerful weapon in the Leviathan armoury. As Stein (1985, p. ii) puts it, 'In America, and the Western world generally, "freedom" is a good word and "big government" is a bad word.' However, just as 'times you liked the best' are likely to vary between individuals, so are conceptions of freedom. Machlup (1969) draws attention in a footnote to Adler, who proposed three notions of freedom. The first is a form of 'inner freedom' and is dubbed the freedom of self-perfection. It involves the freedom to order one's own will, and is independent of external circumstances. The second, the freedom of self-realization, concerns the ability to carry out your own intention without being thwarted by external institutional or social forces. The third is freedom of self-determination, and amounts to saying that individuals are not running in predetermined grooves moulded in a determinant pattern by various external forces or factors. Machlup notes that it is the second of these conceptions that comes closest to the ordinary understanding of the word freedom. Machlup himself favours less heady notions. He is mainly concerned to define liberalism, but in doing so has a great deal to say about freedom. His position is a definite one, that liberalism is essentially about what is described below as negative freedom – the freedom from – rather than positive freedom – the freedom to (Machlup's own terminology is the opposite of this). Additionally, freedom is identified with man rather than nature, so that it becomes the absence of human suppression or restriction. 'Hence, there can be no freedom that it is not the freedom of a person to do specified things – without fear of restraint or punishment by one or more other persons' (Machlup, 1969, pp. 134–5). Apart from identifying freedom with human[3] rather than natural/ environmental restraints or constraints on individual actions, Machlup views negative freedom as that which can be established without government policies. So, in his view of Franklin Roosevelt's four freedoms (of speech, of worship, from want and from fear), the first two are genuine freedoms or liberties as they call for the proscription of public restraints on individual action, whereas the second two require positive prescription for action by government. As part of his argument, Machlup lists[4] some important freedoms, collecting them under the overlapping categories for economic, political and intellectual and moral. It is the economic freedoms that are perhaps most important to this text, but not exclusively so. Interestingly, Machlup concludes that liberals will never agree to any restriction on freedom except as the opportunity cost of securing further freedoms; so that it is illegitimate to champion welfare for the poor and simultaneously call oneself a liberal.

In many ways this conclusion provides a convenient link with more recent discussions of freedom (especially in the *Journal of Social Policy*). First, Sugden (1982) comes to an identical conclusion to Machlup's but by a different route (although it must be admitted that Sugden's identification of liberalism with *laissez-faire* makes him guilty of the sixth of Machlup's seven errors concerning liberalism). Second, discussion has concentrated on freedom with reference to the welfare state, rather than with reference to the public sector as such. Given the above discussion of equity, and that the welfare state is a significant proportion of the public sector, this is not a vital shortcoming. Third, Machlup sees freedom as multidimensional rather than indivisible, and this is part of the more recent contributions.

Generally speaking, the runway for most recent take-offs into discussions of freedoms is Isaiah Berlin's distinction between positive and negative freedom (Berlin, 1958). Berlin makes the distinction between the freedom from something and the freedom to do something. The first represents negative freedom and the second the positive notion of freedom (see Heald (1983) for a convenient summary). It is easy to overdraw the distinction, and MacCallum (1967) argued that essentially freedom involved a triadic set of relationships: the freedom of an actor *from* some constraint *to* do or not do something. Although Goodin (1982) makes use of this format (see below), more can be said of the positive–negative distinction. MacPherson (1973) reinterprets Berlin's negative and positive liberty. Negative liberty becomes counter-extractive liberty and represents immunity from the extractive powers of others, including the state. Positive liberty is redefined as developmental liberty and is equated with an 'individual's' developmental power (a man's ability to use and develop his capacities). Counter-extractive liberty is a necessary prerequisite of developmental liberty.

Apart from the differential role of the government in establishing positive and/or negative freedoms, Goodin (1982) suggests that negative freedom is about the set of available options whereas positive freedom is about the capacity or otherwise to exercise these options. Furthermore, there is a constant sum aspect to negative freedom (an individual's 'freedom from' means another's option has been circumscribed) in contrast with a positive sum aspect to positive freedom. Here Goodin has in mind that freedoms may have different 'values' so their distribution matters. The loss of some freedoms to some individuals

Chart 10.2   Characteristics of negative and positive freedom

Negative freedom	*Positive freedom*
(1) Involves freedom from the actions of others	(1) Involves a broad constraint that includes social structures and institutions
(2) Is available without any extensive government action	(2) Requires government action to make it exist
(3) Involves the set of available opportunities	(3) Involves the capacity to utilize the set of available opportunities open to individuals
(4) Is essentially constant sum in nature (one's loss is another's gain)	(4) Has a positive sum aspect (exchanging freedom between individuals can involve the gainers gaining more than the losers lose)

can be overcompensated for by the extension of liberties to others (the Appendix to this chapter expands on this notion). Chart 10.2 outlines the distinctions made in this section between positive and negative freedom (it is not any specific author's list).

Green (1982) makes a similar distinction in a review article on Field (1981), when he writes of plain freedom and freedom as power. Plain freedom is associated with the desires of individuals to be protected from the injustice of other individuals and the power of central authorities who in upholding individuals' rights must be given power to enact this task, a power which can be abused. Freedom as power correlates with positive freedom above, in that it concerns the use of the power of central authorities to give the 'have-nots' freedom to do things by essentially compulsory redistributive policies. In short, freedom as power can be identified with the desire to solve inequality problems. It is in this way that chart 10.2 can be linked with the third column of chart 10.1. The argument here suggests that those who have an assumptive world that sees individuals as broadly equal in ability should favour negative freedom and (if they are concerned with equity) equality of opportunity policies, whereas those who see individuals as fundamentally different should favour positive notions of freedom and government in-kind and/or cash transfer policies.

Unless the more esoteric is lost sight of, it is worth noting that Goodin (1982) draws attention to both psychological and moral freedom. The former concerns the subjective capacity to take advantage of opportunities (crudely it appears to be the freedom to 'go for it') and the latter the freedom to conform with individually held principles. Perhaps the other end of the definitional scale is represented by Stigler (1978), who equates freedom with wealth and writes 'A wider domain of choice is another way of saying that a person has more freedom or liberty' (p. 214). Given this, it is the efficiency of public policy that matters. 'Let me ask of any proposed or actual policy: will it increase the wealth of individuals in society? If it does, then on balance it will increase the range of options available to the people in that society' (Stigler, 1978, p. 217). If this is accepted, then the relevant question to ask in this context would appear to be, does the welfare state accelerate the rate of growth of the economy? Whatever the answer to this question, to consider it in detail here would be to exclude the contributions of those who have adopted less 'economic' conceptions of liberty (along the lines presented above) and who have contributed the bulk of the discussions on this topic. It is these contributions that are considered in the next section. Recent discussions by economists are reserved for section 10.5.

10.4   ANALYSES OF FREEDOM AND THE WELFARE STATE/REDISTRIBUTION

The substantive section in Goodin (1982) uses MacCallum's (1967) triadic relationship specifically to explore the ways in which the welfare state may affect freedom. The benchmark against which losses and gains of freedom are assessed is the freely working market economy. Below each of Goodin's arguments (summarized in chart 10.3) is briefly considered in turn with the addition of one or two economic arguments (hopefully without doing too much injustice to the complexity of the original arguments).

1. The infringement of individual property rights by the imposition of compulsory taxation at first sight seems an unambiguous freedom reduction; however, there are a number of offsetting arguments. First, the alternative of voluntary charity has only recently come to be scrutinized in detail. Many motives may be involved, not all of which can be associated with voluntarism. So, for example, Keating (1981) and Keating *et al.* (1981) find that employer pressure may account for

Chart 10.3 Goodin's summary account of freedom and the welfare state

	Argu- ment	Impact on freedom (negative or positive)	Of (agent)	From (constraint)	To (actions)
1.	Property rights	Negative	Citizens as taxpayers	Legal constraints	Dispose of property as they please
2.	Uniformity	Negative	Citizens	Legal constraints	Display diverse tastes for public services
3.	Paternalism	Negative	Welfare recipients	Legal constraints	Pursue their own preferences
4.	Red tape	Negative	Welfare recipients	Legal and bureaucratic constraints	Live their lives as they please
5.	Dependency	Negative	Welfare recipients	Psychological and economic constraints	Pursue alternative social and political arrangements
6.	Irreversibility	Negative	Citizens	Bureaucratic and political constraints	Pursue alternative social and political arrangements
7.	Impartiality	Positive	Citizens	Psychological constraints	Display moral impartiality
8.	Moralizing	Positive	Citizens	Psychological constraints	Act upon seriously held moral principles
9.	Poverty	Positive	Welfare recipients	Social and economic constraints	Live their lives as they please

Source: Goodin (1982, p. 172) with very minor alterations.

some contributions to charity. Second, if taxation is a loss of freedom for some, then transfers must represent a gain of freedom for others (see Jones, 1982, below). Third, there are efficiency considerations to be faced. With either interdependent utility functions or non-rivalness problems, individuals will willingly accept compulsory taxation to solve the 'free-rider problem that might arise.

2. The welfare state reduces the freedom of citizens from legal restraints to display diverse tastes for public goods. Again, there are a number of offsetting arguments. Although it is a feature of collective decisions that a common quantity has to be adjusted to, it is only a few 'essential' goods within the welfare state to which this applies. This may correspond to Tobin's (1970, p. 264) specific egalitarianism. Furthermore, the welfare state tends to provide a floor provision rather than a ceiling level. At least this is so for divisible goods which can then be augmented by private purchase. However, where there is indivisibility this is not so, and it is conceivable that in-kind provisions actually decrease the consumption of the good in question. Looking back to section 10.2 it may well be possible to argue that preferences may not be all that different over those in-kind provisions that are part of the welfare state. Goodin himself (1982) accepts this contraction of the choice set of individuals as a reduction in freedom but sees it offset by points 3 and 7 below.

3. This argument deals with the paternalistic or imposed choice aspects of the welfare state. For economists this particular point is usually discussed under the heading of merit wants (Musgrave, 1959) and rationalized by individual lack of information or ability to assess information rationally. The merit want concept has had a chequered history in the literature of economics (see for example Head, 1974), largely because it tends to be at odds with the value judgement that individuals are the best judges of their own welfare. If this is accepted then there is little scope for government intervention to raise the long-term welfare of individuals. Goodin (1982) is not obliged to be part of this framework, and therefore can justify freedom *increasing* paternalistic actions, especially in relation to risk-taking along the lines indicated above. For economists there are at least two theoretical escape routes. First, as Mooney (1979) points out, in relation to health care, it is possible to view individual choice as one of delegation to the 'expert' or government in this case, i.e. the individual preference is to ask the government to choose on his or her behalf. Second, and more subtly, it is possible to employ the Akerloff and Dickens (1982) 'cognitive dissonance' approach. If people have control to some extent over their

beliefs then their beliefs or preferences may not necessarily be interpreted as sacrosanct. Akerloff and Dickens provide examples. Workers in dangerous jobs often believe they work in safe ones and, for example, fail to wear safety clothes even though they are provided. The 'cognitive dissonance' explanation for this is that 'sensible' people do not work in high-risk environments, therefore individuals choose to believe they work in safe ones, and if this is their belief it then makes no sense to wear safety clothes as this action conflicts with their safe-environment belief. Similarly, if individuals dislike thinking of their own old age and choose to believe that they will go on working essentially for ever, then savings for retirement will appear to be a conflicting act. The outcome of both these illustrations is preference maps for individuals that are 'distorted' so that individuals in these cases make inappropriate safety and savings decisions. In this way, a case for government 'paternalistic' action can be justified.

Whether either of these approaches is found convincing is largely a matter of choice. The fact remains that even admitted paternalism need not necessarily represent a decrease in freedom by violating the economists' value judgement that it is individual preferences that are to count.

4. As regards the (red) tape that holds many welfare state packages together, much of it is alleged to be unnecessary. However, to the extent it is there, Goodin develops arguments along two lines. The first of these should find favour with those who emphasize negative freedom. To the extent that welfare recipients voluntarily accept welfare programmes they are as free as other citizens who voluntarily accept market exchanges when they are in desperate economic circumstances. Second, Goodin relies on specifically interdependent utility functions (see Hochman and Rodgers, 1969) to account for the myriad of conditions that may apply to welfare receipt, suggesting for the donees' decreased freedom has a counterpart in donors' increased freedom (from the characteristics of the poor or less well-off that generates the externality). Higgins (1982) refers to this issue, below.

5. That the welfare state reduces freedom of welfare recipients from psychological and economic constraints to pursue alternative social and political arrangements relates to point 4 above. The claim is often made that market economies work by individuals making choices, and to the extent the welfare state obviates the need for this, it creates dependency – 'welfare state junkies'. On this view people who cannot cope in markets are created by the welfare state system rather than existing in the first place. (Goodin, however, develops the point on a number of lines.) Goodin responds that unilateral personal charity may be cold

and soul-destroying but that the impersonal transactions of the welfare state need not be. Furthermore, he draws on psychological arguments that self-reliance as a trait is developed in early contact with family and friends and not later in life. As for the argument that the welfare state helps buy off individuals from potential revolution, he accepts it but assigns little significance to it.

6. This point relates the extent to which the existence of a welfare state presents bureaucratic and political obstacles to citizens decreasing their freedom to follow alternative social and political arrangements. The argument is that, once in place, it is impossible to dismantle the welfare state, so once created, inevitably it curtails future options. Bureaucratic power and Wildavsky (1964) incremental budgeting-type arguments are brought forward as supporting reasoning. As noted in chapter 4, Williamson (1967) suggests that incrementalism may mask a more flexible economic process at work, and therefore more may be going on than meets the eye. Goodin himself responds by suggesting that if the welfare state is a 'good thing', then its irreversibility is a 'good thing'. He adds that rules which say everything is reversible are just as much a freedom-reducer as saying something is irreversible because the first rule precludes the second option of permanency.

7. One of Goodin's three freedom-enhancing arguments relates to the fact that a uniform universalist welfare state encourages impartiality. By having to take part, individuals are constrained to use Hirschman's (1971) voice rather than exit to improve their position, thereby improving institutions for all. The important aspect of this for Goodin is that uniformity frees you from the self-interest constraint that would otherwise shape your behaviour. It allows you to be free to act in a more ethical way.

8. The welfare state enhances citizens' freedom to act on seriously held moral beliefs, freeing them from practical and psychological constraints that would otherwise impede them. This claim concerning freedom centres on the defining boundary of the welfare state, and asks why does it concern itself with increasing the equality of the provision of only some goods and services (those sometimes called 'needs') rather than others. Goodin's response is not centred on the characteristics the goods and services possess, but rather on the non-market nature of their provision. To take something seriously involves isolating it from the ordinary, putting it beyond the meter of money The free play of moral principles can be facilitated only if needs ('higher' concerns) cannot be tainted by the cash nexus. Once they are, moral principles become contaminated so that the freedom to act

on moral principles is 'bought' at the price of excluding other lesser freedoms (the freedom to use the market-place, for instance).

9. This final argument is also a freedom-enhancing one and states that the welfare state increases the freedom of welfare recipients from social and economic constraints to live their lives as they please. Although the welfare state works imperfectly, Goodin finds it undeniable that it makes many individuals free from poverty. *elegant equal,*

On the strength of the argument summarized here, Goodin's conclusion is a strong one. Given that points 7, 8 and 9 are unequivocal pluses, and 1–6 are debatable minuses, the welfare state operates so that 'gains to freedom outweigh the losses' (Goodin, 1982, p. 172). It is noteworthy that this is a result established outside the division between positive and negative freedom outlined earlier, where clearly the welfare state scores well on the positive, and badly on the negative.

Higgins (1982), in facing the question of different types of freedom, initially distinguishes between positive and negative freedom. Positive freedom, the 'freedom to', she sees as underlying the US model of welfare where it is 'doors that are made available rather than 'floors'. 'Floor'-type policies, which she sees as being enshrined in Beveridge's approach to the welfare state, are fundamentally about negative freedom – freedom *from* want and the other four giants (squalor, ignorance, disease and idleness). In the senses listed in chart 10.4, Higgins's assignments should be reversed, as Britain's welfare state has more of the elements under the positive heading and, similarly, America's under the negative heading. The contradiction appears to arise because Higgins is using the terms positive and negative *within* welfare state frameworks and using the 'from' and 'to' in a concrete way, whereas the discussion above is much broader and more conceptual in nature. The main point the author seeks to establish (following Roosevelt) is that many freedoms are secondary (of choice, of disposition, etc.) and contingent on the primary freedom which relates to the economic security. In this light, Britain's recent macro-economic policy appears as a main weapon destroying freedom for British residents. Additionally, Higgins suggests that over time there has been an increase in economic standards and hence an increase in freedom. However, above this base it is evident that taxpayers' freedom has been maintained largely at the expense of welfare recipients who, in receiving 'public money', are induced to conform with behaviour and spending patterns set by government acting on the taxpayer's behalf.

Welfare recipient pipers must play the tune of the taxpayers, and this represents a freedom loss, in her view.

Loevinsohn (1977) adopts a narrow conception of liberty on which only coercion counts as its curtailment, and then tries to argue that redistribution is to be preferred to any non-redistribution option on libertarian grounds. The crux of his argument involves recognition that a non-redistributive option available to government prevents individuals, other than those with the current property rights, from access to goods, whereas a redistributive option prevents individuals having access to goods which they currently own, i.e. either course of action necessarily involves some curtailment of liberty. The next step is to employ what the author calls the 'importance to the agent' principle, which tips the balance in favour of libertarian redistribution. The argument is that transfer recipients have a greater desire to consume the goods than do the producers, so that less damage is done to liberty by allowing them access via redistribution.

Jones (1982), in a similar economic vein, takes issue with those who argue that redistribution (his discussion centres on cash transfers) is inimical to freedom. Jones wishes to use an empirical notion of freedom, and in doing so, at its simplest identifies material resources as freedoms. If this is accepted then a redistribution say from well off 'pike' (see note 8 and appendix 10.1A) to less well off 'minnows' represents a transfer of freedoms. Pike lose resources and hence freedoms, whereas minnows gain resources and freedoms.[5] He further argues if the minnows' gains are alternatively viewed in terms of purchasing power, opportunity, etc., then by the same token pike's losses are losses of purchasing power, opportunity, etc. (i.e. losses of freedom cannot occur only on one side of the redistributive process). Jones defends his position against a number of possible objections. Two are presented here for illustration. The argument that market transactions are voluntary, but that redistributive transfers are coercive, is opposed by essentially viewing the transfer as a redistribution of freedoms (and unfreedoms) before market exchanges begin. In this case redistribution does not drive out voluntarism but allows it to be developed from a different base. The second concerns Hayek (1960), who identifies what government is free to do as being determined by the rule of law, and further argues that laws that single out certain groups are discriminatory and infringe the freedom of the coerced group. An example of such infringement would be progressive taxation, as it discriminates against the rich as a group. Jones responds by suggesting that freedom is not infringed because the law is a general one in that it will apply to anyone lucky enough to become rich (a prospect held out more often in the *laissez-faire* rather than other literature).

Green (1982) casts doubt on the possibilities of a redistributive road to freedom, especially in relation to Field's (1981) plea to establish freedom as power. Green argues the implied fiscal costs to those on below-average earnings would be significant, so that to enact Field's extensive redistributive programme 'would almost certainly reduce the freedom of choice already available to the great majority of workers by virtue of their pre-tax incomes' (Green, 1982, p. 243).

However criticism of a different order of magnitude is directed at Goodin (1982) by Van Den Brink-Budgen (1984). The prongs of the attack are two. First that Goodin's account of the context of the welfare state is 'myopic' (p. 33) and second that his definition of freedom is a portmanteau one that needs to be unpacked. For Van Den Brink-Budgen the welfare state is a multidimensional phenomenon[6] which in part is captured by the following schema:

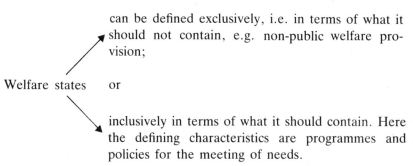

can be defined exclusively, i.e. in terms of what it should not contain, e.g. non-public welfare provision;

Welfare states   or

inclusively in terms of what it should contain. Here the defining characteristics are programmes and policies for the meeting of needs.

Having chosen a definition it has to be recognized that the welfare state is a series of programmes:

A	within *each one* there are	
B	dimensions of choice	
C	(i) over allocation (receipts)	and many
D	(ii) over its nature (cash or in kind)	different
E	(iii) delivery system	responses
F	(iv) finance (contributions,	within each
	rates etc.	dimension

.

.

.

etc,

Finally there is the question of whose perceptions of the programmes are to be considered, e.g. providers or recipients.

Without the introduction of great specificity, it is argued, it is impossible to say how the welfare state has an impact on freedom. The more aggregated view of Goodin is seen as simply not subtle enough for the problem at hand. Similarly the argument is that Goodin's definition of freedom is a conflation of four different elements: negative freedom; opportunity; autonomy (the agent's evaluation of the choice at his or her disposal) and paternalism (merit wantism). If these disaggregating corrections are accepted then a whole new and large matrix of possibilities present themselves. Van Den Brink-Budgen goes on to re-evaluate each of Goodin's nine claims in turn, concluding that it 'is much less certain' (p. 37) whether gains to freedom from the welfare state outweigh the losses.

In some respects there is a parallel here between redistributive studies of the impact of the entire government budget, and much more micro-studies of the redistributive impact of particular programmes. Some analysts are happy to contemplate the former, whereas others suggest only the micro-studies are valid, and these never allow you to answer the big question of how 'the' budget affects redistribution. Part of Goodin's (1984) response to Van Den Brink-Budgen captures this point when he argues that the excessive concern with 'micro'-discussions which may overlap in all manner of ways would imply that an overall assessment of the impact of a given institution on freedom would be impossible or largely meaningless. Additionally Goodin comments that this study was concerned with the question of whether a welfare state can conceivably increase freedoms, so that selective examples are sufficient to establish his case. His analysis was not intended as an exhaustive empirical account of whether Britain's welfare state actually does this today. Finally Goodin suggests that Van Den Brink-Budgen fails to appreciate that any mechanism that excludes or shuts out an otherwise internal compulsion may increase your freedom. Your freedom can be enhanced because you are not left in a position where you will feel compelled to follow narrowly, self-interested behaviour.

10.5 ENTITLEMENT AND POSITIVE-RIGHTS GOODS

Any discussion of the connections between provision of goods and services and welfare, broadly defined to include freedom, must make mention of the contributions of Sen (1981) on entitlements, and

Dasgupta (1986) on the provision of positive-rights goods. Sen would object to the economic definition of Stigler (1978), introduced in section 10.3 above, on the grounds of its apparent narrowness of focus on the market wealth of individuals which misses the much broader concepts of 'entitlements' and the 'capabilities' that flow from them. Entitlements are seen by Sen as the set of alternative commodity bundles individuals can command when making full use of all their rights and opportunities. Whilst in a pure market economy Stigler's wealth and Sen's entitlement approach converge, in actual economies 'the totality of rights and opportunities' (Sen, 1983, p. 754) is a much more subtle and comprehensive concept. Entitlements generate capabilities, e.g. the ability to be well-nourished, the ability to read and write, etc., which centre on what individuals can do. 'When we are concerned with such notions as the well-being of a person, or standard of living, *or freedom in the positive sense*, we need the concept of capabilities' (Sen, 1983, p. 755; emphasis added). Dasgupta (1986) links the major concern of this book – government provision – with the achievement of freedom directly. He similarly emphasizes a positive notion of freedom, and in particular the provision of what he calls positive-rights goods. These are goods necessary to positive freedom, e.g. basic food and shelter, primary education, medical care, sanitation, etc. One of the questions discussed is the way in which positive-rights goods may be provided for individuals. Because of differences of age, physiology, location, etc., individual *needs* for positive-rights goods are seen to vary. In the example set up by Dasgupta (drawing on Weitzman, 1977) the government has a positive-rights commodity it wishes to distribute according to need. However the government has incomplete information on both the income and needs of actual individuals, and given this uncertainty offers equal allocation across individuals. The problem is whether to (1) offer the commodity in-kind with prohibition of resale or (2) provide exchangeable coupons. The solution to the problem depends on the relative degree of dispersion of individual incomes and needs (assumed for simplicity uncorrelated). Chart 10.4 sets out the features of the two cases. In Case 1 the spread of incomes is greater than the spread of needs, so that individuals with large needs could, under the coupon option, end up with less of the positive-rights commodity than those with high income and low needs. Under these circumstances in-kind provision is to be preferred.

In Case 2 the reverse is true. With the spread of incomes less than the spread of needs, those with large needs under an exchangeable coupon system will be able to adjust their holding of the positive-rights

Chart 10.4　Income and needs uncertainty and government intervention

	People have broadly similar incomes	People have broadly similar needs	Form of provision
Case 1:	No	Yes	In—kind with no resale
Case 2:	Yes	No	Exchangeable coupons

commodity accordingly, via the price mechanism, because of the fact that incomes are similar. Here it is the distribution of exchangeable coupons that is attractive. In short, in a world characterized by incomplete information, marked income inequalities, similar needs and concern with a positive notion of freedom, in-kind provision of positive-rights commodities is the appropriate policy for government.

10.6　SUMMARY AND CONCLUSIONS

Having acknowledged the extra economic value judgement nature[7] of the topic it is not surprising that there is little in the way of a strong conclusion to offer. In large measure it is sufficient for the purposes of this book that the 'road to freedom' is not all one-way traffic. That the arguments discussed do not accord with everyone's definition of freedom will not be surprising. However their 'true' categorization may be irrelevant, it is the fact that they are discussed in this connection that is most important.

Although there may be no necessary link between freedom and equality it is the case that they are commonly (often implicitly) associated. The link that has been suggested here is via people's assumptive worlds concerning individual abilities and preferences. For those who believe that people have similar basic talents, especially in relation to the market-place, then it is likely they will place all the emphasis on negative freedom, as defined here; hence the impact of a large public sector will be detrimental to freedom in their view. A similar conclusion will be reached by those who do not think that people are similar in their level of talents, but that they are largely unconcerned with equity. For individuals who see individuals as different in their abilities, then if they are concerned with equity they should tend to favour positive notions of freedom. Here a number of conclusions are tenable. First, that when the welfare state is attempting to achieve equity it actually serves to increase freedom. Second, it may be that on balance the welfare state decreases freedom, but this cost is compensated for by other positive achievements of a large public sector. Third, it may be argued that, without more detailed analysis of the individual programmes that are a part of the public sector, then whether freedom is increased or decreased remains an open question. Finally a strong case can be made for government in-kind provision of positive-rights goods in a world of incomplete information.

10.1A APPENDIX: FREEDOM, PIKE AND MINNOWS[8]

The question arises in at least two of the contributions to the 'freedom and welfare state' debate as to the welfare- or utility-maximizing distributions of freedom (Goodin, 1982, p. 154; Jones, 1982, pp. 226–7). Although, as Jones writes, 'measuring freedom itself and comparing different conditions with respect to freedom is notoriously problematic' (Jones, 1982, p. 227), something may be gained, if only in terms of fixing ideas, by treating freedom like income and discussing rationales for different distributions.

There are a number of possibilities to be considered. The actors are labelled pike and minnows, and the cases described involve different responses to the following questions:

1 Do pike and minnows have the same utility from freedom curves?
2 Do utility functions exhibit diminishing marginal utility of freedoms?
3 Do we know who are pike and who are minnows?
4 Are all freedoms identical in their ability to affect utility, or is there a hierarchy of freedoms some of which can be relegated to minor importance.
5 Are freedoms rival so that any transfer from, say, minnows to pike necessarily involves the minnows losing what the pike gain?

In the following figures utility of freedom is notionally measured on the vertical axis and freedom for pike on the left (of the vertical) and freedom for minnows on the right (of the vertical) along the horizontal axis. It must be emphasized that the framework offered here is a pedagogic device (familiar to economists) and it is not suggested that freedom and associated marginal utilities can be quantified and parcelled out in any neat fashion.

Freedom Rival with Pike and Minnows Different

In figure 10.A1 it is assumed that pike and minnows have different utility of freedom functions, hence the different position of the marginal utility curves labelled MUp (pike) and MUm (minnows). Here the welfare-maximizing allocation of freedoms is unequal with OP_2 going to pikes and OM_2 to minnows ($OP_2 > OM_2$). At this allocation marginal utilities are equalized and hence $P_2a = M_2b$. An equal allocation of freedoms would involve losing P_2acP_1 in utility from pike and gaining only M_2bdM_1 for minnows. Total utility would clearly fall. Here then, to the extent that a large public sector or welfare state equalizes freedom, it reduces utility.

Freedom Rival with Pike and Minnows Different but cannot be Identified (MUp may be MUm and vice-versa)

This is the Lerner (1944) uncertainty case for equal redistribution, that given diminishing marginal utility curves, if it is impossible to know

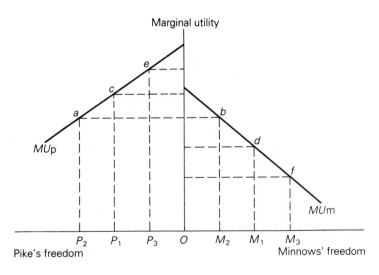

Figure 10.A1 Pike and Minnows: different utility functions

who has the higher marginal welfare curve, then the expected value of total welfare is maximized by equal distribution of freedoms. Here, to the extent a large public sector or welfare state equalizes freedoms, it increases expected welfare. This type of argument is in good measure consistent with the Rawlsian 'veil of ignorance' perspective.

Using figure 10.A1 a movement from equality OP_1, OM_1 towards inequality OP_2, OM_2, would involve a gain of P_2acP_1 for pike and a loss M_2bdM_1 for minnows, the difference between the two areas being the net benefit to inequality of freedoms. Suppose, however, because of uncertainty pike were minnows and minnows were pike. The gain from inequality would be M_1dfM_3 and the loss P_1ceP_3, the difference between these two trapezoids is much greater than the difference between P_2acP_1 and M_2bdM_1, so on the principle that you are just as likely to be right as wrong you have half a chance of a small gain and half a chance of a large loss; hence expected utility is maximized staying with an equal division of freedoms.

Freedom Rival with Pike and Minnows the Same

This case is illustrated in figure 10.A2, and requires that freedom be distributed equally for utility to be maximized ($P_1a = M_1b$ when $OP_1 = OM$).

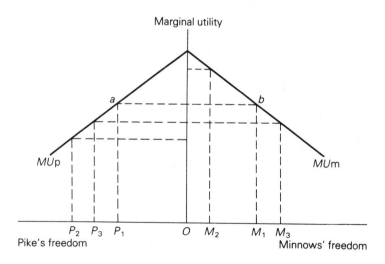

Figure 10.A2 Pike and Minnows: same utility functions

Should freedom be rival, but all utility of income schedules exhibit constant marginal utility of freedom, the above arguments would all be modified. Lerner's uncertainty case for equal distributions would fail. Additionally any allocation of freedom would maximize utility in figure 10.A2 as the effect on the figures of constant marginal utility of freedom would be to make them horizontal. As for the case where pike and minnows are different, all freedom would be given to the pike as they would always have a constant MUp curve above the MUm. In this respect having a decreasing marginal utility of freedoms curves is important (if the objective is utility maximization).

One way of retrieving the arguments above would be to reply yes to question (4) above and to view freedoms as hierarchical. Higgins (1982) takes this view, discussing primary and secondary forms of freedom. In the context of the framework presented here this suggests guaranteeing primary freedom for minnows is to be preferred to conferring more secondary freedoms on pike. In terms of the figures, even with constant marginal utility curves you would no longer be adding equal numbers of 'units of freedom' depending on which side of the vertical axis was being considered. With a hierarchy of freedoms and diminishing marginal utility of freedoms the arguments presented above would tend to be reinforced.

The final question above relates to rivalness or non-rivalness of freedom.[9] In figures 10.A1 and 10.A2 a constant volume of freedom has been allocated. Is it possible for changes in the distributions of freedom to alter its sum total in the same way that so-called Pareto optimal redistribution of income can raise the utility of the donor and donee? This seems to be one way of viewing points 7 and 8 on Goodin's summary (chart 10.3). 'Citizens' freedoms are enhanced by taking part in the welfare state (not just welfare recipients). In terms of figure 10.A2 a move to equalize freedom from pike to minnows say OP_2 to OP_1 and OM_2 to OM_1 increases the set of freedoms[10] so that $OP_3 + OM_3$ becomes the new total compared to OP_1 plus OM_1 previously. Again it must be emphasized that it is not suggested that freedom can be metered and satisfactorily captured in this mechanistic framework. Rather it may be the case that the structure of the arguments that are being forwarded can be usefully summarized like this, and areas of agreement and disagreement established.

NOTES

1 See LeGrand (1982) for an analysis of this question in relation to the UK.
2 Interdependent utility functions of course obviate this need to some extent, but imply a limited donor-orientated concept of equity.
3 Stigler (1978) agrees that it is not really possible to distinguish between coercion by other men and other limitations on choices.
4 Machlup's (1969) list of economic freedoms includes freedom of work, enterprise, trade, travel, migration, contract, purchase and sale, entry to an industry, consumption, occupation, association (where the object is not to harm others).
5 This seems to capture what Loevinsohn (1977) has in mind when he writes 'In general, there will be at least a *prima facie* libertarian case for redistribution whenever the following condition holds: by redistributing property, a government can decrease the overall extent to which people's desire for material goods go unsatisfied, so that overall it will become less important to people to use or consume property from which they are legally barred' (Loevinsohn, 1977, p. 239).
6 Friedman and Friedman (1980) are also critized here for viewing the welfare state with a single level of relevant analysis, the source of finance.
7 Institutional economists have a much broader notion of efficiency than that presented here, so that the issues raised in this chapter gain more prominence. Klein (1984), for example, writes 'a role for the public sector in providing for national defence is seemingly beyond dispute. Here we argue that all economies also reflect at any time some economy-wide attitude toward freedom, equity, and compassion. In precisely the same way in which an economy can be judged with respect to narrow efficiency or security, all economies can be compared with respect to those other qualities, which together form a significant part of emergent value. The higher efficiency refers to the extent to which the economy structures choice so as accurately to reflect fully the amount of attention to these other characteristics that the participants in the economy would choose if they were truly and fully free to choose' (Klein, 1984, p. 61).
8 The use of pike and minnows is taken from Tawney's (1952, p. 164) 'Freedom for the pike is death for the minnows' statement (quoted in Goodin, 1982, p. 154).
9 Goodin (1982) has a discussion that is seemingly at odds with this presentation. He views negative freedom as constant sum in nature, and argues that it then makes little sense to talk of maximizing it because of its fixity of nature. However maximizing and equalizing positive freedom is appropriate because freedoms can be ranked by their worth and lesser ones sacrificed, by Pike, in our example, will be more than compensated for by the gains for Minnows. An egalitarian distribution of freedom is

then justified by diminishing marginal utility of freedom and the desire to maximize total utility. This account appears to confuse three issues we have tried to isolate: the volume of freedoms; the marginal utility associated with additional freedom (which may or may not be viewed as varying between individuals) and qualitative differences in the nature of freedoms.

10 This analogy is misleading to the extent that Pareto optimal redistribution does not affect total income but raises the utility derived from it.

REFERENCES

Akerlof, G. A. and Dickens, W. T. (1982), The economic consequences of cognitive dissonance, *American Economic Review*, vol. 72, no. 3 (June), pp. 307–19.

Berlin, I. (1958), *Two Concepts of Liberty*, Oxford: Oxford University Press.

Dasgupta, P. (1986), Positive freedom, markets and the welfare state, *Oxford Review of Economic Policy*, vol. 2, no. 2, pp. 25–36.

Field, F. (1981), *Inequality in Britain*, London: Fontana.

Friedman, M. and Friedman, R. (1980), *Free to Choose*, London: Secker & Warburg.

Goodin, R. E. (1982), Freedom and the welfare state theoretical foundations, *Journal of Social Policy*, vol. 11, pt 2 (April), pp. 149–76.

Goodin, R. E. (1984), Freedom and the welfare state: a mini-dimensional solution, *Journal of Social Policy*, vol. 13, pt 2 (April), pp. 203–5.

Green, D. G. (1982), Freedom or paternalistic collectivism, *Journal of Social Policy*, vol. 11, pt 2 (April), pp. 239–44.

Hayek, F. A. (1960), *The Constitution of Liberty*, London: Routledge and Kegan Paul.

Head, J. G. (1974) *Public Goods and Public Welfare*, Durham, NC: Duke University Press.

Heald, D. (1983), *Public Expenditure*, Oxford: Martin Robertson.

Higgins, J. (1982), Public welfare: the road to freedom, *Journal of Social Policy*, vol. 11, pt 2 (April), pp. 177–99.

Hirschman, A. O. (1971), *Exit, Voice and Loyalty*, Cambridge, Mass.: Harvard University Press.

Hochman, H. M. and Rodgers, J. D. (1969), Pareto optimal redistribution, *American Economic Review*, vol. 59, pt 3–5, pp. 542–57.

Jones, P. (1982), Freedom and the redistribution of resources, *Journal of Social Policy*, vol. 11, pt 2 (April), pp. 217–38.

Keating, B. (1981), United way contributions: anomalous philanthropy, *Quarterly Review of Economics and Business*, vol. 21, no. 1 (Spring), pp. 114–19.

Keating, B., Pitts, R. and Appel, D. (1981), United way contributions: coercion, charity or economic self-interest? *Southern Economic Journal*, vol. 47, no. 3 (January), pp. 815–23.

Klein, P. A. (1984), Institutionalist reflections on the role of the public sector, *Journal of Economic Issues*, vol. 18, no. 1 (March), pp. 45–68.

LeGrand, J. (1982) *The Strategy of Equality*, London: Allen & Unwin.

Lerner, A. P. (1944), *The Economics of Control*, London: Macmillan.

Loevinsohn, E. (1977), Liberty and the redistribution of property, *Philosophy and Public Affairs*, vol. 6, no. 3, pp. 226–39.

MacCallum, G. (1967), Negative and positive freedom, *Philosophical Review*, vol. 76, no. 3, pp. 312–45.

Macpherson, C. B. (1973), *Democratic Theory*, Oxford: Oxford University Press.

Machlup, F. (1969), Liberalism and the choice of freedoms, pp. 117–46 in Streissler, E., Haberler, G., Lutz, F. A. and Machlup, F. (eds), *Roads to Freedom – Essays in Honour of Friedrich A. von Hayek*, London: Routledge & Kegan Paul.

Mooney, G. H. (1979), Values in health care, pp. 23–44 in Lee, K. (ed.), *Economics and Health Planning*, London: Croom Helm.

Musgrave, R. A. (1959), *The Theory of Public Finance*, New York: McGraw-Hill.

Sen, A. K. (1981), *Poverty and Famines: An Essay on Entitlement and Deprivation*, Oxford: Clarendon Press.

Sen, A. K. (1983), Development: which way now? *Economic Journal*, vol. 93, no. 372 (December), pp. 745–62.

Stein, H. (1985), Foreword to Plaut, S. E. *The Joy of Capitalism*, London and New York: Longman.

Stigler, G. (1978), Wealth and possibly liberty, *Journal of Legal Studies*, vol. 7, no. 2, pp. 213–17.

Sugden, R. (1982), Hard luck stories: the problem of the uninsured in a laissez-faire society, *Journal of Social Policy*, vol. 11, pt 2 (April), pp. 201–16.

Tobin, J. (1970), On limiting the domain of inequality, *Journal of Law and Economics*, vol. 13, no. 2, pp. 363–78.

Van Den Brink-Budgen, R. (1984), Freedom and the welfare state: a multidimensional problem, *Journal of Social Policy*, vol. 13, pt 1 (January), pp. 21–39.

Weitzman, M. L. (1977), Is the price system or rationing more effective in getting a commodity to those who need it most? *Bell Journal of Economics*, vol. 8, no. 2 (Autumn), pp. 517–24.

Wildavsky, A. B. (1964), *The Politics of the Budgeting Process*, Boston: Little, Brown.

Williamson, O. E. (1967), A rational theory of the federal budgetary process, *Public Choice*, vol. 2, pp. 71–89.

11

Conclusion

The central objectives of this book were to acquaint the reader with those arguments of government failure which cast the public sector in the role of a Leviathan, and to provoke a critical response with respect to some of these allegations. In part I we reviewed many criticisms of government. It appears clear that government intervention will seldom be costless, and in certain cases will prove welfare-reducing. This conclusion appears incontrovertible and we applaud those public choice developments which have enhanced the understanding of such government failings. Our defence of Leviathan is therefore not a plea of 'always innocent' but rather of 'innocent on some charges' and 'not proven' on some others. The charges laid against the public sector have, then, in our estimation, been over-emphasized. To the extent that an *impression* of government activity rests solely on this Leviathan literature, we are in danger of adopting policies which are the consequence of fear rather than of reason.

The arguments of part I are consistent with the possibility of the public sector emerging as a Leviathan; it is another matter, however, to argue that in all or most instances an unbridled injurious monster *has* emerged. In part II the Leviathan arguments are re-examined but in a context in which other considerations are relevant. This re-evaluation yields a number of more qualified conclusions. These include:

1　within a majority voting rule, risk-aversity on the part of individuals may itself induce a defence against 'excessive' taxation given a scenario in which voters are tempted to allocate tax costs to their peers;

2　'fiscal ignorance' *per se* may be realistic but not necessarily biased solely towards tax costs; it is not clear that individuals know more about the benefits of expenditures;

3   bureaucrats may be unlikely to be allocativley inefficient to the extent of twice the social optimum, except in extreme conditions – moreover it is possible that in certain instances bureaus produce 'too little';

4   even if it is accepted that the public economy over-provides its goods and services, 'micro-level' crowding out is a powerful mitigating response;

5   'privatization' is ill-advised on the basis of 'faith'; the comparison of public and private efficiency is invariably more difficult and a case-by-case response seems appropriate;

6   the position that tax rates are currently so high that revenues would expand were they reduced is not easily reconciled with a government which efficiently maximizes revenue – estimates of the welfare costs of taxes still remain to be shown as prohibitive;

7   whilst a large public sector intervention may be inimical to negative freedom it may be a requirement of positive freedom.

While not exhaustive this list is sufficient to cast doubt on the damning criticism levelled at public sector provision. This outcome emerges as a result of a deliberate change of emphasis. For example, with reference to chart C.1 it is possible to argue that individuals suffer large welfare losses because they do not respond to the expenditure programmes of government but alter their behaviour quite radically in response to the finance instruments (e.g. taxation) applied by government. In questioning the Leviathan position our approach has been to consider the alternative asymmetry, i.e. individuals not responsive to taxation but responsive to public economy expenditure. In good measure this emphasis is apparent in chapters 7 and 9. It is not our position that asymmetry actually exists in this form; indeed a high degree of fiscal ignorance, with symmetry on both sides, may plausibly exist. It is our position, however, that to base the Leviathan case on deliberate asymmetry must be argued and such bias shown to exist. Chart C.1 is clearly an over-simplification designed to indicate one aspect of the nature of the debate.[1] If individual expenditure programmes and financial instruments differ substantially then discussion must focus on a micro-appraisal of programmes rather than a macro-consideration of two sides of the budget.

   That the Leviathan position is called into question is important. If doubt exists as to the validity of the case then this is *itself* an important

Chart C.1 A simple taxonomy of positions

	Expenditure programmes	Finance instruments
Individuals responsive	No	Yes
Individuals responsive	Yes	No

conclusion. Certainly the public sector is guilty of failings, as indeed would be true of the private sector in a world in which perfect markets are not evident. However, that the case against the public sector has been proven beyond reasonable doubt can be contested.

The importance of this conclusion rests in terms of resistance to decisions which may be taken on the basis of an impression. The case for a tax constitution (Brennan and Buchanan, 1980) is a response to a world in which individuals are prey to a revenue-maximizing government. The constitution proposed would, on occasion, reverse that advice, which usually stems from the standard literature on public finance. For example, whilst selective taxation has typically been criticized because of the excess burden it creates, tax constitutionalists would welcome such taxation to the extent that it emphasized an awareness of government.

We do not deny that this policy advice is sound within a model which perceives government as a danger to the interests of individuals, and wherein it is the welfare of individuals (apart from government) which is the maximand. However, in contesting this unproven allegation of the current situation we would take issue with the automatic acceptance of such constitutional proposals.

Moreover we would question the ability of a constitution to deal with such a problem even if it were the case that Leviathan fears were genuine. In a recent study of constitutional economics (McKenzie, 1985) contributors addressed the problems inherent in constraining government. The establishment of a constitution provides a normative basis for evaluating different outcomes. However, the question arises as to how such a set of constraints are agreed upon. To dismiss voting procedures as inefficient mechanisms for decision-taking begs the question of how constraints are to be agreed upon. Complete unanimity may not always prove an acceptable rule (Buchanan, 1986) but common agreement and consent on constraints would need to be obvious if they have any normative appeal. If constraints effectively prevented powerful groups from realizing rents it is arguable that they may be socially destabilizing (e.g. see the debate between Davidson and Olson in McKenzie, 1985). To the extent that constraints impose costs on government (e.g. the need to insure adequate compensation for any infringement, however minor, of individuals' rights) there will inevitably be transactions (administrative) costs (Tullock, 1985). The enactment of the constitution will presumably be the responsibility of a court to which appeals against government may be addressed. Yet if the offices of government (bureaux, etc.) fail as individuals pursue self-interest, is there reason to believe that a similar public choice analysis of courts and judges will not unearth imperfections?

The work which has advanced on constitutional economics has obvious roots in a sincere attempt to protect individual liberties. We question that the threat of government is as pervasive as such analysts maintain and that, even if their arguments were accepted, the safeguard of constitutional constraints is an easy remedy. Those who research these issues clearly acknowledge the inherent difficulties (e.g. Brennan and Buchanan (1980, p. 10) note 'We do not deny that major problems of constitutional enforceability may emerge').

The main thrust of this book is that governmental as well as market failures do exist, but that the pendulum of criticism has swung 'too far' against the public sector. The book has attempted to, at least, raise some of the essential theoretical and empirical issues that need to be confronted by those, perhaps few, individuals not committed firmly to one view or another.

Some words of Enoch Powell on this subject are appropriate. In answering the question 'How big should government be?' he began his response:

> This is one of those questions which have the appearance of being capable of an experimental or objective answer, but of which, on examination, prove to refer us back to matters of opinion and intent. It is a debating proposition. It is a proposition in a debate which mankind will never conclude and in which the tides and currents will continue to flow back and forth. Those of us who today offer our own answer to the question are borne on those tides and currents and are indicators of their direction. The question is not so much analogous to 'how ought a lunar spaceship to be constructed?' as to 'where is human happiness to be found?' (Powell, 1968, p. 41)

In large part this summarizes the 'message' of this book. The (economic) argument is that it is time for the tides and currents to turn and not to run fully against the public sector – at least for a while. Even for readers who reject this sentiment it is hoped that the general chapters of part I will be of use in themselves, and the remainder will provide sceptics with a chance to question our arguments and thereby sharpen their own positions.

NOTES

1 This taxonomy does not seek to capture the whole of the debate. Clearly within the Leviathan argument is the case that individuals currently do not respond privately to either expenditure programmes or taxation, except in so far as they believe tax costs to be low and vote for additional expenditure. Costs depend only upon subjective evaluation, and if individuals do not themselves respond to tax costs their relevance may be questioned. This aside, the Leviathan case, as currently argued, is broader than the simple taxonomy of chart C.1. Also other authors note the costs of government even when individuals respond to expenditure programmes (e.g. Brennan and Pincus, 1983) and these arguments are answered in chapters 8 and 9.

REFERENCES

Brennan, G. and Buchanan, J. M. (1980), *The Power to Tax: Analytical Foundations of Fiscal Constitution*, Cambridge: Cambridge University Press.

Brennan, G. and Pincus, J. M. (1983), Government expenditure growth and resource allocation: the nebulous connection, *Oxford Economic Papers*, vol. 35, no. 3 (November), pp. 351–65.

Buchanan, J. M. (1986), *Liberty, Market and State: Political Economy in the 1980's*, Brighton, Sussex: Wheatsheaf Books.

McKenzie, R. B. (1985), *Constitutional Economics: Containing the Economic Powers of Government*, Lexington, Mass: Lexington Books.

Powell, J. E. (1968), How big should government be?, pp. 41–61 in Douglas, P. H. and Powell, J. E. (eds), *How Big Should Government Be?* Washington, DC: American Enterprise Institute.

Tullock, G. (1985), Comment, in McKenzie, R. B. *Constitutional Economics: Containing the Economic Powers of Government*, Lexington, Mass.: Lexington Books.

Author Index

Subject Index